IMAGES
of America

LONG BEACH'S LOS CERRITOS

I0900969

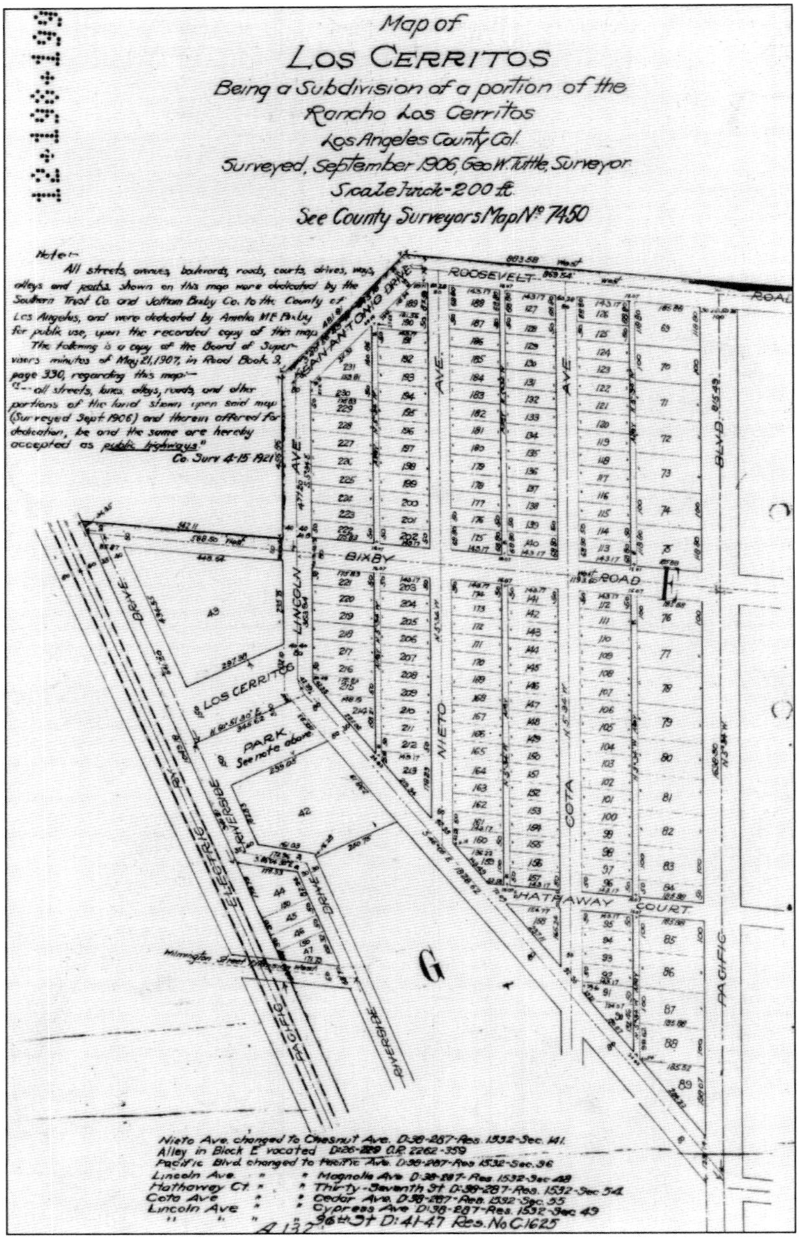

Los Cerritos Subdivision Map, 1906. Jotham Bixby created the Los Cerritos neighborhood in 1906 by subdividing a portion of the Rancho Los Cerritos. This survey, made by George W. Tuttle, shows the boundaries extended from Roosevelt Boulevard on the north to the intersection of Pacific Avenue and Thirty-sixth Street on the south. Cota Street on the map is today called Cedar Avenue; Nieto Street is now called Chestnut Avenue. Country Club Drive is shown on this map as Lincoln Avenue. All streets and parks were dedicated by the Southern Trust Company and Jotham Bixby Company for public use. (Courtesy of Rancho Los Cerritos.)

On the Cover: Going to Long Beach. This is a 1910 photograph of American Avenue (now Long Beach Boulevard) between Wardlow and San Antonio Roads. (Courtesy of the Long Beach Historical Society.)

IMAGES
of America

LONG BEACH'S LOS CERRITOS

Geraldine Knatz

ARCADIA
PUBLISHING

Copyright © 2014 by Geraldine Knatz
ISBN 978-1-4671-3129-2

Published by Arcadia Publishing
Charleston, South Carolina

Printed in the United States of America

Library of Congress Control Number: 2013947215

For all general information, please contact Arcadia Publishing:
Telephone 843-853-2070
Fax 843-853-0044
E-mail sales@arcadiapublishing.com
For customer service and orders:
Toll-Free 1-888-313-2665

Visit us on the Internet at www.arcadiapublishing.com

To the support and continued growth of our neighborhood treasure, the Rancho Los Cerritos, and to my family, John, Patrick, and J.R. Mulvey.

Contents

Acknowledgments

Ellen Calomiris and Steve Iverson of Rancho Los Cerritos provided a great amount of assistance, including reviewing drafts of the book and searching out and scanning photographs. I also want to thank the Long Beach Historical Society, especially Julie Bartolotto, Tim Friden, and Ashley Franks-McGill, for assistance in finding photographs. I am particularly indebted to members of the Vignes family, who gladly shared information, especially Ellen Collins, who had enough faith in me to send me her original photographs for scanning. Margaret Wilkinson Mahannah has lovingly preserved a history of her years at Los Cerritos and shared her collection with me. James G. Craig Jr. assisted in identifying photographs and connecting me with old-timers from the neighborhood. My husband John's photographic skills were instrumental is getting good photographs of homes featured in this book. The Neighbors of Los Cerritos, a loose collection of residents dedicated to making the rancho known to all neighborhood residents, was part of the inspiration for the creation of this book. Begun by Patrick Murphy in 2004, the group hosts events to introduce the rancho to Los Cerritos residents. In 2006, the Neighbors organized a centennial celebration for the Los Cerritos neighborhood. Neighbors were urged to share old photographs. To ensure that the efforts and photographs collected were made available to the widest audience, this book has been prepared. All author royalties will accrue to the Rancho Los Cerritos, whose continued support is vital for our community. Finally, Loretta Berner, a local historian who grew up on the McGill, Smith, Malhardt bean ranch, was the first person I interviewed about Los Cerritos history. She happily shared the results of her previous research with me. She wanted the history of this neighborhood to be preserved and a book written, and she passed that desire on to me. Images provided by the Rancho Los Cerritos Historic Site are labeled RLC; those from the Historical Society of Long Beach are labeled HSLB; images from Virginia Country Club are labeled VCC; and those from Los Cerritos School are identified by LCS.

Unless otherwise noted, all photographs are courtesy of the author.

INTRODUCTION

Los Cerritos is a vibrant, primarily residential community in northern Long Beach. The name *Los Cerritos* means "little hills," reflecting the geography of Signal Hill and the small hills of the surrounding areas, such as Bixby Knolls. Los Cerritos began as a 27,000-acre rancho, operated primarily as a single cattle ranch. It evolved over time into ranches separately operated as part of the rancho. Smaller ranches were sold to create the Los Cerritos Colony; ultimately, land was subdivided into residential lots.

In 1784, Gov. Pedro Fages awarded a large land grant to Manuel Perez Nieto, a leather-jacket soldier who arrived in Alta California around 1771. Nieto's grant stretched between the coastline and the main road leading from Los Angeles to San Diego, and between the Santa Ana and San Gabriel Rivers. When Nieto died, his land was divided into six parcels. Nieto's daughter Manuela Nieto de Cota received 27,000 acres, which became known as the Rancho Los Cerritos. The Cotas built the first adobe structures on the land, known as the Cerritos. No evidence of this adobe currently exists. In 1843, the land was sold to John Temple, a transplanted Easterner who had business operations in Los Angeles. At its peak, Temple pastured 15,000 cattle, 7,000 sheep, and 3,000 horses. The export of hides through the port at San Pedro made Temple a rich man. In the 1860s, however, severe drought caused thousands of cattle to die, and Temple never restocked.

In 1866, Flint, Bixby & Company purchased the 27,000-acre rancho from John Temple for $20,000, about 75 cents an acre. Jotham Bixby became the manager and, three years later, he purchased half ownership of the rancho, organizing the firm of J. Bixby and Company. Living at the rancho for 15 years, Bixby raised his family along with 30,000 head of sheep.

As the sheep operation scaled down, Bixby focused his attention on subdividing his property. Much of the land of the Rancho Los Cerritos was divided into small farms or sold. Some farms were leased to tenants and used to grow grains or operate dairies under the direct supervision of Jotham or his son George H. Bixby. In 1890, George Bixby built a large home that became the center of the ranch management, which today is at 11 La Linda Drive. When Jotham Bixby moved his family from the rancho in 1881, he rented it to William Boyle, who ran a dairy for about 10 years. Boyle left the adobe in 1906, and Oscar King took over the dairy.

Jotham Bixby supported the California Immigrant Union, an organization formed by the San Francisco Chamber of Commerce to promote bringing immigrants and Easterners to California to settle the land. The purpose of the union was to facilitate the subdivision of large land holdings for these new California residents. By 1870, land values in Los Angeles County were $7 per acre and rising, and in 1878, Jotham Bixby began selling off portions of the rancho, including 1,400 acres that became the Wilmington Colony. The Cerritos Colony was part of the Wilmington Colony or, as it was sometimes called, the Wilmington Colony Tract. Bixby made sales to a number of individuals, and these individual sales of small ranches comprised the Cerritos Colony. Many of the buyers were Southern Methodists or members of the Holiness Church. Originally called the Southern Methodist Colony before being renamed the Cerritos Colony, the land was situated three miles east of Wilmington, with Willow Street and Perris Road, now known as Santa Fe Avenue, as its major thoroughfares. In 1867, a major flood caused the San Gabriel River to alter its course and cut through the central part of the rancho, and the low land along the river sprouted willow trees. Because of all the willow trees in the area, the Cerritos Colony was often called The Willows.

Bixby had the land for the Cerritos Colony surveyed into 40-acre farm lots. According to colony resident Katherine Robinson Bushong, the colony stretched from Pacific Coast Highway on the south to Wardlow Road on the north. Colony resident Evelyn Moulton recalls lots of 40, 60, and 80 acres, with 40-acre lots being one-fourth of a mile on a side. A search of deeds from 1870 to 1880 shows Bixby Company sales of farm lots or partial lots to individual colony members as well as a sale of a half-acre by Dennis Rogers to the trustees of the Holiness Church.

By 1878, the Wardlow, Parris, Kincade, Hayes, and Teel families had established themselves on small ranches of 20 to 80 acres. They were joined by the Valentine, Moulton, Robinson, Lewis, Hass, Holaday, Stewart, Martin, Saunders, Wilhoit, Tolle, Loper, Thompson, Schrode, Shaw, and McDonald families. A notice in the *Los Angeles Times* in 1882 noted that the colony consisted of 20 families on the southeast side of the Old San Gabriel River, which by this time was renamed the Los Angeles River.

Elijah Teel, his son George Marion Teel, and other Teel family members traveled by wagon train from Texas to California in 1869. This wagon train was made up of a group of devoutly religious people who, according to George Teel's diary, wasted no time making themselves available for service and for places of responsibility within their churches once they arrived in California. Some were Methodists, but the Teel family became associated with the Holiness Church when in California. The Teels lived first in Garden Grove but then acquired land in the Cerritos Colony in the late 1870s. Walter Case, in his book *The History of Long Beach*, indicates that Elijah Teel purchased 80 acres of the colony from Jotham Bixby around 1878. No direct purchases from Jotham Bixby or the J. Bixby Company to any Teel family member was found in county records for the period 1875 to 1880, but there were sales of land to George Milton Teel, son of Elijah Teel, in 1878 by Alfred Robinson, and sales between other individuals with the Teels, including B.F. Townsend.

Elijah's son George Marion Teel led Holiness meetings under a tent at the Cerritos Colony. The Methodists also held camp meetings in the colony. Washburn, in his *History and Reminiscences of the Holiness Church*, describes the September 18, 1889, Cerritos camp meeting: "The Lord is saving the people; Brothers Rogers and Morgan are in charge, Brother Holdridge assisting, pouring in red hot shot that makes sinners tremble." Teel's May 18, 1897, diary entry states: "Moved to Long Beach to take pastoral care of the Cerritos Holiness Church. Rented house to A.M. Morgan for $1.50 per month." A.M. Morgan is Alfred Marion Morgan, who married George Teel's sister Susan California "Callie" Teel. George Teel was actually moving back to Los Cerritos, having lived there as a young man when the colony started in the late 1870s.

By the 1880s, the residents of the Cerritos Colony had diversified their land use to a mix of agricultural purposes. G.M. Holaday promoted the area in the *Los Angeles Times*, noting the availability of water, soil good for pumpkins and corn, the Cerritos School under the management of Prof. W. Bailey, and the Methodist Camp meetings. Capt. Charles Parris had started a small orchard. In 1885, Holaday joined Cerritos Colony residents H.C. Bailey, R.B Robinson, W.W. Schrode, and S.W. Tolle to form a water district to service the residents of the colony. Also living in the area at that time were the Finley, Owen, and Wallace families. There were alfalfa, hay, and barley fields, citrus orchards, dairies, and horse ranches. The diversity of operations found in the small farms of the Cerritos Colony was significant, reflecting a dramatic change from the large, single-purpose sheep or cattle ranches of the previous era. More important, this diversity made the colony self-sufficient. In 1887, the *Los Angeles Times* reported that a number of the most reliable gentlemen residents declared that "the Willows can now be called a town."

The colony families petitioned the county for the establishment of a school. L.T. Hayes, who purchased 40 acres from Jotham Bixby in 1880, donated one acre on July 7, 1881, for the school.

The first trustees were Messrs. Robinson, Saunders, and Lewis. The site was approximately one acre and thick with willows. The willows were cleared, and a one-room, wood-frame building was erected on Willow Street that became the first Cerritos School, later called the South Cerritos School. In 1948, former colony residents who attended the school came back for a reunion. At the event were Callie Teel Morgan, Mrs. James A. Teel, Fannie Clarke Teel, Elnora Kincade Martin, Nettie Saunders Lewis, Elizabeth Lewis Gimmell, Katherine Robinson Bushong, Frank E. Cook, Sarah Ellison Garrison, Birdie Bailey Schilling, and John Lewis, all children who grew up in the colony.

Being so close to the Los Angeles River was a precarious situation for many of the colony ranchers. In 1887, the Lewis family fled their ranch to higher ground to wait out the rains. The Cerritos school was often closed due to bad weather. Despite the vagaries of the river's course, the community thrived. Although the colony was building up fast, one *Los Angeles Times* article in 1887 reported that the only drawback was the colony's lack of "men with energy," but that a new class of people was coming in and "taking hold with energy." The colony residents even established a brass band in late 1886. The band's members were N. Roach; J. Inman; Arthur, Samuel, and Altia Thompson; B. Lyster; and C. Rolston. Their leader was Prof. Arthur Thompson.

The beginning of the Los Cerritos neighborhood as it is known today began with the first residential subdivision in 1906. Many of the first residents who purchased lots in the subdivision came from the surrounding farms, such as the King family and the Vignes family, or moved in from the colony ranches, such as the Lopers and the Moultons.

In 1890, John Louis Vignes and his wife, Mary Kent Marcellus, moved from Los Angeles to Long Beach. Vignes was the grandnephew of Don Luis Vignes, a French immigrant to Los Angeles in 1831 who was responsible for the establishment of the first commercial vineyard in Los Angeles and for whom Vignes Street in Los Angeles is named.

The Vignes family moved first to a home that had been occupied by George H. Bixby at Third Street and Cedar Avenue. Vignes listed his occupation as a stockman and his residence as Long Beach when he registered to vote on September 23, 1890. Vignes farmed with the Watson brothers on the Dominguez property, and he worked the dairy on the Watson property on the northeastern corner of Alameda Street and Wardlow Road. The strong relationship between the Watson and Vignes families was evidenced by Vignes serving as a pallbearer for the funeral of Francisca Ferrer de Watson in May 1903. After several years, the family moved to the Dominguez property before becoming one of the first homeowners in the Los Cerritos subdivision in 1910. Their home was the center of social activity in the early days of the Los Cerritos neighborhood.

Because the Vignes family believed its five daughters should be educated, they were instrumental in the establishment of schools where they lived, first as part of the Cerritos School District, then the Dominguez school when they lived on Watson land, and finally with the expansion of the Cerritos School District to serve the 1906 subdivision when they moved back into Los Cerritos. Their five accomplished daughters and their husbands represent a significant part of the early history of Los Cerritos.

Historically, the colony was the primary residential community of this area prior to the 1906 subdivision, which created the neighborhood today called Los Cerritos. Areas no longer part of Los Cerritos but part of the Cerritos Colony were portions of West Long Beach and the Wrigley District. However, well into the 20th century, West Long Beach and the Wrigley District were considered part of the Los Cerritos precinct for voter registration and federal census records.

Today, the concrete channel of the Los Angeles River separates West Long Beach, which was part of the historical residential district of the Cerritos, from the place now called Los Cerritos. The area of the Cerritos Colony that is currently east of the river and south of Wardlow Road is now called the Wrigley District. Although the physical area that was called Los Cerritos has changed significantly over time, what is left today represents the core of a community that is significant for several reasons. First, the families that developed the small farms and dairies organized themselves into a community and established a school district and water district prior to the establishment of the City of Long Beach. The survey that planned the Cerritos Colony was completed at least five years before the survey started in 1882 for Willmore City, which later became Long Beach. Second, Los Cerritos residents fought to maintain their independence from Long Beach for as long as possible. It was the invasion by oil-drilling interests that led residents to finally flee to the safety of incorporation into the City of Long Beach. But when the Long Beach School District sought to include the two Los Cerritos Schools within its district, only the "south" Los Cerritos School on Willow Street joined. On March 10, 1922, 102 registered voters of Los Cerritos signed a petition objecting to joining the Long Beach School District, and so the "north" Los Cerritos School on San Antonio Drive kept its independence for a few more years. Third, the neighborhood reflects the shifting demographics of the greater city of Long Beach, from a start where deeds limited ethnicities of residents, to an economic stratification most obvious in the housing stock from north to south reflecting the influence of the Virginia Country Club, to today's more diverse and eclectic population.

One can speculate that the reason for the fierce independence shown by Los Cerritos residents over the course of history is geography. Bounded on the west by the Los Angeles River and the north by the Rancho Los Cerritos and then the large expanse of the Virginia Country Club golf course, Los Cerritos is not a community one can "drive through." Access is limited to the south and eastern edges. Looking at a map today, the area shows as a dense green in the crater bounded by the 710 Freeway and the 405 Freeway. This limited access has resulted in a close-knit neighborhood rarely found in a "bedroom community" of the greater Los Angeles region. It is small, compact, and walkable, with its own school, park, and historic site. It is a place where families that move in tend to move to other homes within the neighborhood rather than leave.

While geography may have molded the current independent streak of the neighborhood, its real independent roots lie in actions of the people who occupied the historical boundaries of the residential area that was Los Cerritos. The small colony ranchers developed a self-sufficient community, with its own school and water districts, even its own brass band. They toyed with the idea of becoming an independent city. In 1922, during the battle over succession into Long Beach, there was an unsuccessful attempt to create a separate City of Willowville that included the area from Willow Street north to the Virginia Country Club. Today, the residents of these areas, West Long Beach and the Wrigley District, might not recognize their shared history with Los Cerritos, yet they share a continuation of that independent spirit.

One

Rancho Los Cerritos and the Ranch Era

A single drawing exists that shows the rancho during the cattle-ranching operation of John Temple. Most photographic material is from the Jotham Bixby era of sheep ranching and tenant farm operations. As the sheep business wound down, Bixby focused on managing smaller ranches and subdividing and selling his property. The Mitchell Ranch consisted of about 1,100 acres, including Los Cerritos and Bixby Knolls. After the year 1900, this ranch was divided into smaller ranches, and the operation was turned over to R. "Ray" Chester Andrews and a resident foreman, Colby Clarke. Other ranches included the McGill 1908 leasehold between Cherry Avenue and Long Beach Boulevard, which later transferred to Smith and then Malhardt. Robert Wardlow operated a small farm and dairy two blocks east of Santa Fe on Wardlow Road, close enough to the first Los Cerritos school to supply the students with milk. From Wardlow Road south to Willow Street and between the Wardlow Ranch and Atlantic Avenue, was Modesto and Ruth Moreno Romero's ranch. Oscar King took over the dairy started at the rancho adobe by William Boyle and moved it to Linden Street and Forty-fifth or Forty-sixth Streets. Later, his dairy was taken over by Paul Lussman, one of the Swiss dairymen who had been working there. Howard King had a ranch just to the west of his brother Oscar's ranch. Just across the river from the existing Los Cerritos School was the Encinas Ranch. Several of these ranch operators purchased lots in the new Los Cerritos subdivision when it opened in 1906. Nellie Menke King, daughter of Howard King, recalls living on her father's ranch from 1907 until 1913, when they built the fifth house in the new subdivision. She recalls walking to the old adobe on Sundays through fields of mustard and lupine. The adobe door was always open, the children felt welcome, and the Mexicans living there would play music and cook beans and tortillas. Today, the rancho still welcomes kids of all ages with numerous public events.

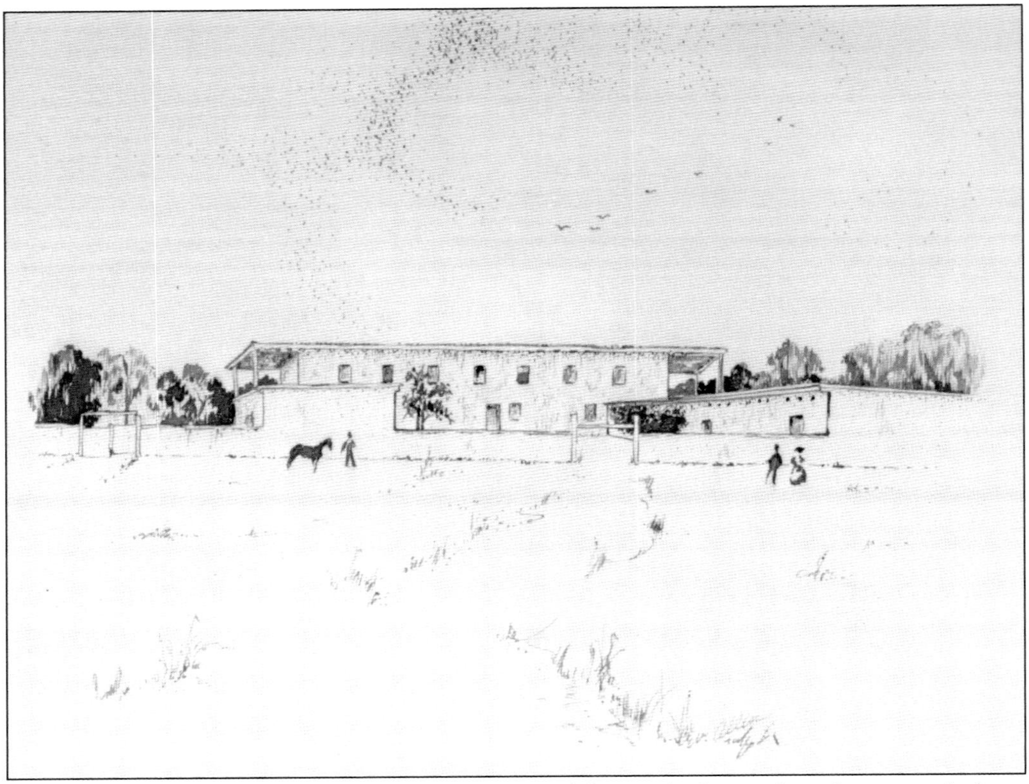

Los Cerritos Rancho House. This early drawing of the rancho house shows how it might have looked when it was built by John Temple. This drawing reflects the appearance during the 1850s and 1860s but is a more recent re-creation, based upon 1872 photographs. The house originally had a flat roof. (RLC.)

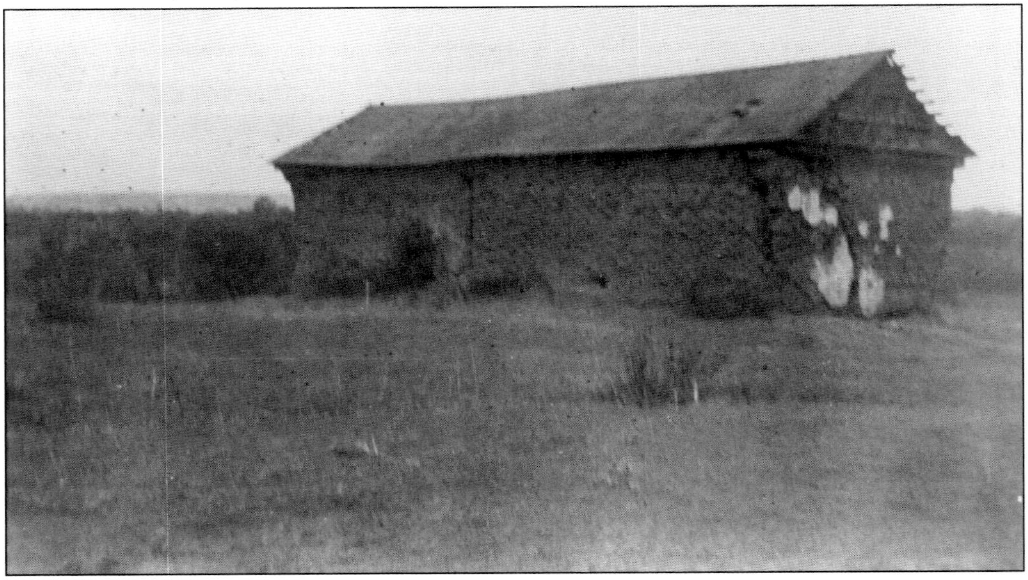

Cota Adobe. This old adobe west of the rancho house was probably built by the Cota family around 1835. The adobe was later called the "flea house." This photograph probably dates from 1915 or earlier. (RLC.)

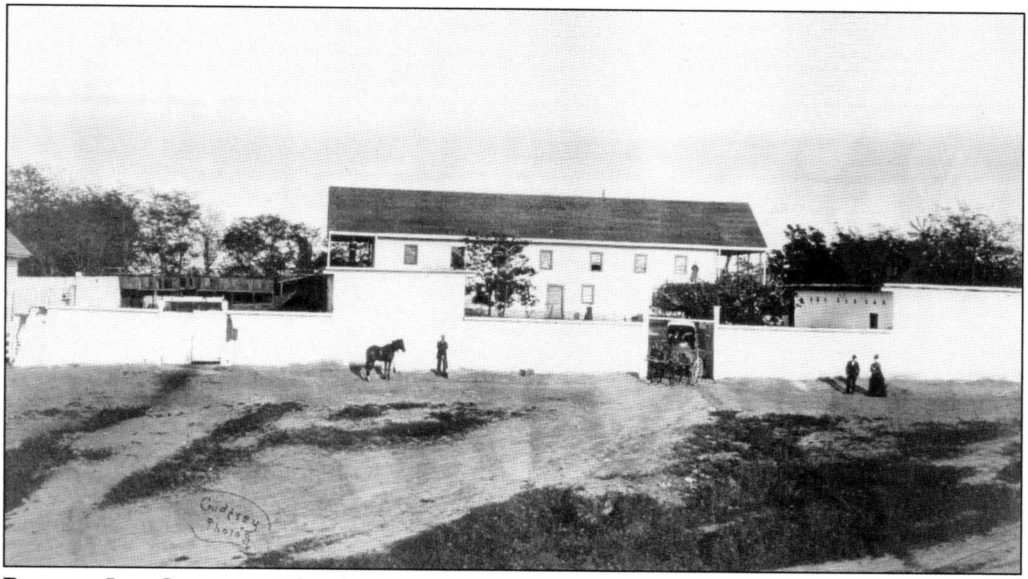

Rancho Los Cerritos. This front panoramic photograph of the rancho was taken at spring shearing time in 1872 by Los Angeles photographer William Godfrey. (RLC.)

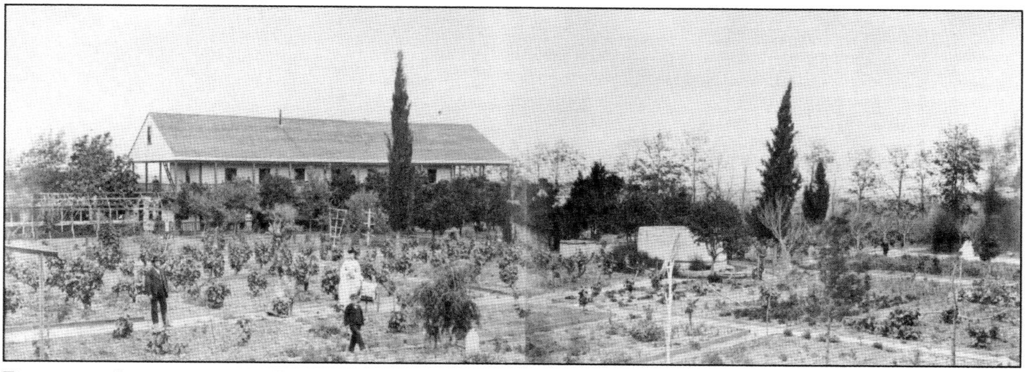

Rancho Gardens and Bixby Family. The gardens of the rancho were used as an orchard. Jotham Bixby is on the left side of the photograph. His son George is in front of his mother, who holds son Harry on her lap. To the right of George H. is the grave of his sister Mary. The water reservoir is shown in the center of the photograph. (RLC.)

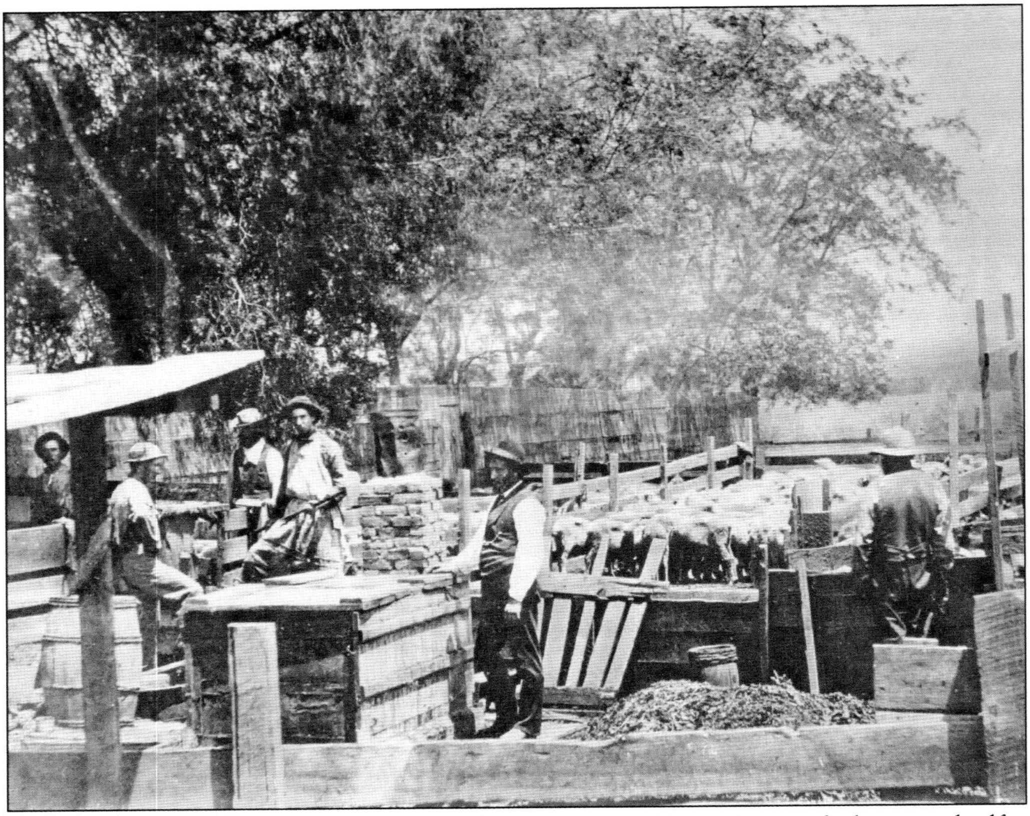

Sheep Dipping at Rancho Los Cerritos. Sheep were dipped in a mixture of tobacco and sulfur to protect them from insects and parasites. In the center of the photograph is Jotham Bixby, with his hand on a crate holding a large iron kettle, which is still at the rancho. (RLC.)

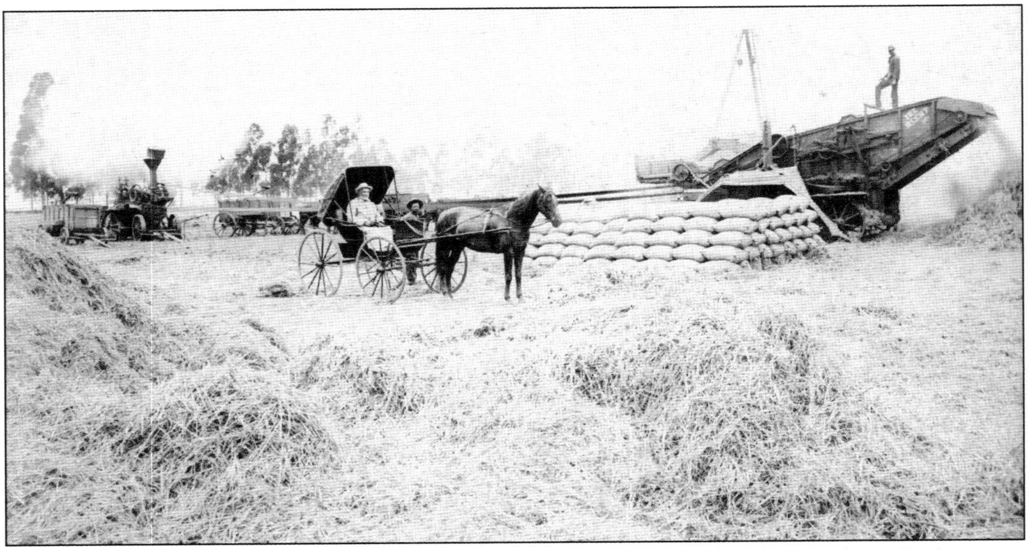

Jotham Bixby in Horse-drawn Buggy. Ranch employees described how Jotham Bixby came out in a buggy to survey the ranches on Los Cerritos land. Fred King, the blacksmith, is standing next to the buggy, and Jim Wardlow is standing on top of the thresher. This photograph was taken around 1907. (RLC.)

BIXBY GUSHER. This photograph, published in the *Long Beach Press* in November 1918, shows the "Bixby Gusher," an artesian well dug to 671 feet on rancho property. (RLC.)

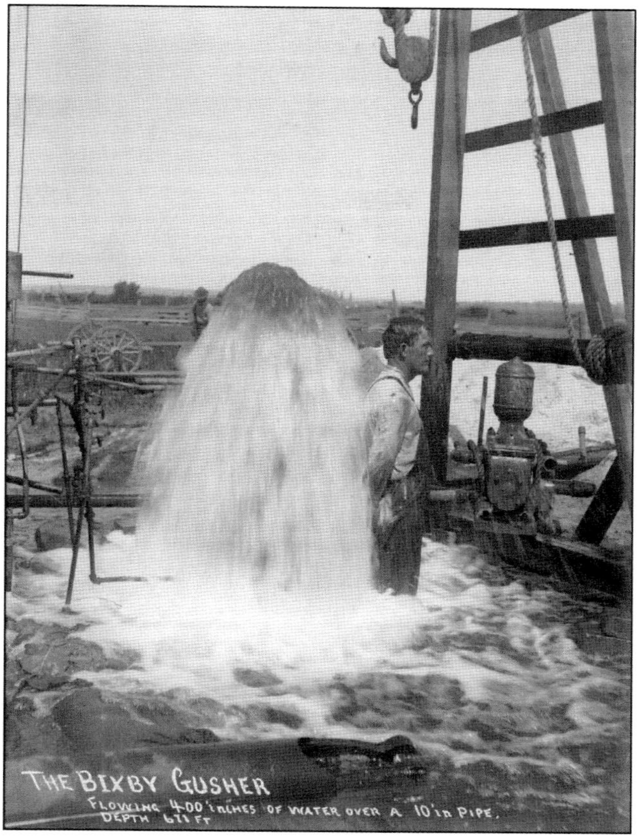

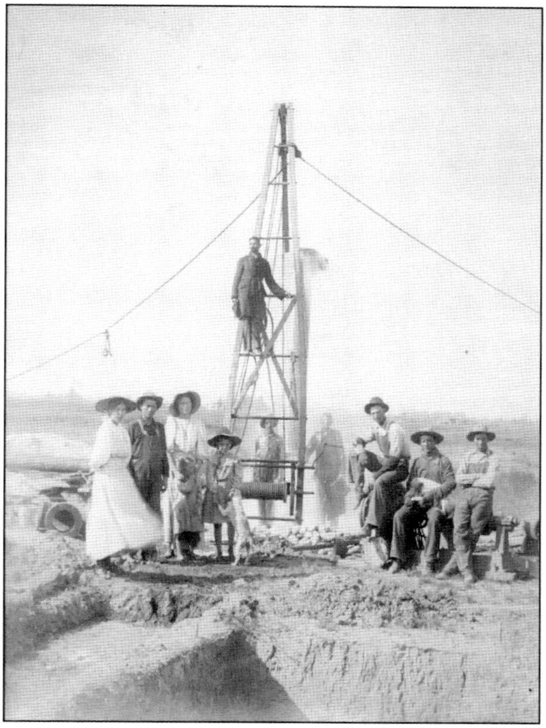

ARTESIAN WELL. At least 10 artesian wells were dug on rancho land. By 1880, the rancho had a steady supply of water. This well is near San Antonio Drive and Orange Avenue on the Mitchell Ranch. On the left of the well are, from left to right, Viola Eschom, unidentified, and Mrs. Fred Beckett with two children: Josephine and Alta Andrews. Bill Ealey is on the ladder. Colby Clarke holds a dog on his lap. (RLC.)

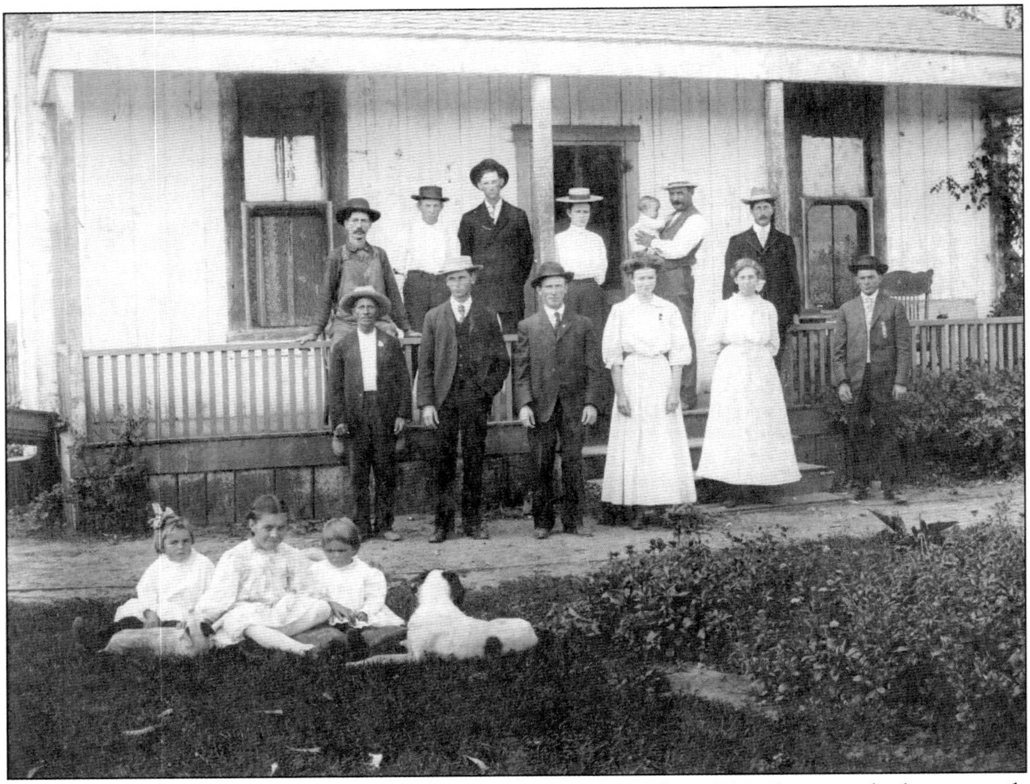

Ranch Families at Mitchell/Andrews Ranch House. This 1908 photograph shows ranch families on the side porch of the Mitchell/Andrews house. Those standing are, from left to right, (first row) Shorty Montoya, Charles Casseris, Colby Clarke, Bertha Ralph, Viola Eschom, and unidentified; (second row) Bill Ealey, Ed Clarke, Harry Andrews, Mrs. Magner (cook), Chet Andrews (holding Chester), and unidentified. Two of the children sitting on the lawn are Alta and Nellie Andrews. (RLC.)

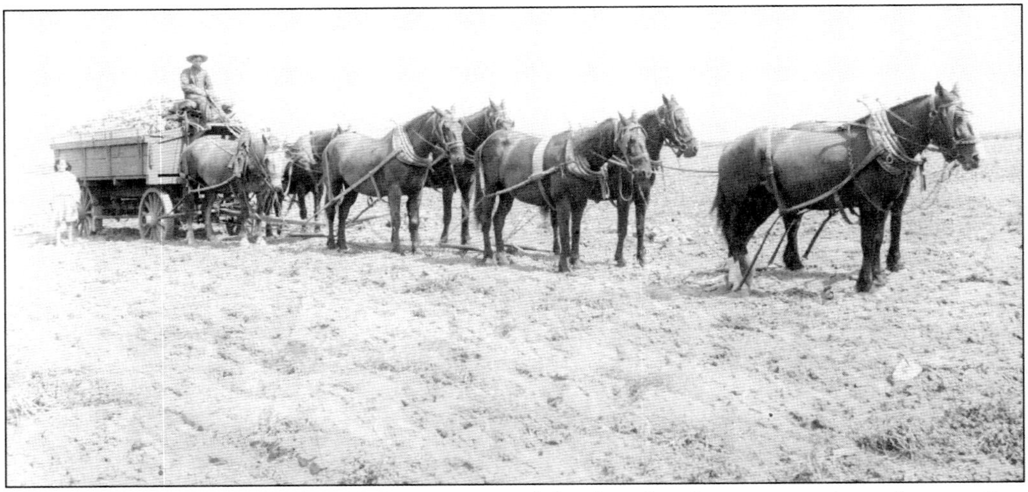

Howard King Ranch. The Kings were one of the first families to move into the new Los Cerritos subdivision. Here, a team of eight horses and a wagon are hauling sugar beets on the ranch around 1920. King and his wife, Mina, had four daughters and one son. The girl standing beside the wagon may be daughter Florence. (RLC.)

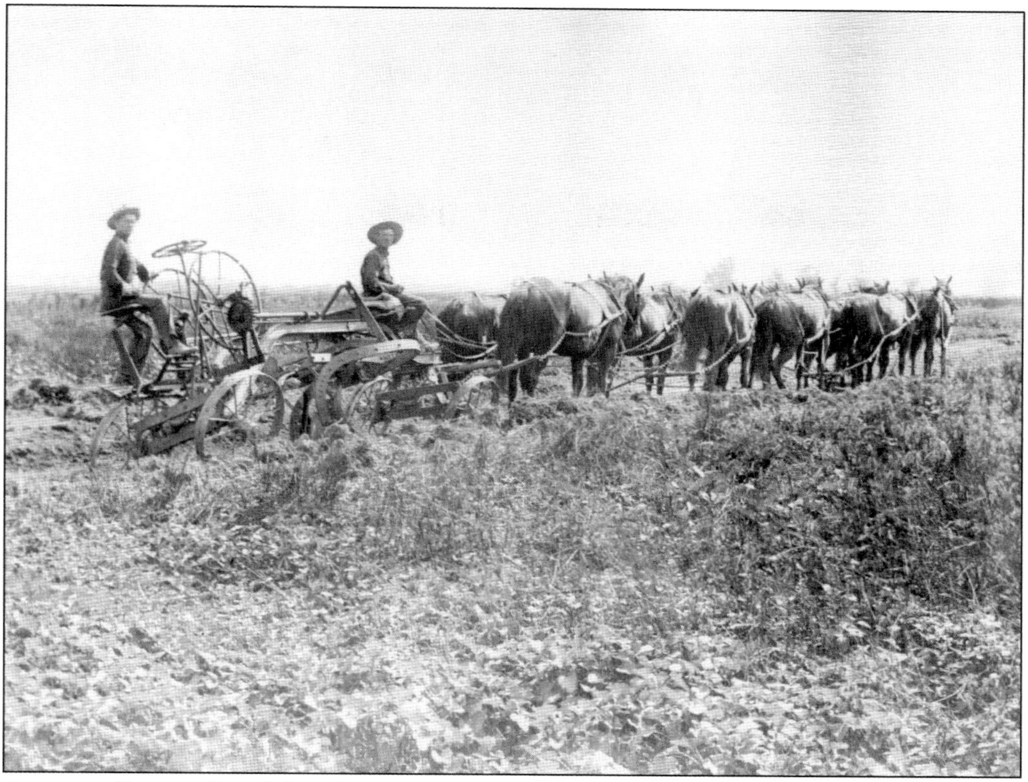

ANDREWS RANCH. Ranch hands are operating a disk plow, pulled by six teams of horses on the Andrews Ranch. (RLC.)

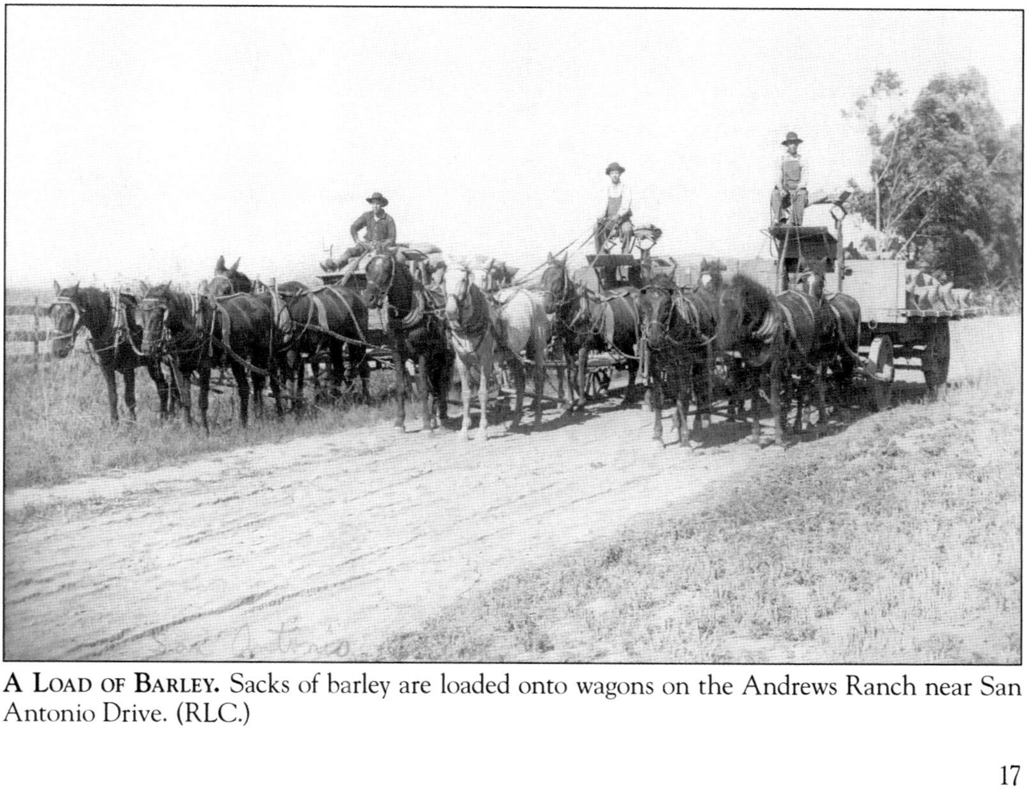

A LOAD OF BARLEY. Sacks of barley are loaded onto wagons on the Andrews Ranch near San Antonio Drive. (RLC.)

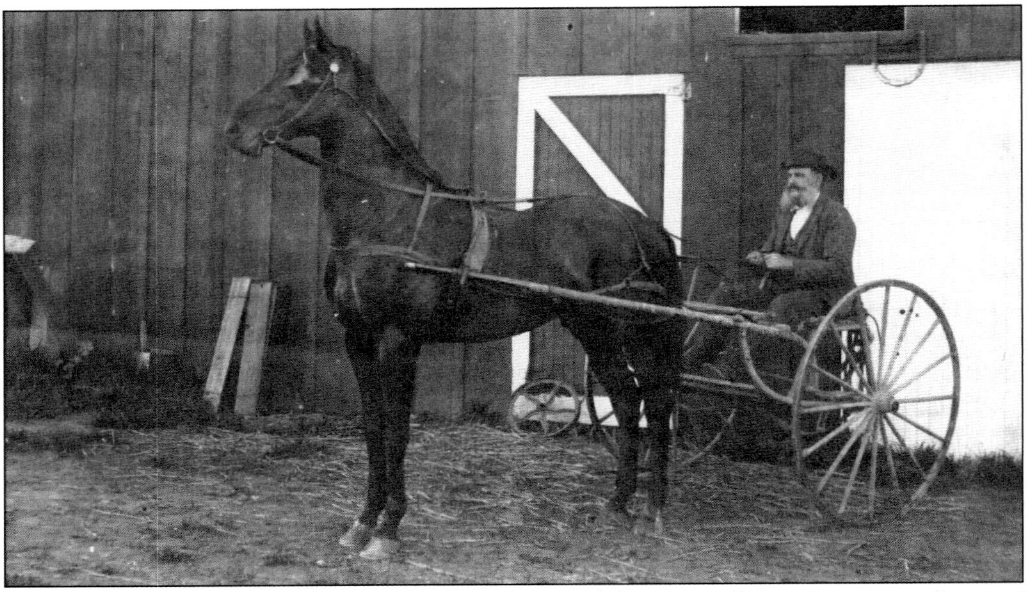

Charles Edward Mitchell. Mitchell, shown here with his trotter Dairyman, was a relative of Jotham Bixby from Maine. Mitchell operated the Bixby cheese dairy at Clearwater. He lived at the rancho around 1884 while the cheese factory was being constructed. (RLC.)

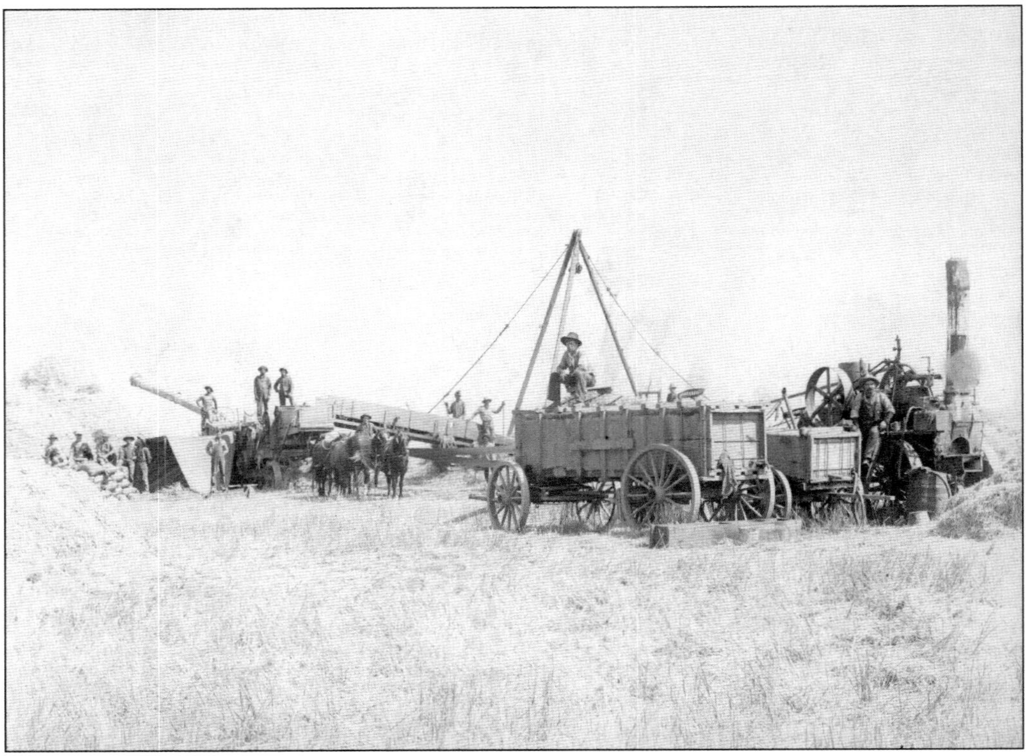

Threshing Crew. Ranch hands are shown with wagon and machinery in a field on the Andrews Ranch near San Antonio Drive and Atlantic Avenue. (RLC.)

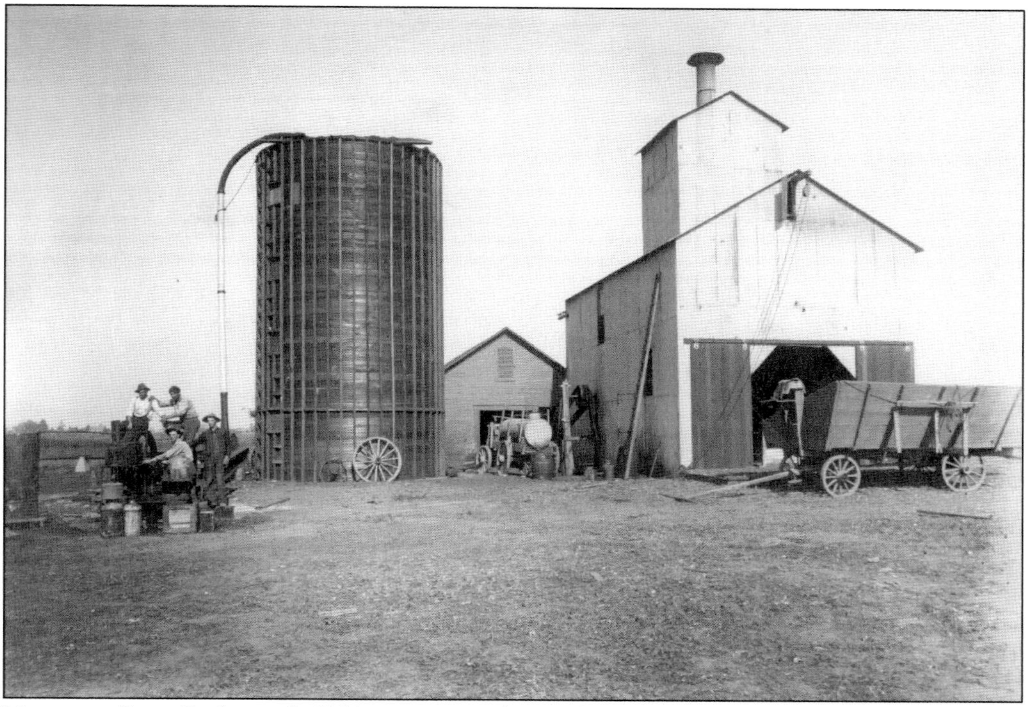

Mill and Silo. Barley and alfalfa were ground, mixed with molasses, and sacked for horse feed on the Mitchell/Andrews Ranch, shown here. (RLC.)

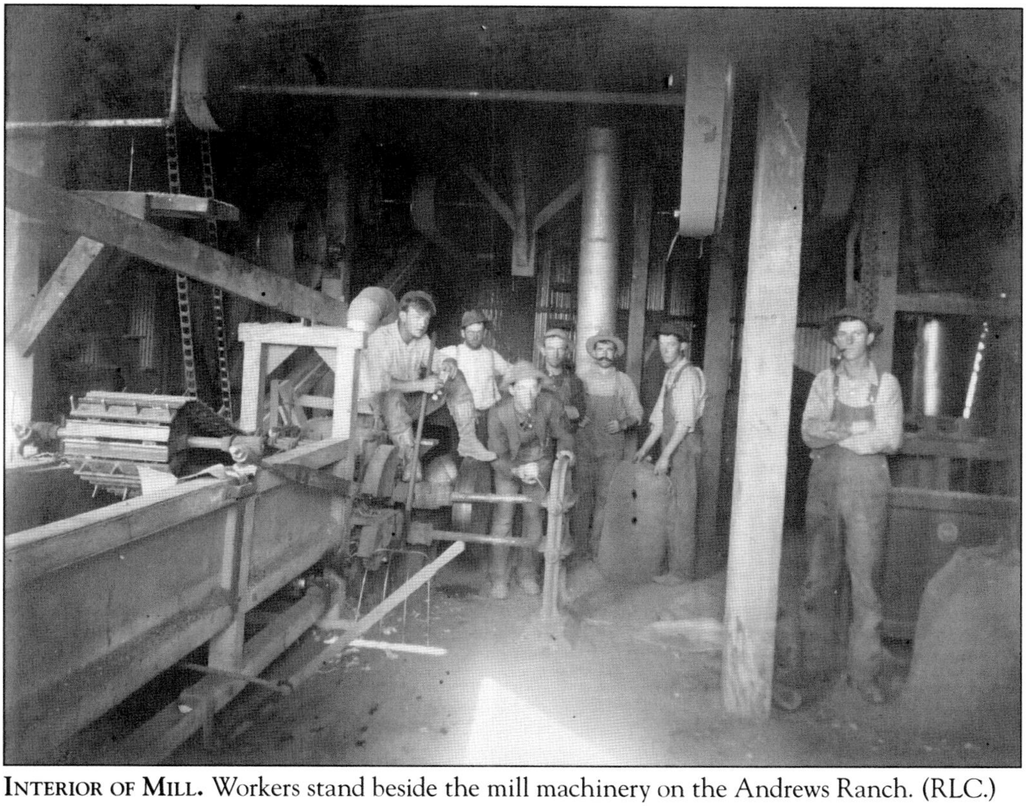

Interior of Mill. Workers stand beside the mill machinery on the Andrews Ranch. (RLC.)

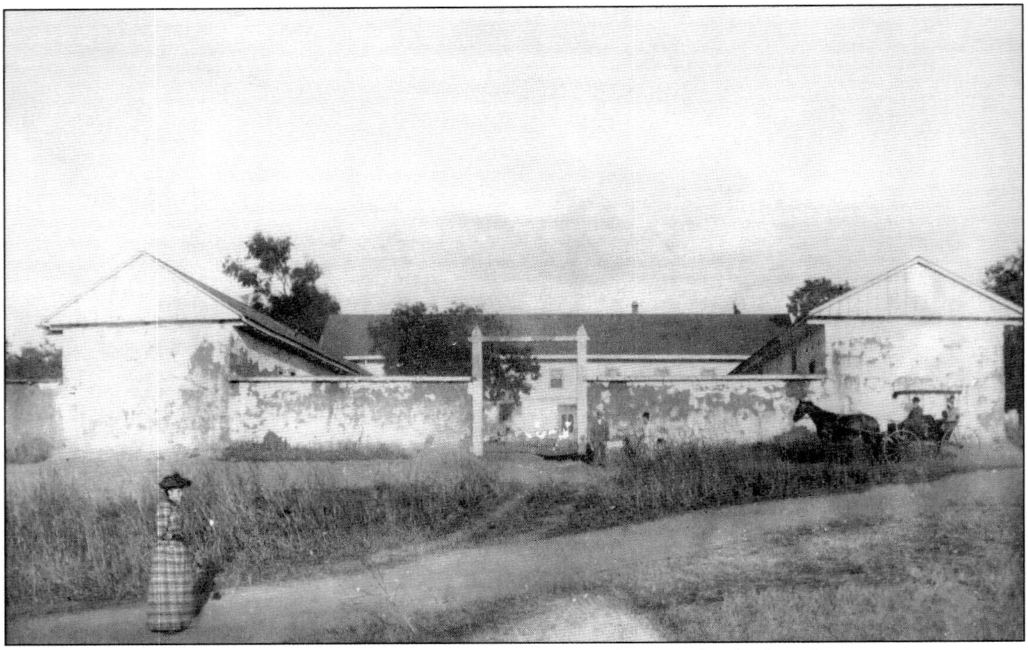

RANCHO ADOBE. This c. 1895 photograph shows the rancho as it looked at the time it was being used as a dairy. (RLC.)

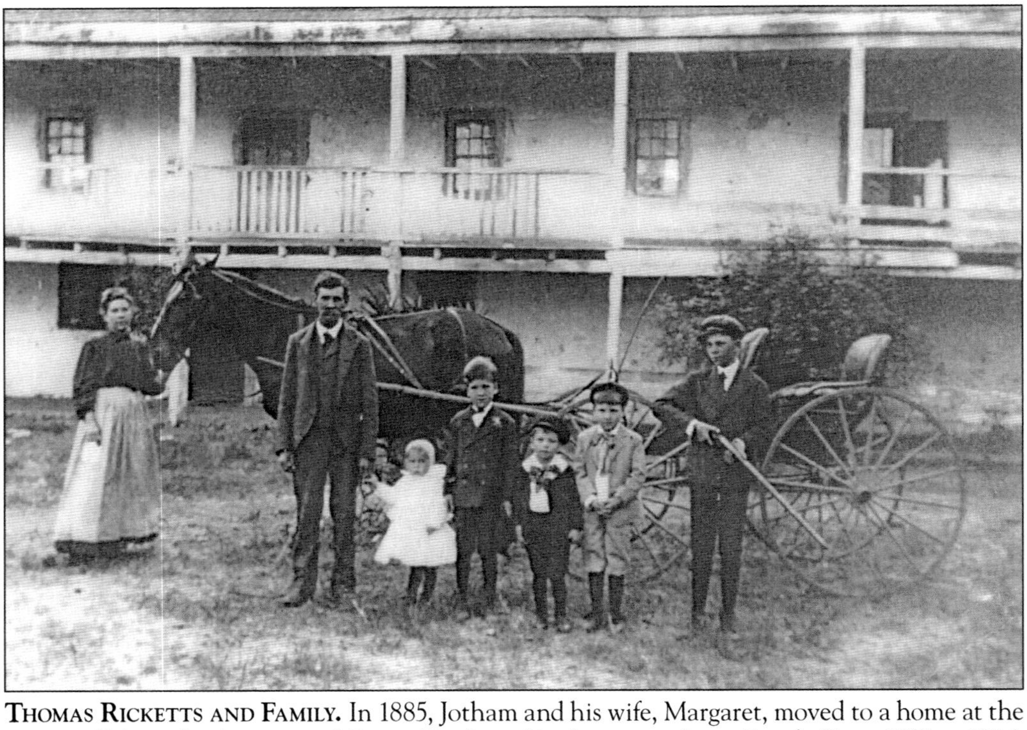

THOMAS RICKETTS AND FAMILY. In 1885, Jotham and his wife, Margaret, moved to a home at the corner of Magnolia Avenue and Ocean Boulevard in downtown Long Beach. From 1898 to 1906, William Boyle and his son Johnny lived at the rancho, operating a dairy with 150 cows and five to six milkers. Thomas Ricketts and his family lived there from 1908 to 1910. (RLC.)

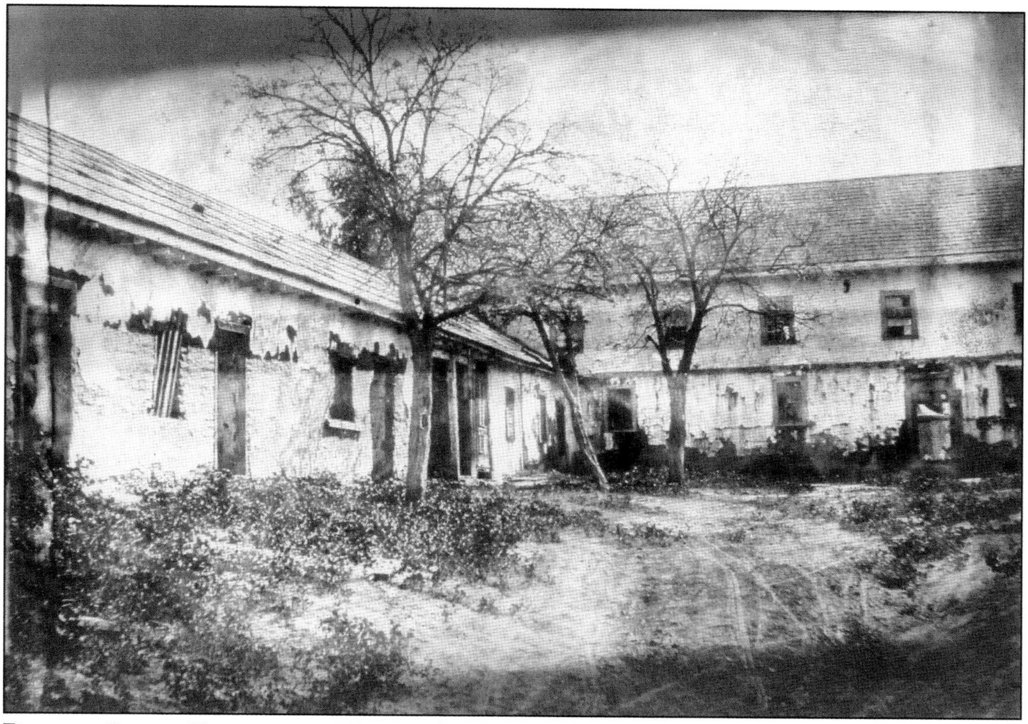

Rancho Inner Courtyard. The rancho was not well maintained during the succession of tenants. Occupancy by the Ricketts family was followed by the Rosales family, the Lerg family, the Coronado family, and a number of boarders. This c. 1905 photograph shows how the inner courtyard of the ranch house had deteriorated. (RLC.)

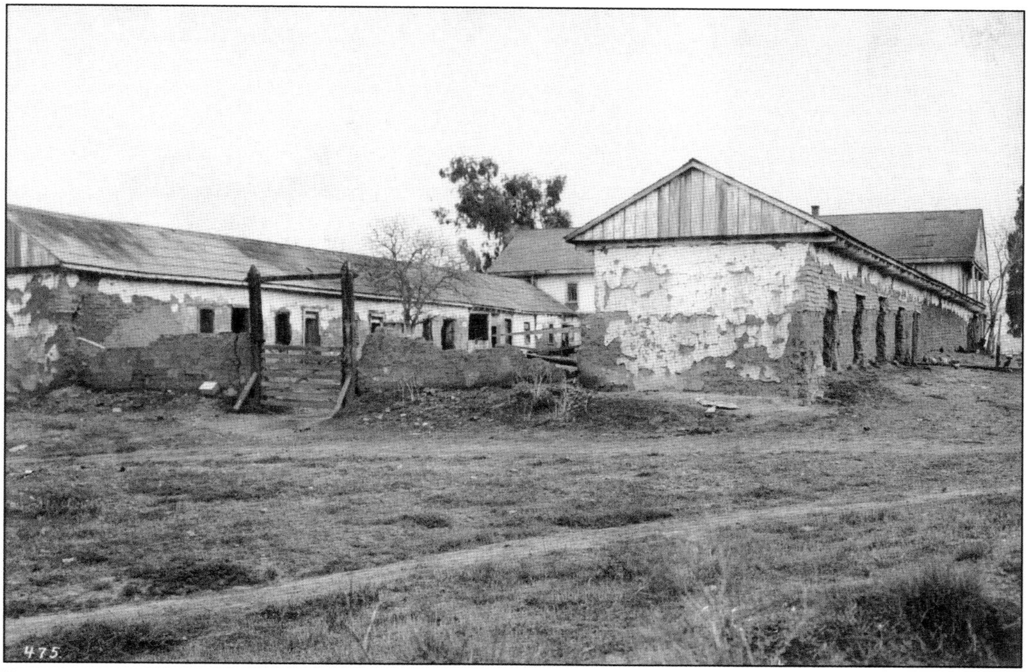

Deteriorated Adobe. This photograph, believed to have been taken around 1915, shows the deteriorating condition of the adobe during its tenant period. (RLC.)

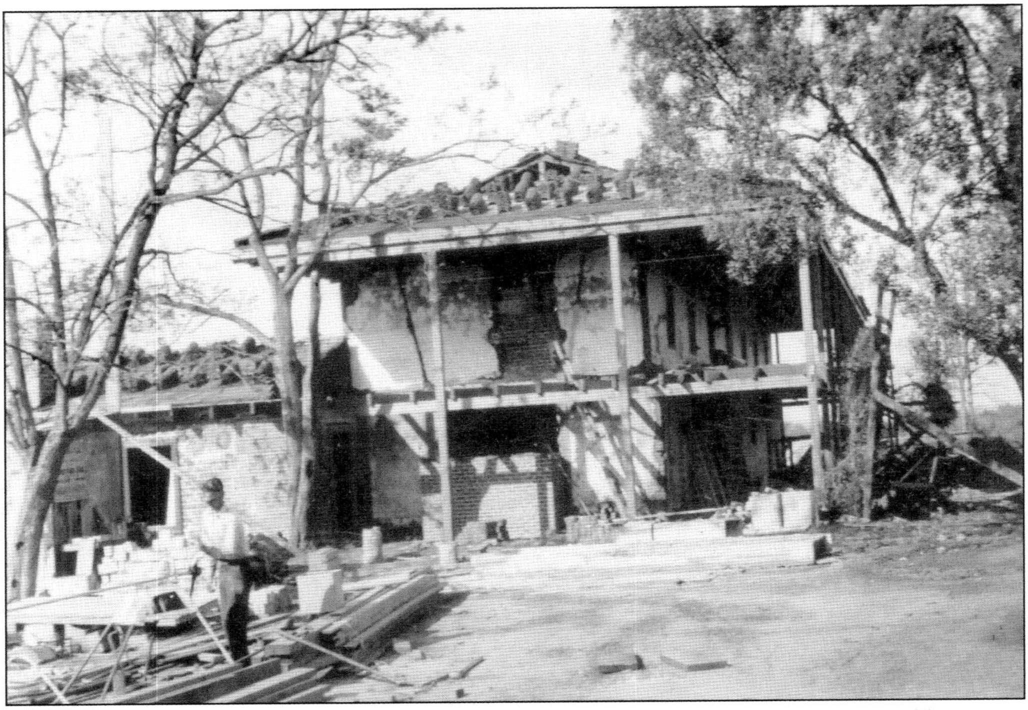

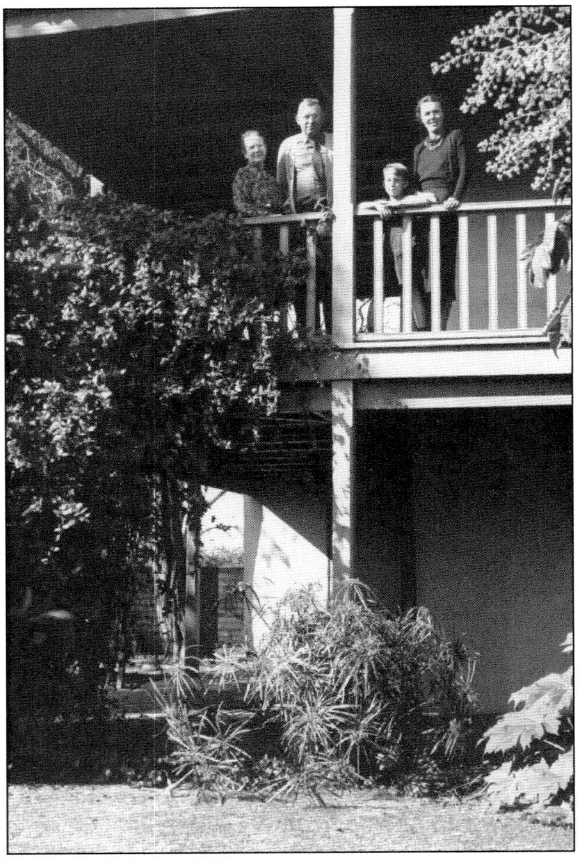

Rancho Renovation. In 1930, the Jotham Bixby company sold the rancho, along with 4.7 acres, to Llewellyn Bixby Sr. for $1. Bixby contracted with C.T. McGrew & Sons and architect Kenneth Wing for a restoration plan. The design combined elements of the original Monterey Colonial with a simplified Mission Revival style. Ralph D. Cornell, a well-known landscape architect, was retained to design the gardens. (RLC.)

Bixby Family Members. Llewellen Bixby Sr. moved into the rancho with his wife, Avis, and his son Llewellyn Jr. in March 1931. Pictured from left to right are Avis Bixby, Llewellen Bixby Sr., Paul H. Dudley Jr., and Avis Bixby Dudley. Llewellen Bixby Sr. and Avis lived in the house until Llewellen's death in 1942. (RLC.)

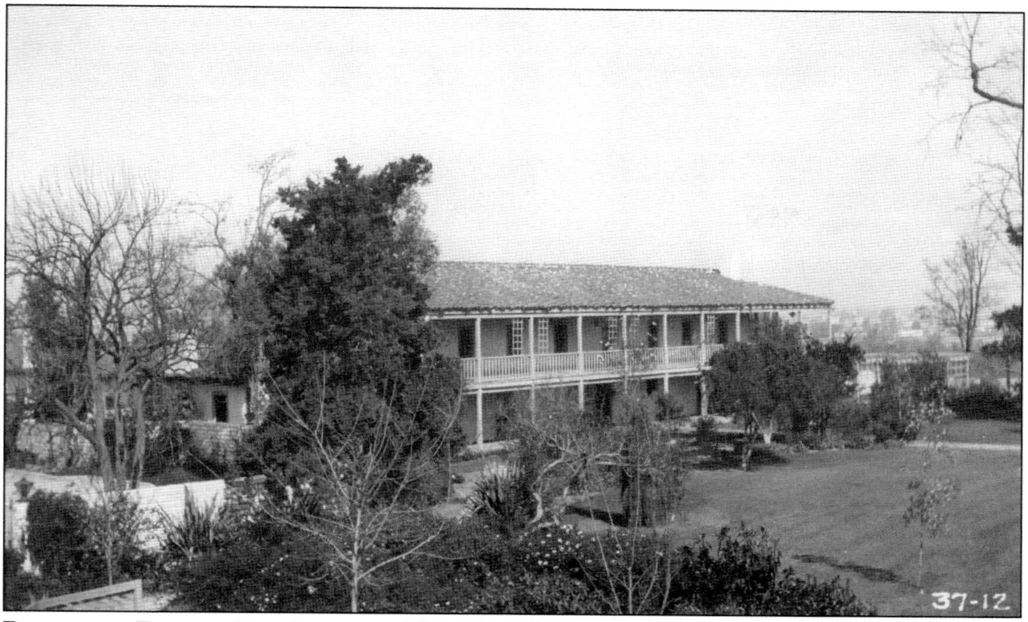

Renovated Rancho Los Cerritos. This 1934 photograph by Daniel Cathcart was part of the Historical American Building (HABS) survey undertaken by the Department of the Interior. In 1943, the City of Long Beach began efforts to purchase the rancho as a historic site, library, and park. The sale was completed in September 1956 for $82,400. In October 1970, Rancho Los Cerritos was designated as a National Historic Landmark. (RLC.)

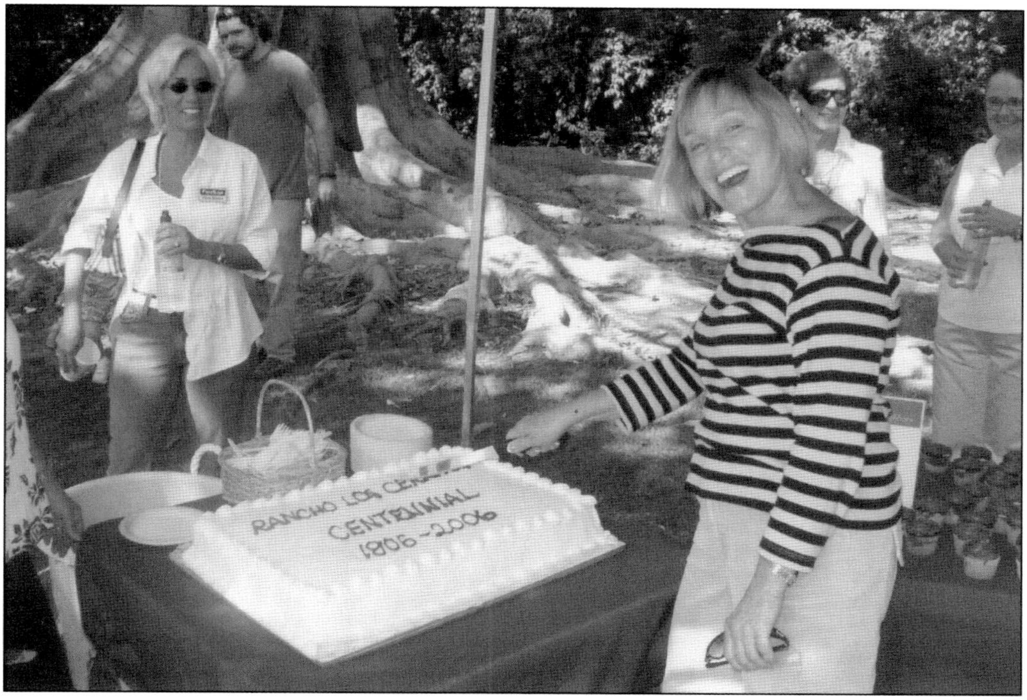

Los Cerritos Centennial. Long Beach City councilwoman Rae Gabelich cuts the cake at the 100th anniversary of the Los Cerritos neighborhood in 2006. The event attracted over 300 residents to the rancho for neighborhood tours and history-themed booths. (RLC.)

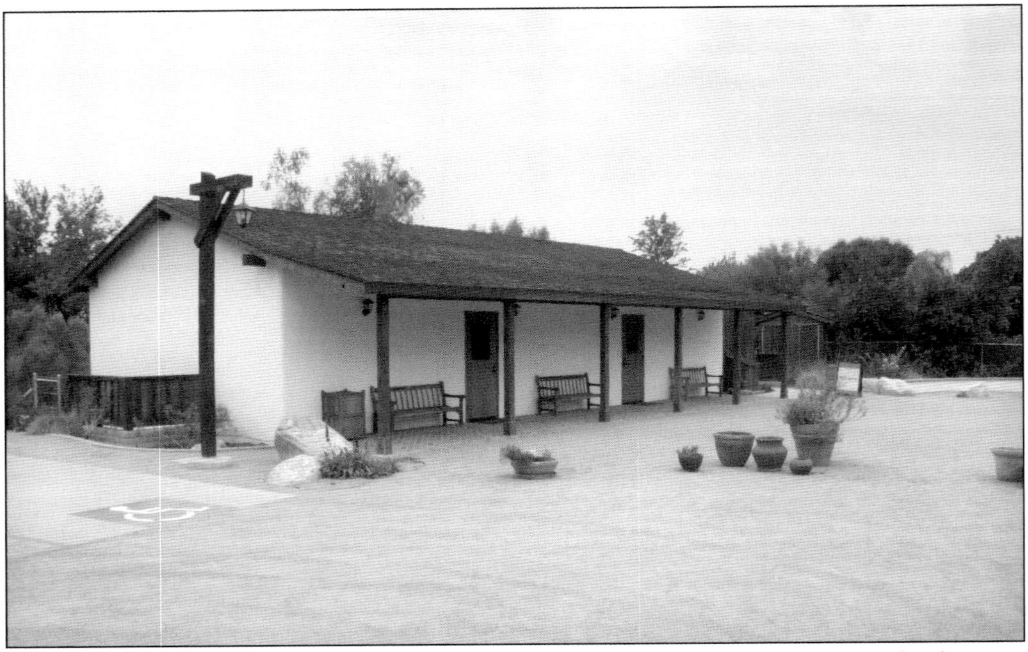

Visitor Center. A 25-year master plan prepared in 1999 serves as a guide for the site's development and interpretation to enhance the visitor experience. Phase II of the plan included the construction of a visitor center, modeled on the two-room adobe structure built at Rancho Los Cerritos by Guillermo and Manuela Cota around 1835. The center opened in 2012. (Courtesy of John Mulvey.)

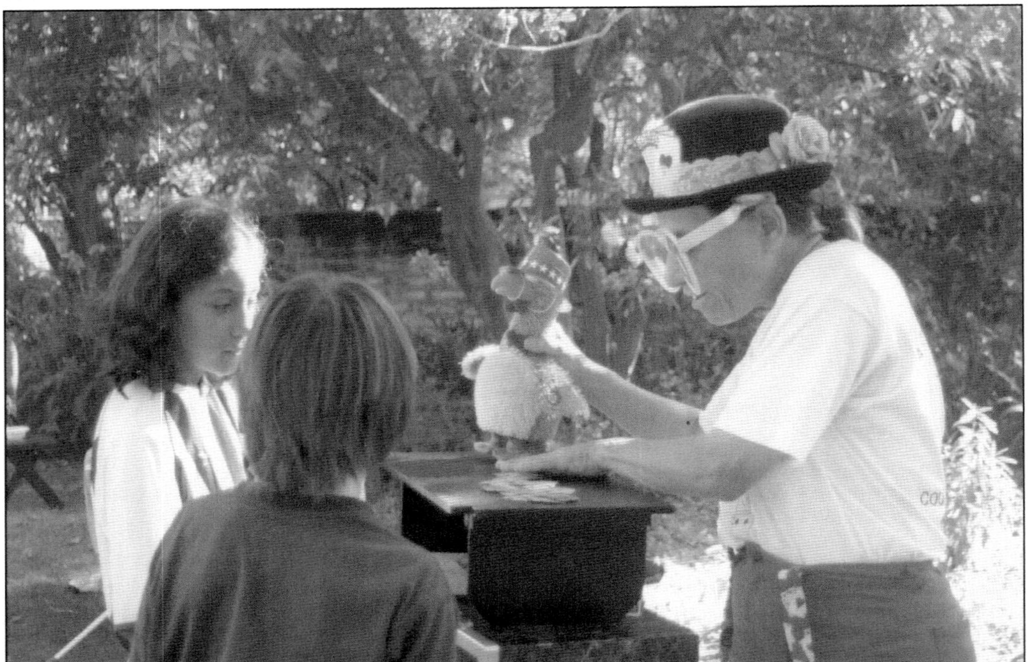

Neighborhood Activities. Today, Rancho Los Cerritos is a center of activity for Los Cerritos and all of Long Beach. Marcia Lee Harris, a rancho volunteer and author of *Fanny Bixby Spencer, Long Beach's Firebrand*, shares magic tricks with young visitors. Harris also plays the role of Fanny Bixby Spencer in reenactment performances. (RLC.)

Two

Early Residents in the Cerritos Colony and 1906 Subdivision

Jotham Bixby began selling off small ranch lots for the establishment of a colony in 1875. The Cerritos Colony, or the Willows, became a self-sufficient farming community comprising approximately 20 families. In 1912, a *Daily Telegram* reporter visited Los Cerritos and described a "5 acre fairyland" created by Samuel and Edna Lasell, who turned a barley field into land yielding full-grown pepper trees, black acacias, oranges, and apples in a mere three years. The Lasell home was called an example of the possibilities of home life in Los Cerritos. The 1910 census lists Mr. Lasell on Perris Road (today's Santa Fe Avenue, the heart of the Cerritos Colony). For many, the lure of cement sidewalks and oiled streets was enticing, and by 1916, the Lasells, like other colonists, moved further north into the Los Cerritos subdivision. The 1906 subdivision offered large lots of 50-by-250-feet backing up to a 16-foot-wide alley. One of the first lots sold was to Mary Kent Vignes, wife of John Louis Vignes. Part of a well-known Los Angeles family, John Louis Vignes is the grandnephew of Don Luis Vignes, a French immigrant who developed the first commercial winery in Los Angeles and for whom Vignes Street in Los Angeles is named. John and Mary Vignes had five daughters. Although the Vignes family is not found in Los Cerritos today, the family had a major influence on the development of Los Cerritos. Oscar King, who operated the Cerritos adobe dairy, also became one of the first residents. The 1913 Long Beach directory lists Oscar and his brother Howard King as residents of the Cerritos tract, on the Pacific Electric right-of-way north of the Willowville station. Additional subdivisions were created by Jotham Bixby's daughter, Amelia Bixby, and the heirs of the George H. Bixby family in 1911 and 1912. The residents in the late 1920s can be found on a Krenek Investments map, along with census and voter registration data.

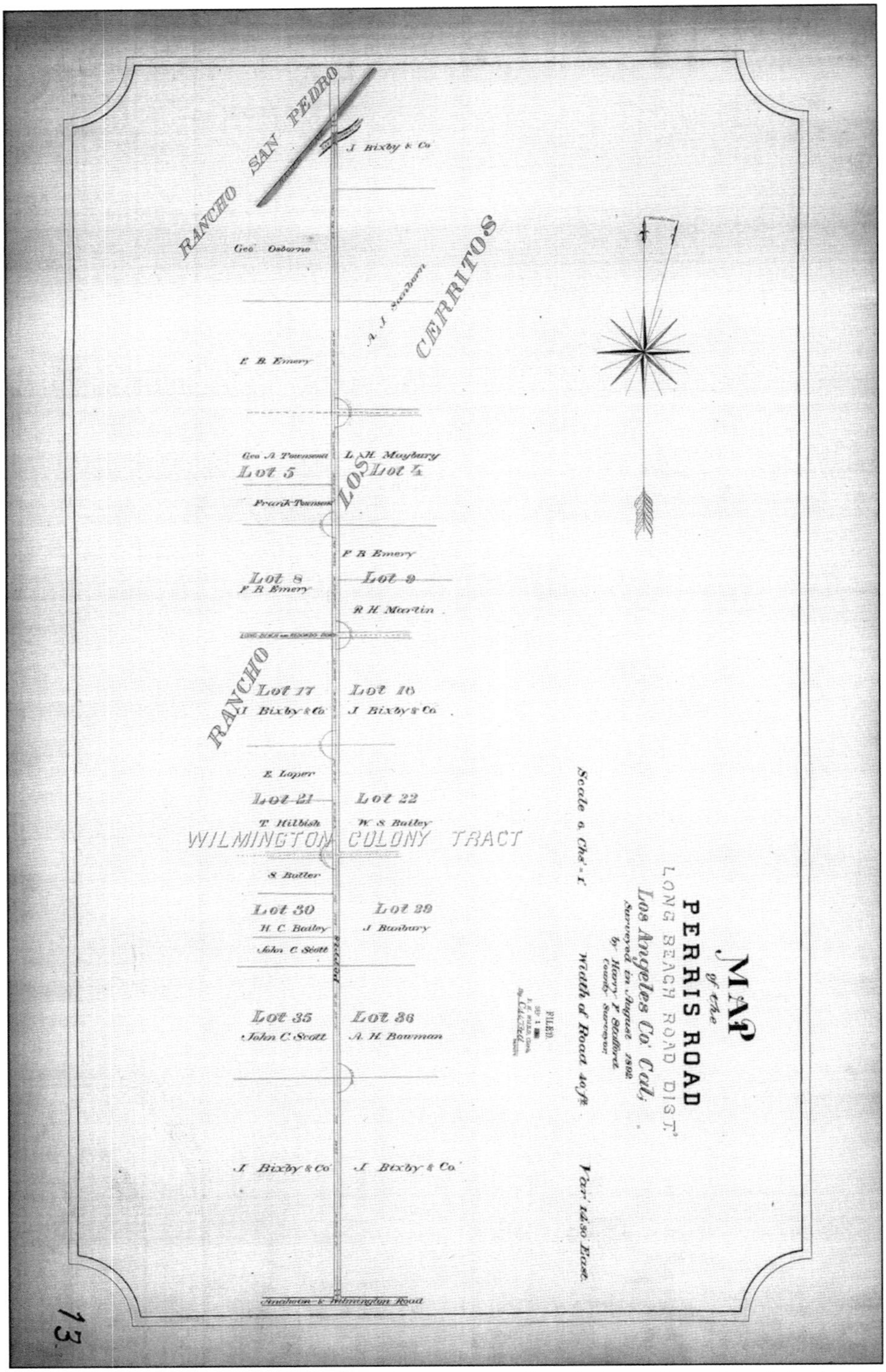

Perris Road Map. This 1892 map lists the owners of land along Perris Road (today's Santa Fe Avenue) in the Cerritos Colony. The Long Beach and Redondo Road is Willow Street, and the street between lots 21 and 30 is Hill Street. (Courtesy of Huntington Library, L.A. County Assessor's Road Map Collection.)

George Marion Teel. Teel (1854–1926) married Mary McCoy in 1885 at the Methodist Episcopal Church in Cerritos Colony. He later affiliated with the Holiness Church and was assigned responsibility for a tent, where he preached at camp meetings in the colony. He died a member of the Church of Nazarene.

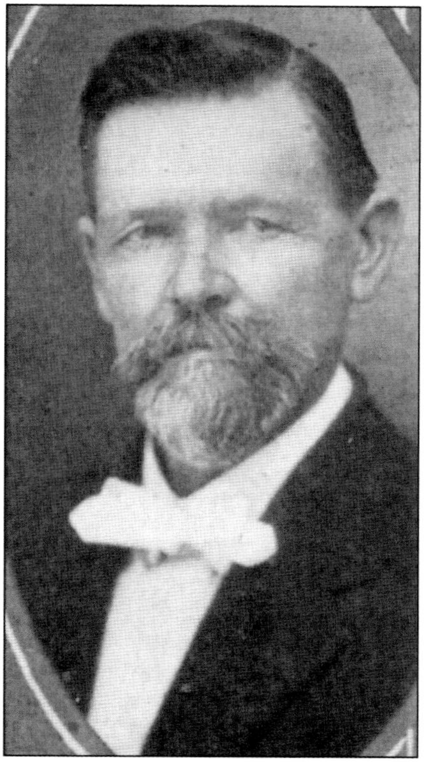

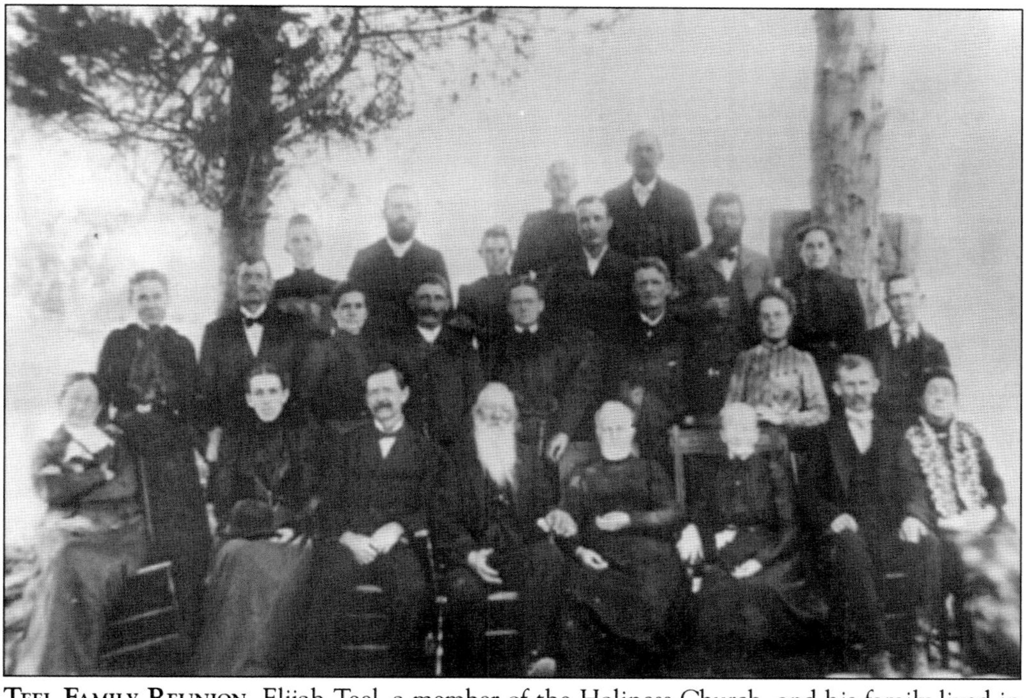

Teel Family Reunion. Elijah Teel, a member of the Holiness Church, and his family lived in the Cerritos Colony in the late 1870s and 1880s. This photograph shows the Teel family reunion in 1902. Elijah Teel is seated in the center with the long white beard. To his right is his wife, Martha. On his left is his son George Marion Teel. (Courtesy of Sherri Lentz.)

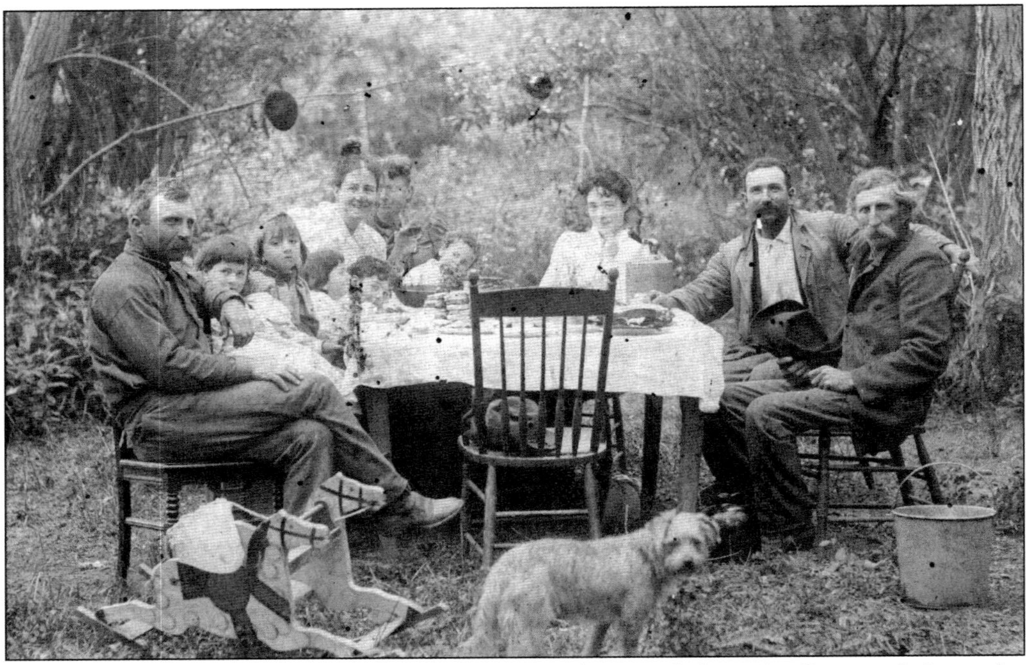

Picnic in the Ranch in the Willows. This 1897 photograph from the Cerritos Colony, also known as the Willows, includes, from left to right, ? Harris (a neighbor), Harris's two daughters, Mary Kent Vignes with her three daughters, Miss Lester (nanny), Amy Marcellus (Mary's sister), John Louis Vignes, and ? McQuillus (ranch hand). (Courtesy of Ellen Collins.)

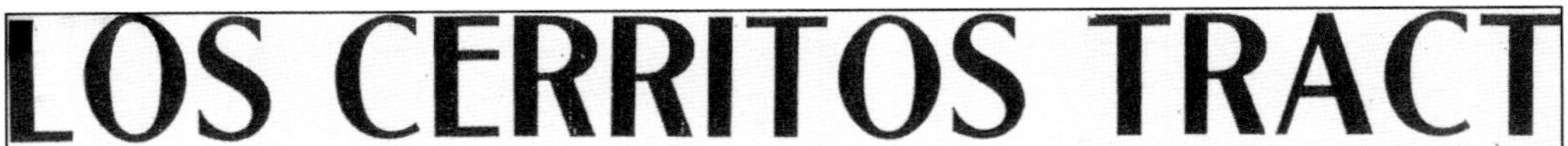

LOS CERRITOS TRACT

The New Subdivision Beautiful Just Opened

Ideally located on high ground with magnificent panorama of mountains, city and sea, Los Cerritos will logically become the place for fine homes in Long Beach. Its superior natural advantages and strategic location assure its future.

We want you to see it now. Arrange to go out with us. Buyers who want the best home site for their money will come in scores. YOU should be among the number and give Los Cerritos Tract your serious consideration.

A Wilshire District of Surpassing Beauty

LB. COLL

IMPROVEMENTS—Los Cerritos Tract is to be highly improved. The owner, George H. Bixby, has devoted much energy to seeing that nothing but the highest and best should enter into the development work. Street work, curbs and sidewalks are partially completed; water is on the tract; gas and electricity are soon to be put in. Ornamental shrubbery, including palms, pepper trees and acacias will adorn certain parts of the tract and be a distinctive feature of this subdivision.

CAR SERVICE—Los Cerritos Tract is on both the Los Angeles-Long Beach and Huntington Beach lines. Cars make regular stops. The station on the property is only a few minutes' ride from the heart of the business district and a short ride from Los Angeles. Business men, professional men and men of wealth and culture will find Cerritos most accessible. The Long Beach-Los Angeles Boulevard and Whittier Boulevard can be used by automobilists.

Attractive Residences Planned

LONG BEACH PUBLIC LIBRARY

Building is getting under way in Los Cerritos Tract. Some very attractive residence plans are now being prepared for immediate construction. These homes are to be of substantial construction and an ornament to the tract. Protective building restrictions call for nothing but harmony and beauty.

The moderate prices and satisfactory terms will particularly interest YOU. Only 6 per cent interest asked on deferred payments. Taking into consideration the improvements, the view, the location and the surroundings, every lot is priced way below its true value.

INTERESTING PRICES

In a short time, Long Beach will be built up solid to Los Cerritos. Prices now are not what they will be then. Your opportunity is now, before the complete up-building of the entire surrounding region. When fine lots like those in Los Cerritos Tract are scarce, something invariably happens to the price.

This community has a beautiful future before it. A future of upward and onward character which will carry the wise investor along with it. Don't wait! We will gladly take you out at any time.

Long Beach Improvement Co. — Corner First and Locust — Home Phone 710, Sunset 125

Long Beach, Cal.

C. H. WINDHAM — 127 East First Street — Sunset Phone 452, Home Phone 45

Long Beach Improvement Company Advertisement. This 1912 *Daily Telegram* advertisement for a lot in Los Cerritos notes that "protective building restrictions call for nothing but harmony and beauty." Early deeds not only limited ethnicity of purchasers and residents but also required a dollar amount be spend on the home's construction. Charles H. Windham was the sales agent taking visitors from Long Beach to visit Los Cerritos.

THE LITTLE CLUB. Women on this roster came together in 1930 to create the Little Club to alleviate some of the suffering the country experienced in 1930. Half of the women on this list were part of the "Over Here Girls" who made surgical dressings and raised funds for the Red Cross during World War I. The Little Club made infant layettes and was active until 1965.

MEMBERS

FRANCES SINGLETTON ABLE	MRS. MILTON MCGREW
MRS. C. B. BELLOWS	MRS. FREEMAN MCKENZIE
MRS. JOHN BOUL	MRS. C. C. MCWHINNEY
MRS. HARRY BUFFUM	MRS. RUTH CRAIG MERRELL
MRS. JOHN CLOCK	MRS. WILLIAM NESTLE
MRS. JAMES CRAIG	MISS SUSANNE NETTLEMAN
MRS. JOHN CRAIG II	MRS. W. M. REAGAN
MRS. HOWARD DEEMS	MRS. DAVE SMITH
MRS. HENRY DUNN	MRS. LESLIE STILL
MRS. KEITH ENLOE	MRS. PHIL SWAFFIELD
MRS. L. T. EDWARDS	MRS. ROLAND SWAFFIELD
MRS. WILLIAM GORDON	MRS. GLEN TRESSLAR
MRS. NED GRIFFIN	MRS. LAURENCE UPDIKE
MRS. ATALA HANBERY	MRS. HERBERT WAITE
MRS. PERCY HIGHT	MRS. MATE WALKER
MRS. GREGG HOSKINS	MRS. MAX WALLACE
MRS. W. H. HOSKING	MRS. GEORGE WALDVOGEL
MRS. KARL KUMPE	MRS. ROBERT WILCOX
MRS. HAL MCGREW	MISS HAZEL WORK

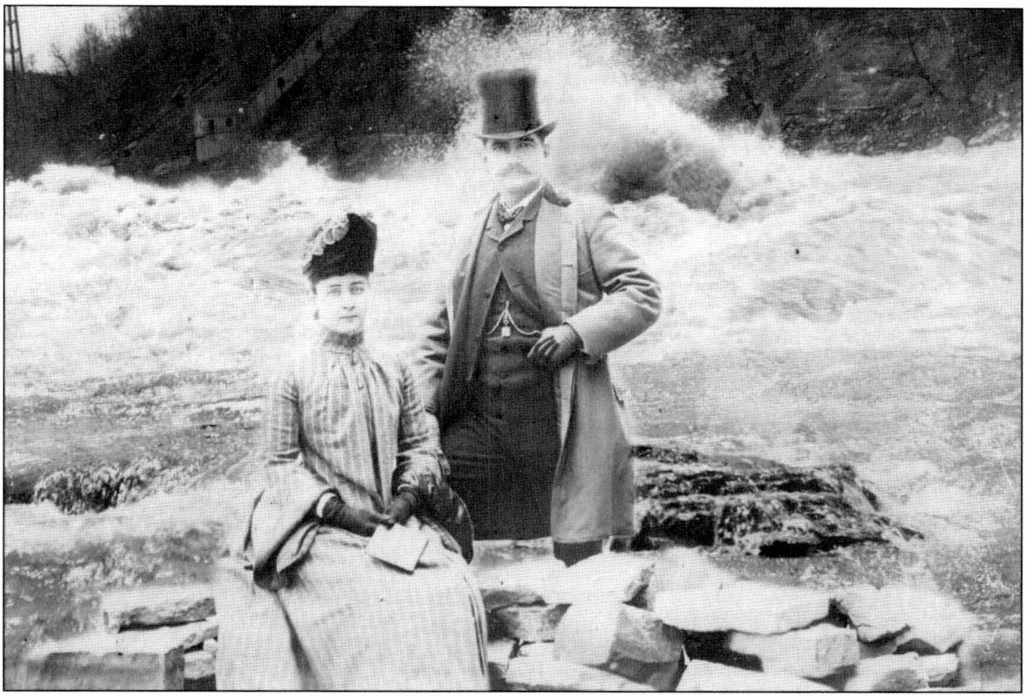

MARY KENT MARCELLUS AND JOHN LOUIS VIGNES. The Vigneses moved into the Los Cerritos subdivision in 1910. They were civic leaders instrumental in the founding of the Los Cerritos and Dominquez School Districts. (Courtesy of Ellen Collins.)

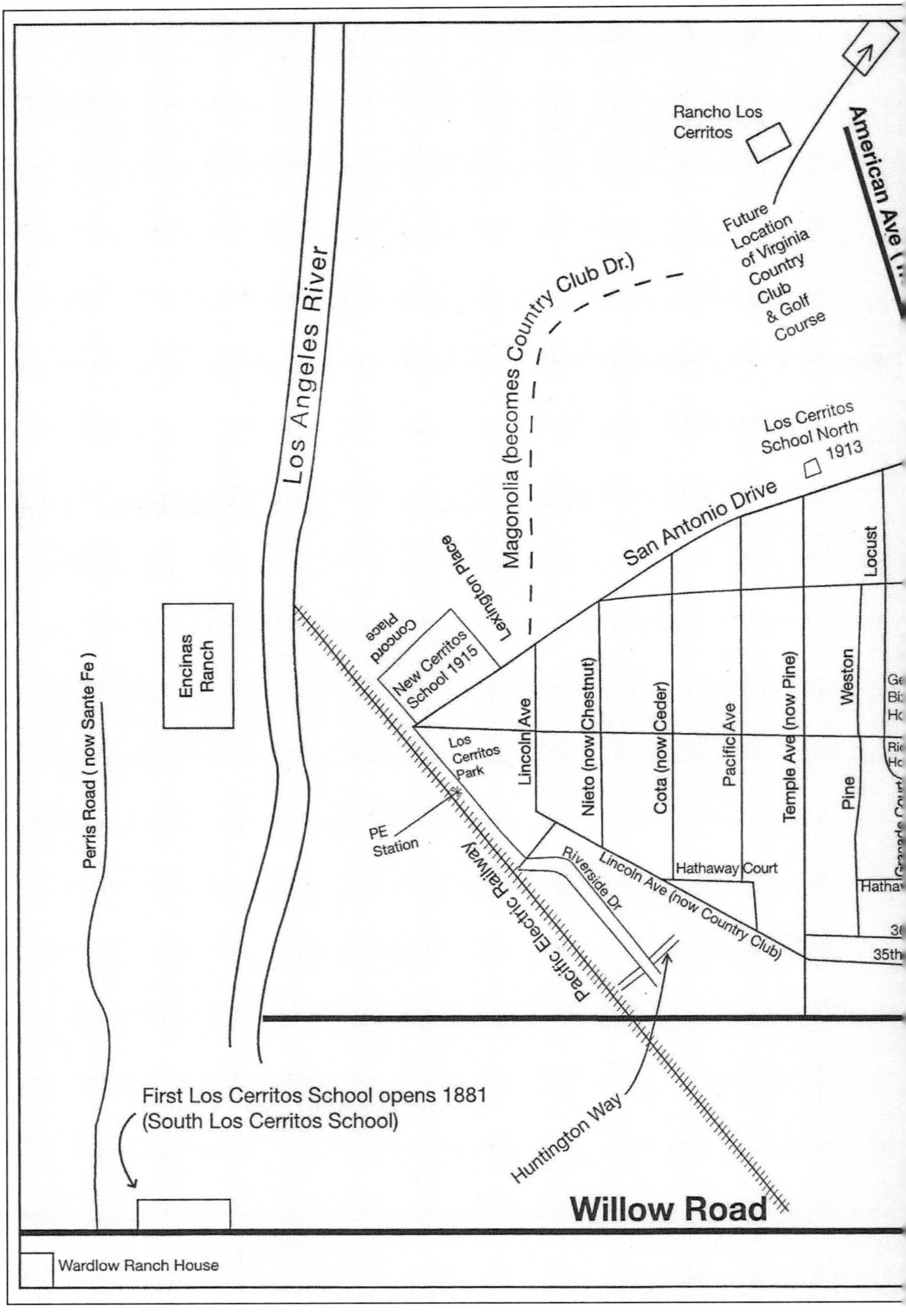

Rancho Los Cerritos
American Ave
Future Location of Virginia Country Club & Golf Course
Magonolia (becomes Country Club Dr.)
Los Angeles River
Los Cerritos School North 1913
San Antonio Drive
Locust
Lexington Place
Concord Place
New Cerritos School 1915
Encinas Ranch
Perris Road (now Sante Fe)
Los Cerritos Park
Lincoln Ave
Nieto (now Chestnut)
Cota (now Ceder)
Pacific Ave
Temple Ave (now Pine)
Weston
Pine
PE Station
Pacific Electric Railway
Riverside Dr
Lincoln Ave (now Country Club)
Hathaway Court
35th
Huntington Way
First Los Cerritos School opens 1881 (South Los Cerritos School)
Willow Road
Wardlow Ranch House

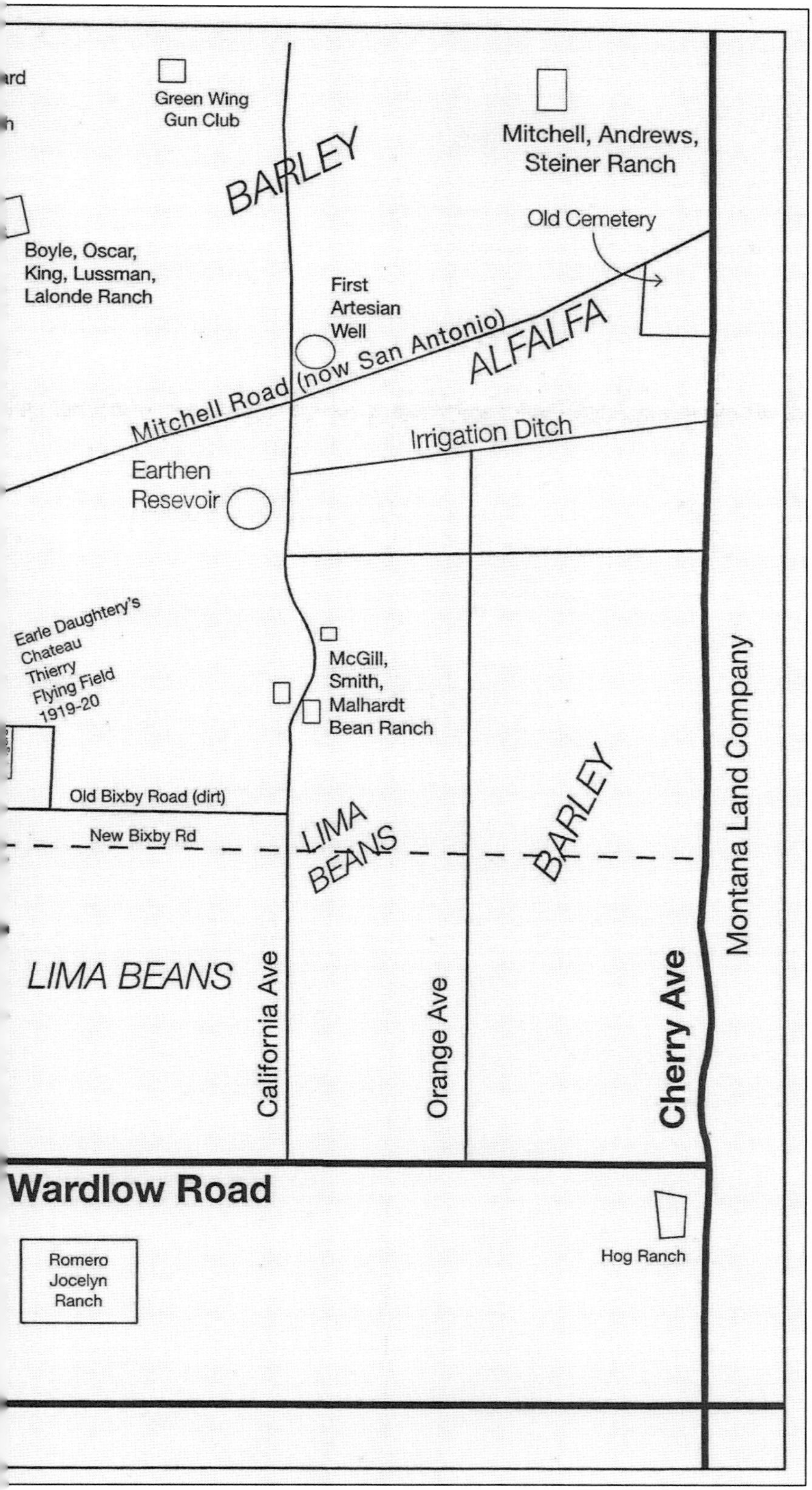

MAP OF LOS CERRITOS BEFORE 1920. This map, compiled from several made by Loretta Berner, with some revisions by the author, identifies the original street names in the Los Cerritos subdivision along with the surrounding ranches, and it illustrates the proximity to the Cerritos Colony. The locations of the George H. Bixby and Richard Bixby homes are also shown. (Map illustrated by Joseph Maldonado.)

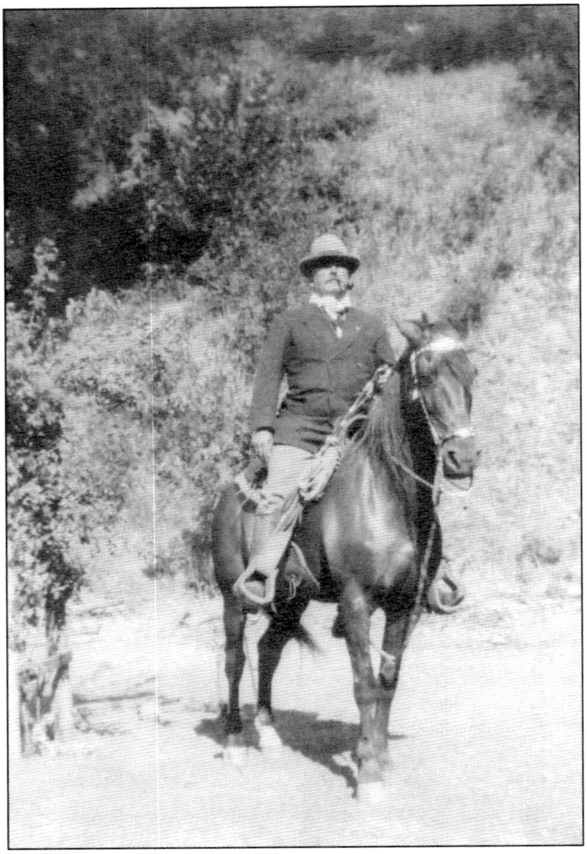

John Louis Vignes. Vignes was a rancher and a dairyman. He also served on the grounds committee for the 1910 Dominguez air meet, along with Dick Ferris, a Los Angeles promoter, W.K. Bixby, William Humphreys, and Arthur W. Kinney. (Courtesy of Ellen Collins.)

Vital Vignes Family. This c. 1875 photograph shows Vital Ferdinand Vignes, the father of John Louis, and his wife, Emma Lecroq, and their children. In the first row are Julia (left) and Ferdinand (in Vital's lap). Standing in the second row are, from left to right, Adella, John Louis, and Helen. Upon hearing of the birth of his son John's fifth daughter, Vignes wrote, lamenting, "all hope was lost to have a descendent of the Vital Vignes family." (Courtesy of Ellen Collins.)

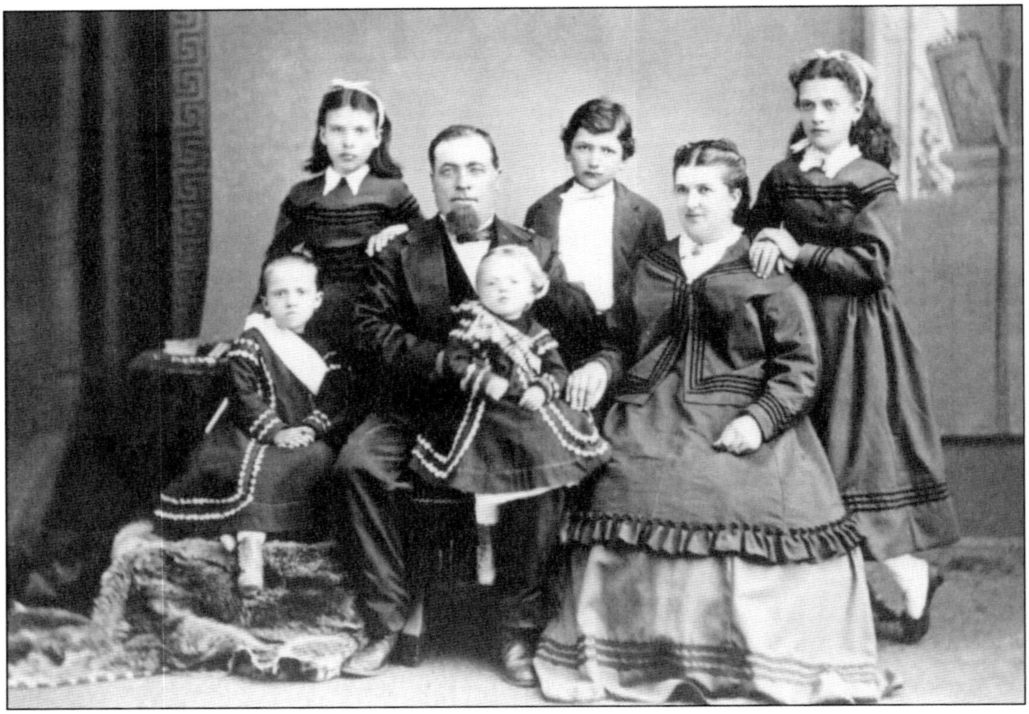

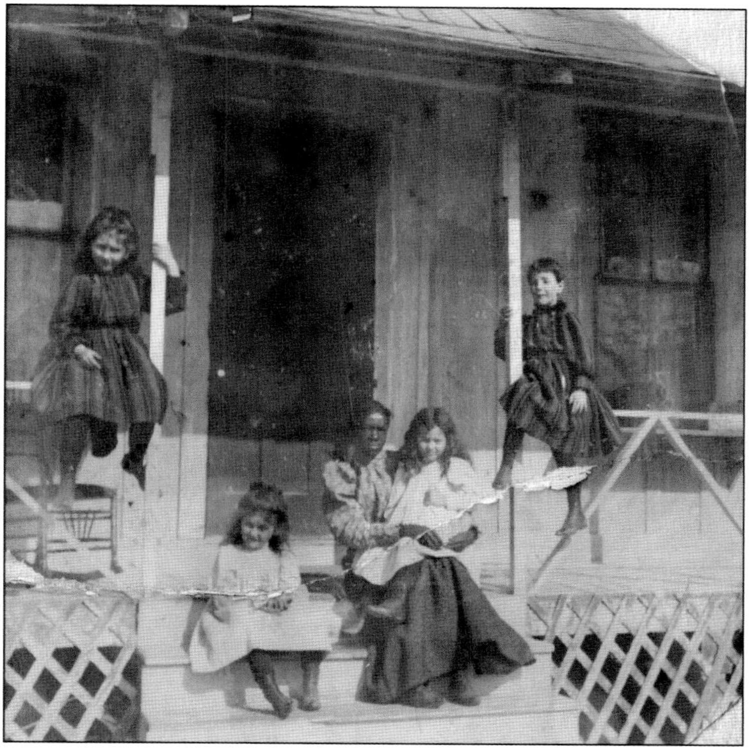

Vignes Children. This c. 1896 photograph of the children of John and Mary Vignes is labeled "Rancho Los Cerritos," although the exact location is uncertain. Shown here are, from left to right, Marguerite, Marie, Antoinette (in nanny's lap), and Edwine. (Courtesy of Ellen Collins.)

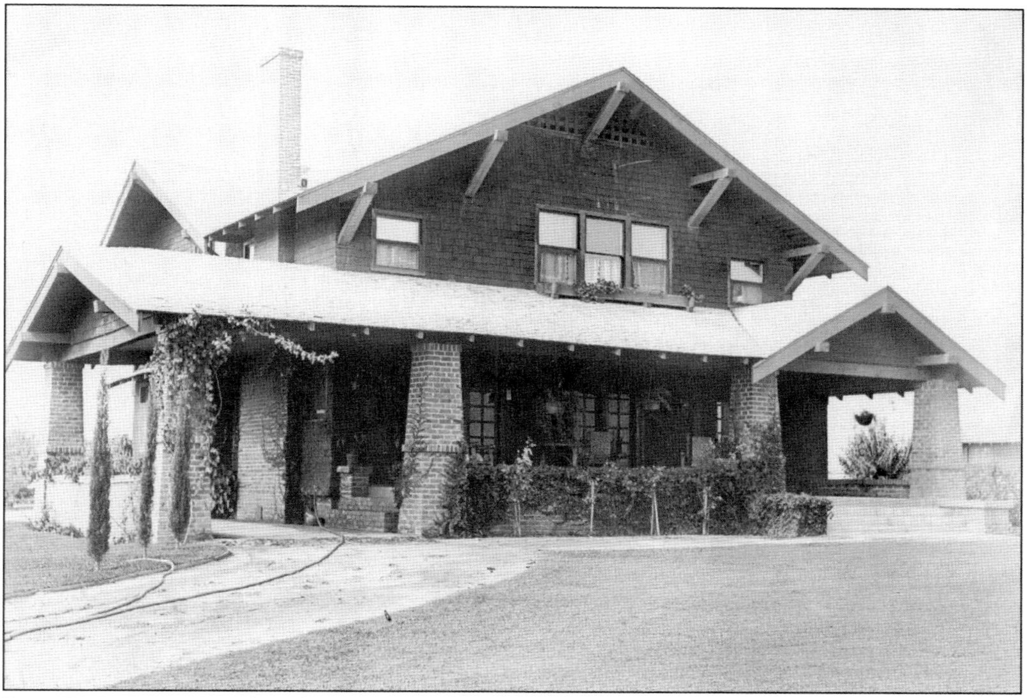

John Vignes Home. The John Vignes home was located at the southwest corner of Temple and Court Streets, which today would be Pine and Thirty-seventh Streets. The home was designed in the Maybeck style, after architect Bernard Maybeck. It was moved to 4045 Virginia Road and later demolished. This photograph was taken in 1910. (Courtesy of Ellen Collins.)

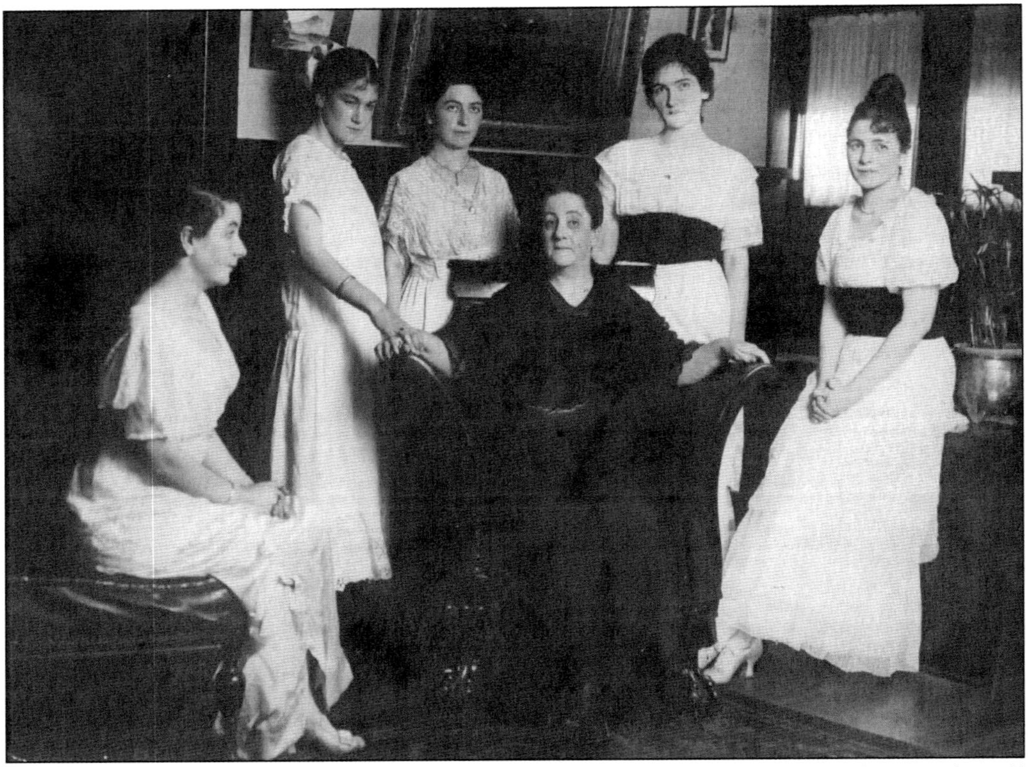

VIGNES DAUGHTERS. John and Mary Vignes had five daughters. Vignes was adamant that all his daughters be educated and that their spouses provide a proper home for them. Although the Vignes family name is no longer found in Long Beach, his daughter's families were active in civic affairs. Surrounding their mother, Mary, are, from left to right, Edwine, Amelia, Marguerite, Marie, and Antoinette. (Courtesy of Ellen Collins.)

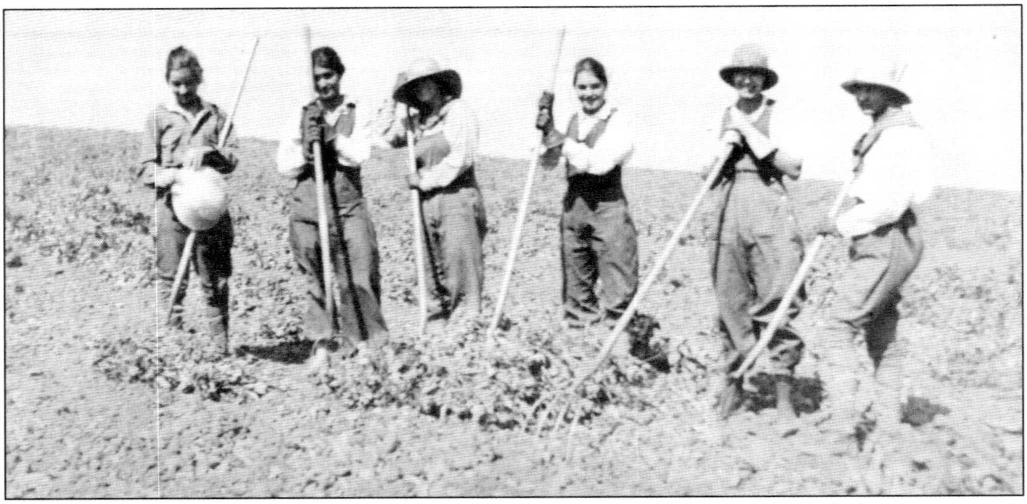

YOUNG WOMEN FARMWORKERS. A shortage of men during World War I to work the farms meant that young women from Los Cerritos and neighboring farms were "drafted" as farmworkers. Nicknamed "farmerettes," those pictured here in November 1918 are, from left to right, Lena Reuther, Dorothy Andrews, Amelia Vignes, Josephine Andrews, Mabel Shaw, and Florence Reuther. (RLC.)

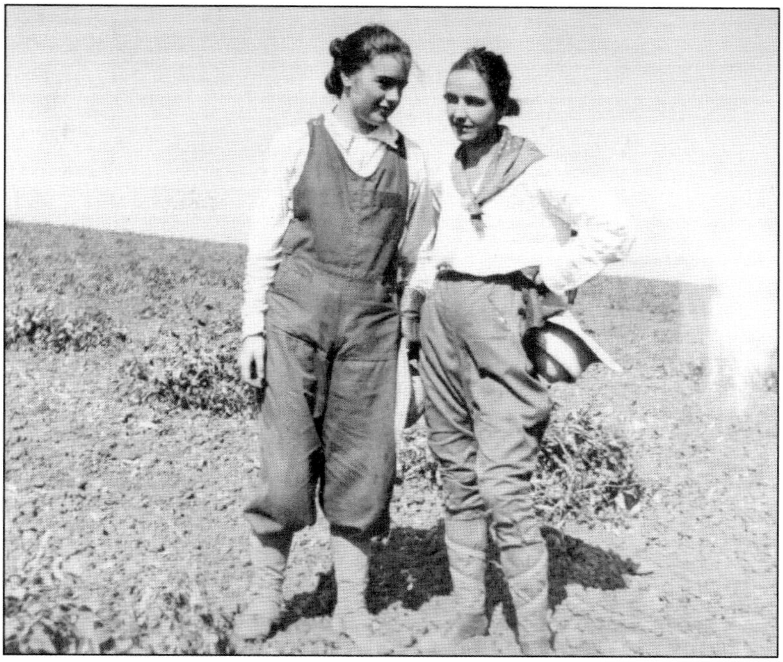

JOSEPHINE ANDREWS AND FLORENCE REUTHER. Boot-clad and with puttees (leather worn for protection on the legs), ranch hands Josephine Andrews (left) and Florence Reuther, married later to George Buehn, pose for a photograph. (RLC.)

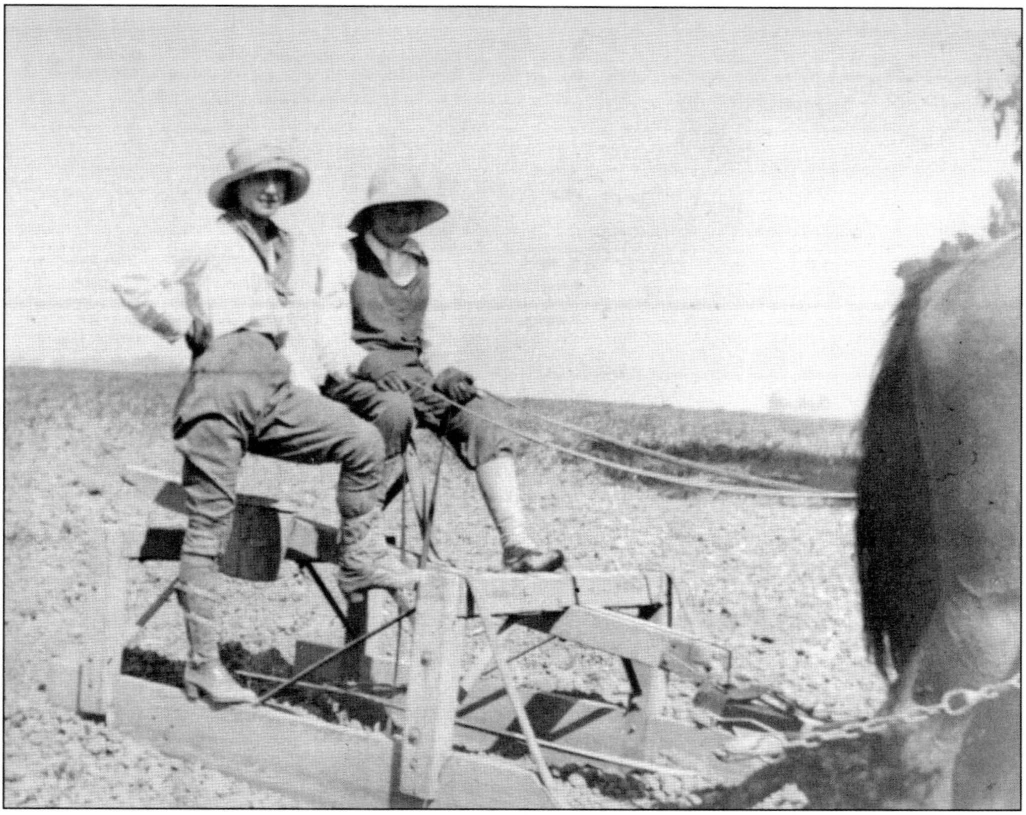

FLORENCE REUTHER AND AMELIA VIGNES. Florence Reuther (left) and Amelia Vignes pause during plowing. Josephine and Dorothy Andrews were the daughters of R. "Ray" Chester Andrews, who took over the operation of the Mitchell Ranch. (RLC.)

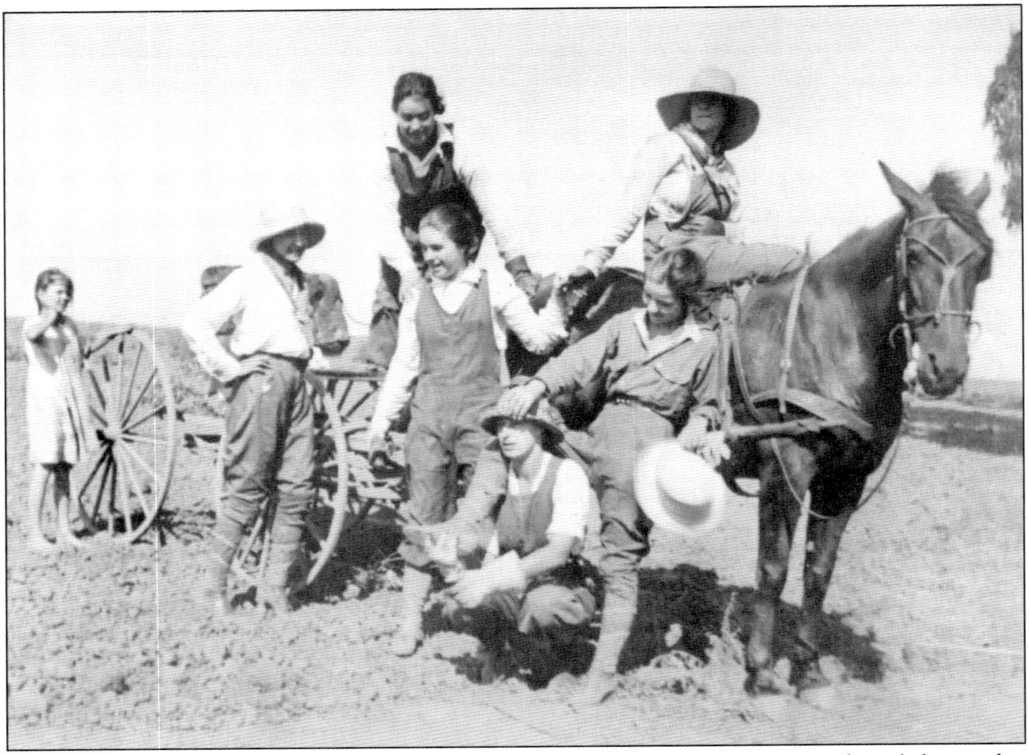

FARMERETTES WITH LORETTA BERNER. Taking a break at the water wagon are, from left to right, Loretta Berner, Amelia Vignes, Dorothy Andrews (on wagon), Josephine Andrews, Florence Reuther (crouching), Lena Reuther, and Mabel Shaw (on horseback). Future historian Berner, 10 years old, drove the water wagon with a 10-gallon milk can of drinking water. (RLC.)

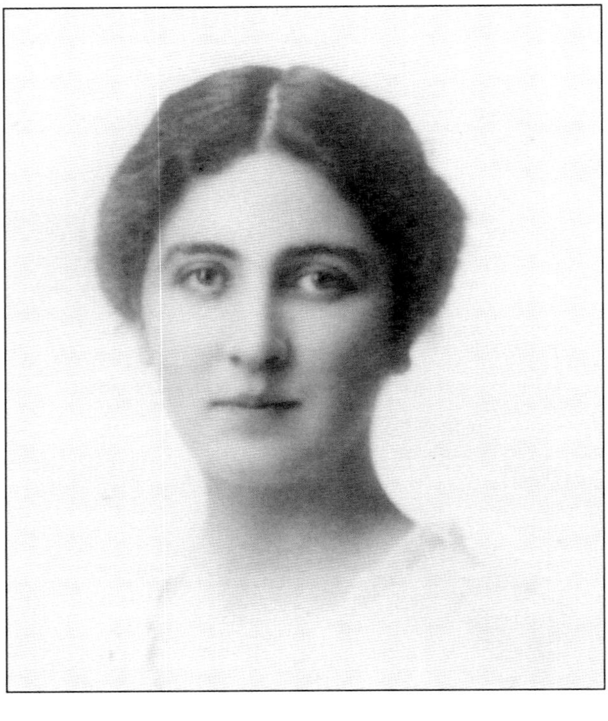

MARGUERITE VIGNES. Marguerite Vignes graduated from the University of Southern California College of Fine Arts in June 1911. She taught art and made greeting cards, often using homes in Los Cerritos as her subject matter. Her work was exhibited in Long Beach and Los Angeles. (LCS.)

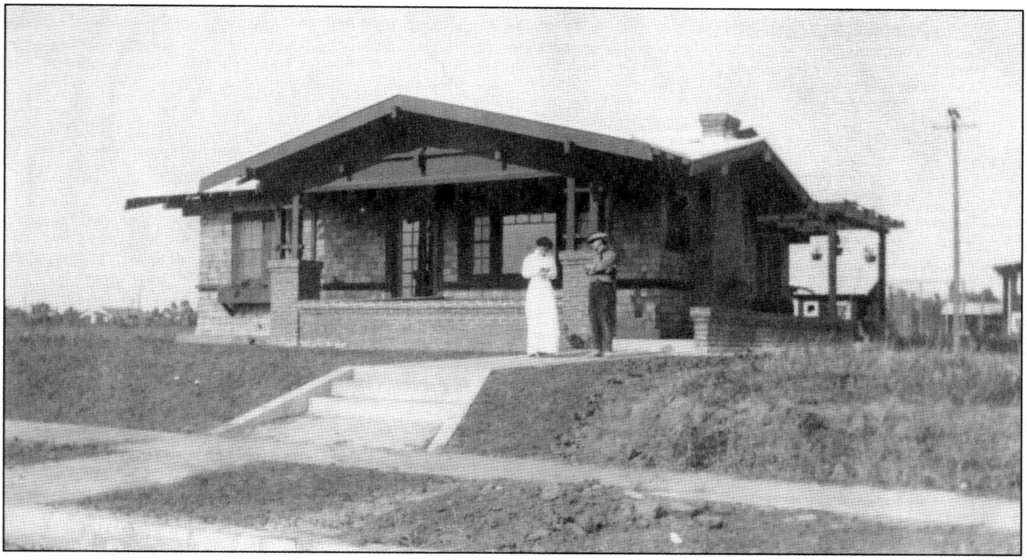

Walp Residence. Marguerite married Bertine James Walp, who built a home for his new wife in Los Cerritos at 3808 Cota Street (now Cedar Avenue), not far from her parents' home. The Craftsman-style, one-story home was constructed in 1914. When her husband, Bert, died in 1933, she became the director of arts and audio visuals for the Long Beach School District. (Courtesy of Ellen Collins.)

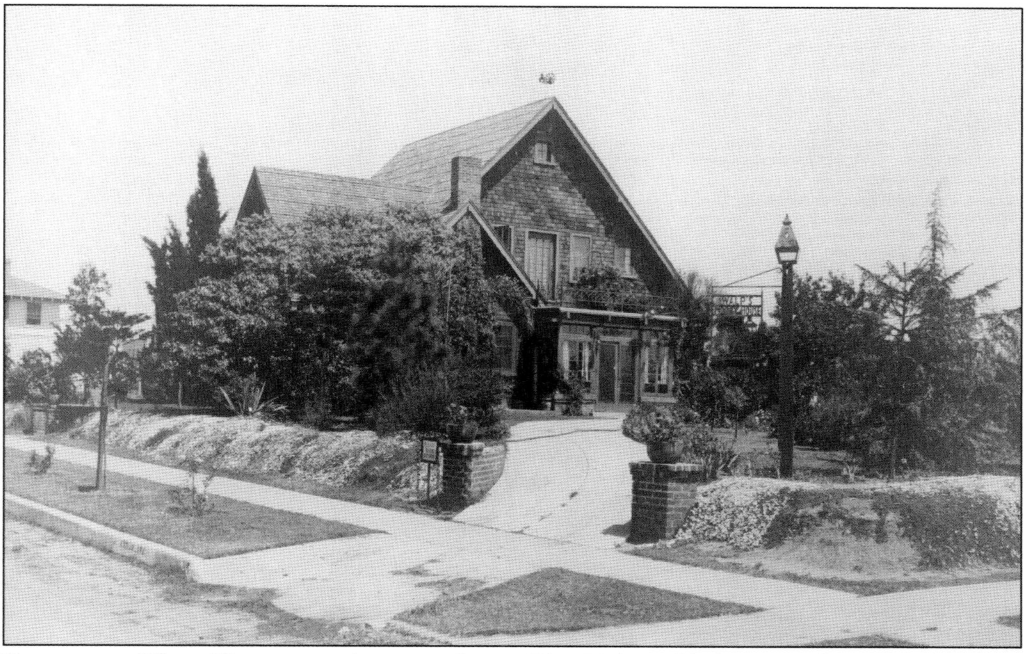

Remodeled Walp Home and Antique Shop. The Walps added a second story and started an antiques business, Hobby House, from their home. The sign is visible in the photograph, hanging from the lamppost. Their pursuit of early American furniture took them on numerous trips. The home is currently being restored by owners Maureen and Aaron Price. (Courtesy of Ellen Collins.)

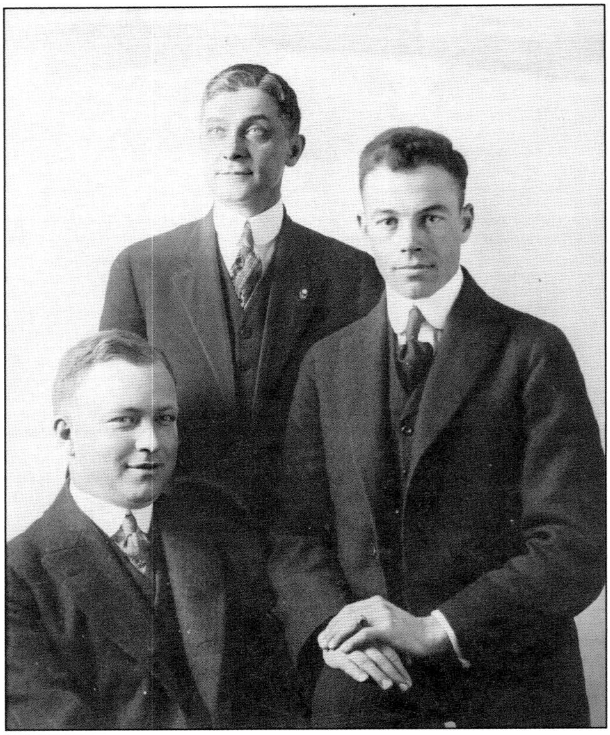

Walp, Reynolds & Dodd, Tailors. Posing here are, from left to right, Bert Dodd, Bert Walp, and Edward W. Reynolds. Together, they opened up a gentlemen's clothing business on West Third Street in downtown Long Beach. All three were associated with the Hansen clothing company at Pine Avenue and Third Street prior to striking out on their own. (Courtesy of Ellen Collins.)

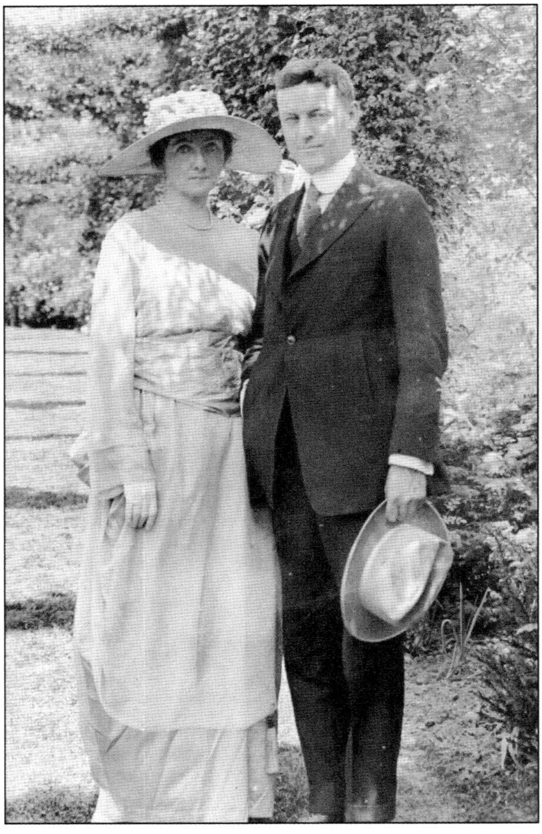

Marie Vignes and Frederick San Souci. Louis Vignes's daughter Marie was the first teacher at the "North" Los Cerritos School. The Los Angeles State Normal School Bulletin for 1914 lists Marie Kent Vignes as a graduate on June 26, 1913, of the General Professional Course. She married Frederick San Souci, who was killed in a car accident in 1947. Marie was injured but survived. She never remarried but continued to teach. (Courtesy of Ellen Collins.)

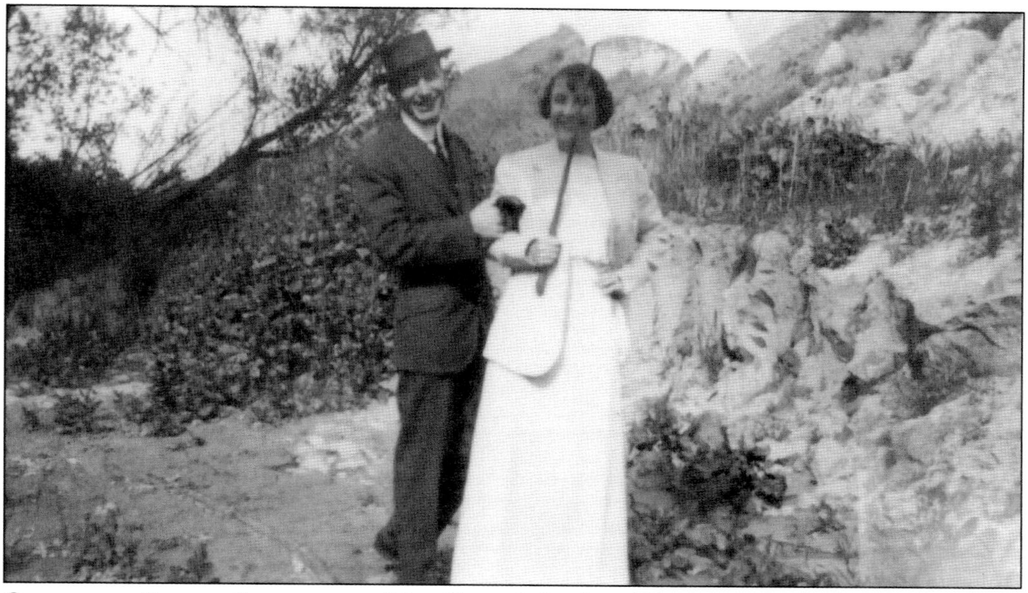

Oliver and Edwine Sweningsen. John Vignes's daughter Edwine married Oliver Sweningsen. Edwine graduated from the University of Southern California Conservancy of Music as a pianist. In 1907, Sweningsen and his family relocated to California, and his father operated a general store at Anaheim and American Avenue (now Long Beach Boulevard). Oliver worked as a laborer, then an electrician for Craig shipyard, before moving on to work for the Bell Telephone Company. This photograph was taken in the summer of 1914. (Courtesy of Ellen Collins.)

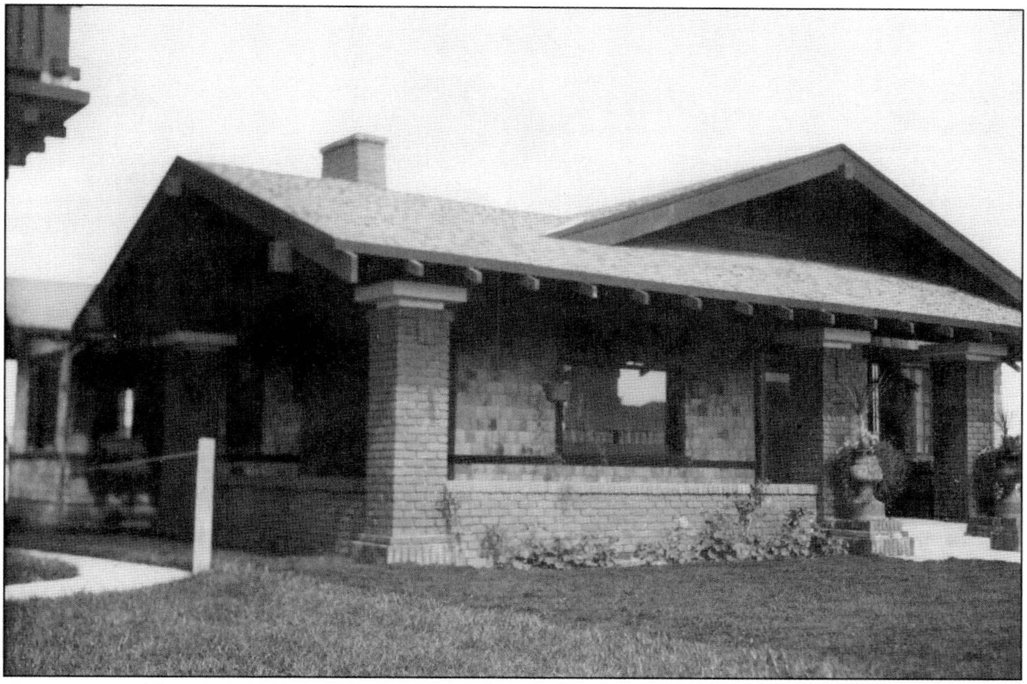

Sweningsen Home. The Sweningsens moved into their new home at 3819 Chestnut Avenue in 1914. The couple was married only four months after her sister Marguerite was wed. John Louis Vignes required that all prospective sons-in-law have a home, and this house is very similar to the Walp residence. (Courtesy of Kurt and Edwina Barats.)

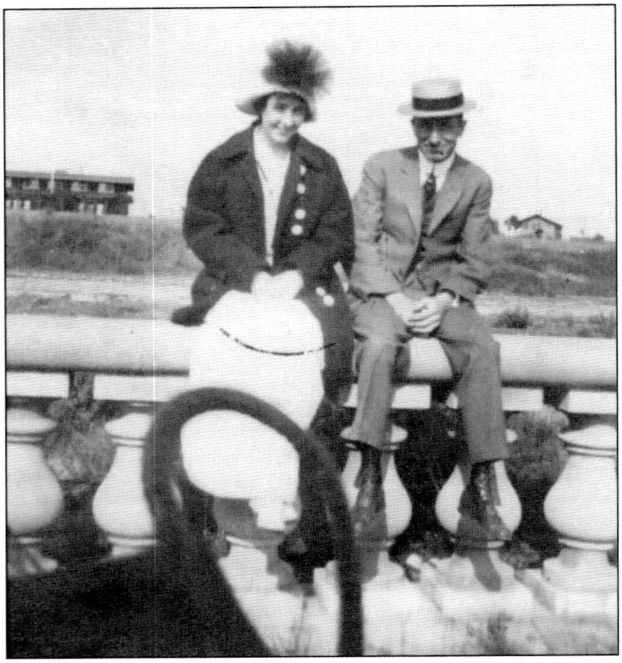

The Sweningsens at the Cerritos Station. Edwine and Oliver Sweningsen await a train at the Cerritos Station on the Pacific Electric line. The station adjoined the Cerritos Park on the west side. The steps that led down to the station still exist. In the background is the El Rodeo Club, which had a prominent location overlooking the park. (Courtesy of Kurt and Edwina Barats.)

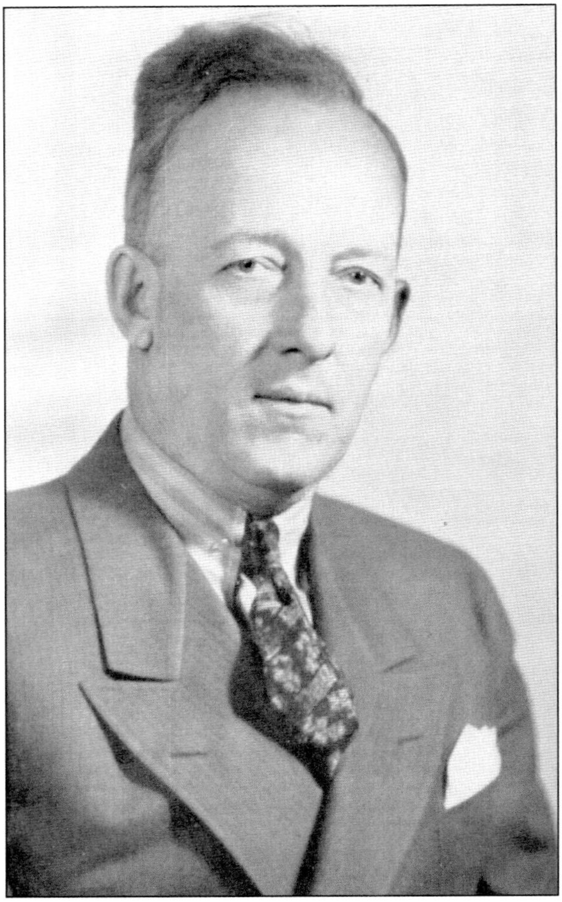

Will J. Reid. A prominent Los Cerritos resident was Will J. Reid, who provided insurance coverage for commercial fishing vessels before he invested in the Hancock Oil Company. A community leader and philanthropist, Reid was a hunter who became an avid conservationist and president of Ducks Unlimited. Reid published the history of the Los Cerritos Gun Club.

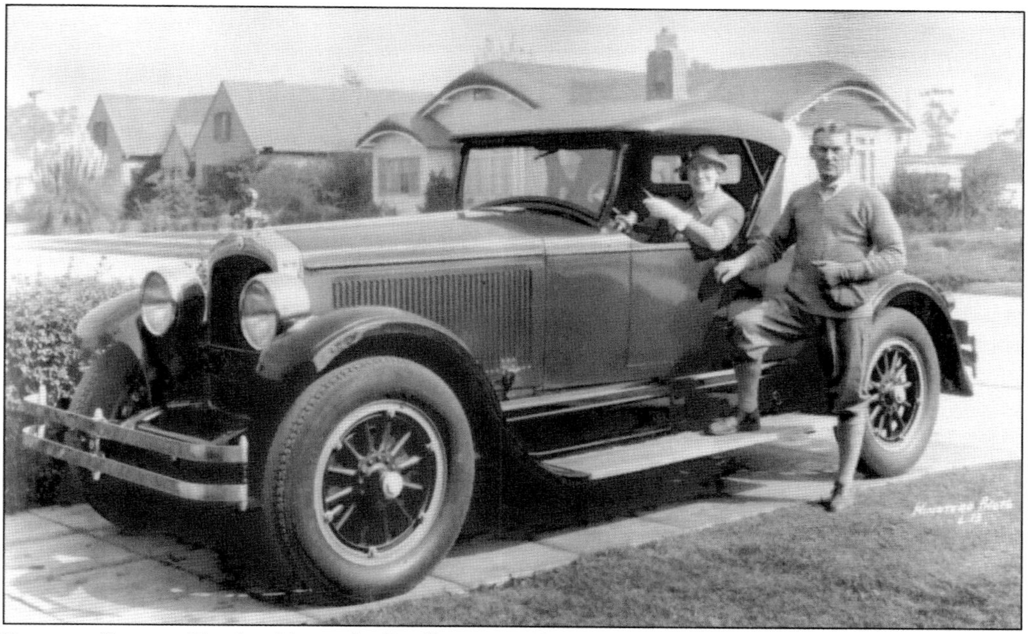

Bradley Family. Charles Alexander Bradley Sr. and his wife, Clara Belle Farrell, are in the driveway of their residence at 3829 Weston Place with their 1925 Jordan Roadster. In the background is 3838 Weston, built in 1924 for Charles Z. Walker. Next to the Walker house is 3846 Weston Place, built in 1921, occupied by C.W. Freeman of Standard Oil Company, then by Will J. Reid. (Courtesy of Pat and Mary Bradley.)

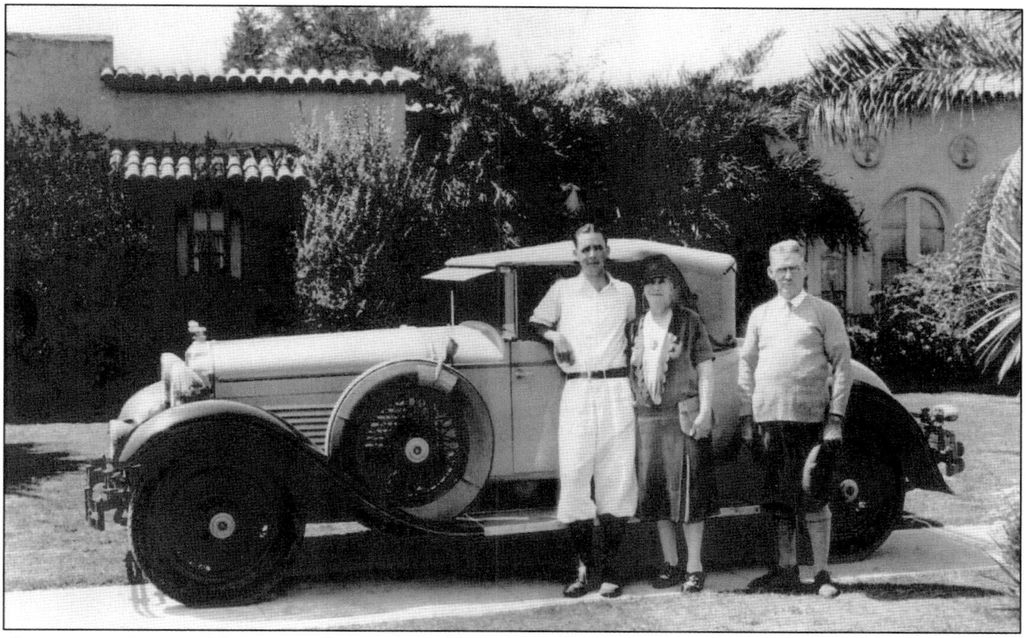

Changing Street Numbers. Between February 1924 and November 1925, the street numbers on Weston Place and possibly other streets were changed. This photograph shows Charles Alexander Bradley Jr. with his parents and their 1929 Stutz Cabriolet in front of 3615 Weston Place, which is today 3829 Weston Place. The house still stands. Bradley Sr. was caught in a flash flood and flipped the Stutz. (Courtesy of Pat and Mary Bradley.)

INDEX TO REGI

9th Congressional District
33rd Senatorial District
70th Assembly District
4th Supervisorial District

Cerritos

LOS ANGELES CO

No.	Name, Address, Occupation and Party

A

157 Adair, Mrs Hazel N, hswf, 2619 Pasadena av, D
4 Allam, Frank D, grdnr, Pepper dr, Vista Del Mar tr, R
3 Allam, Mrs Orpha, hswf, Pepper dr, Vista Del Mar tr, R
158 Allen, Charles A, dntst, Arlington & Long Beach bld, NS
2 Allen, John, rtrd, American av, NS
159 Almy, J Eben, dnst, 2662 Pasadena av, NS
5 Almy, Mrs Martha R, hswf, 2662 Pasadena av, P
1 Ayers, Thomas P, lbr, Hathaway & Pacific, D

B

162 Baird, John E, rlrdr, 2613 Pasadena av, NS
164 Baird, Mrs Susan, hswf, 2613 Pasadena av, NS
6 Barbour, Goodrich H, pltry rnch, Columbia & Linden, R
7 Barbour, Mrs Elida B, hswf, Linden av & Columbia, R
160 Barbour, Miss Hattie, cshr, Columbia & Linden, NS
161 Barbour, Miss Theresa, clk, Columbia & Linden sts, NS
8 Beach, Mrs America A, hswf, Canton & Long Beach blvd, NS
9 Beach, John D, rtrd, Canton & Long Beach blvd, NS
19 Bixby, George H, frmr, Bixby rd & American av, R
17 Bode, Arnold G H, mnstr, Cota av, NS
16 Bode, Mrs Lucy Dyott, hswf, Cota st, S
10 Bogue, William N, crpntr, Eldridge st, D
166 Bottorff, Mrs Anna L, hskpr, 2660 Pasadena av, R
165 Bowles, Walter A, rl est, Los Cerritos, R
163 Brown, George S, lmbr wkr, Linden av, R
11 Brown, William M, mnfctr, Pasadena & Willow, R
12 Brown, Miss Grace E, stngrphr, Willow & Pasadena, R
13 Brown, Miss Vesta, stdnt, 2607 Pasadena av, R
14 Brown, Miss Rhoda S, pno tchr, Linden nr Columbia, R
15 Brown, Mrs Sarah B, hskpr, Linden av nr Columbia, R

C

26 Carlson, Mrs Ethel Y, hswf, Perris rd, R
25 Carlson, Charles J, tlr, Perris rd, R
20 Carlson, Ralph W, rnchr, Perris rd & Willow st, R
21 Carlson, Chester H, rnchr, Perris rd & Willow st, R
35 Christensen, Chris A, cntrctr, Locust & San Antonio, R
33 Christensen, Mrs Mollie B, hswf, Locust st, R
22 Clinton, Ned M, mlkmn, Bixby rd & Nieto av, NS
23 Clinton, Miss Charlotte J, stngrphr, Nieto av, NS
24 Clinton, Mrs Elizabeth, hswf, Nieto av, R
167 Compton, Mrs Sarah M, hswf, 2604 Pasadena av, NS
31 Conn, Sidney, crpntr, 2628 Linden av, NS
32 Conn, Mrs Mollie, hswf, 2628 Linden av, R
29 Conway, Frank L, rtrd, Crest dr, R
30 Conway, Mrs M Lillian, hswf, Crest dr, R
34 Cook, William M, bnkr, Pacific av, R
27 Cook, Mrs Ethel S, hswf, Pacific av, R

D

38 Daly, James H, atty, Weston pl & Bixby rd, R
37 Daly, Mrs Lorene, hswf, Los Cerritos, NS
41 Darling, Miss Jennie E, hskpr, 2652 Pasadena av, NS
36 Davis, John F, hg rsr, Warlaw av, NS
39 Diffenderfer, Mrs Caroline E, rtrd, Temple st, D
40 Diffenderfer, Miss Laura M, hskpr, Temple st, R

E

168 Edwards, Andrew J, mnstr, 2705 Elm av, Pro
169 Edwards, Mrs Mary A, hswf, 2705 Elm av, Pro
42 Ethridge, Mrs Mary, hswf, Pacific av, D

No.	Name, Address, Occupation and Party

F

43 Frank, John W, plc ofcr, Pepper dr & American, R
44 Frank, Mrs Mary Maude, hswf, Pepper dr & America av, R

G

48 Gephart, Fred A, blcksmth, 2615 Pasadena av, Pro
47 Gephart, Mrs Edith, hswf, 2615 Pasadena av, R
52 Gillett, Mrs Mabel Q, hskpr, American av, R
54 Gillett, Mrs Lizzie, hskpr, American av, R
46 Gillett, Homer E, dlvrymn, American av, R
138 Gillett, Eugene, ret, American av, R
56 Goff, Mrs Lola M, hswf, Lincoln & Locust av, NS
55 Goff, Edward H, cnty rd frmn, Lincoln & Locust, R
51 Graves, Asa P, cbntmkr, 2627 Linden av, D
50 Graves, Mrs Marion R, 2627 Linden av, Pro
170 Grisham, Hugh, rnchr, Locust av, D
49 Grisham, Otto S, pntr, Locust av, D
53 Grisham, Mrs Susan I, hswf, Locust av, D

H

176 Haffner, George, grdnr, Los Cerritos, NS
59 Hall, John D, slsmn, Bixby & Lincoln avs, D
63 Hancock, Mrs Willis M, hswf, Bixby rd, NS
57 Harding, Hiram B, rtrd, American av, R
175 Harris, Lloyd A, ret, Pacific & Roosevelt sts, R
62 Harryman, Mrs Margaret A, hswf, Elm av, S
61 Harryman, George W, lbr, Elm av, S
174 Hayes, Harry G, drymn, Wardlow st, R
173 Hayes, Harvey, drymn, Wardlow st, R
172 Hickok, Mrs Alice M, hswf, Lincoln av, NS
64 Hill, Miss Addie M, hskpr, American av, R
177 Hodge, Mrs Anne F, hswf, Los Cerritos, R
171 Hodge, Frederick M, loans, American & Whittier, R
178 Hoffner, Mrs Alice, hswf, San Antonio & American, N
179 Howard, Mrs Florence, hswf, Elm av, NS
180 Hussey, Mrs Florence M, hswf, Elm av, NS
60 Hussey, James M, lbr, Columbia & Elm, R

J

67 Jaques, Duane H, slsmngr, Hathaway ct & Cota, R
182 Johansing, Harry G, ins, American & Parker pl, NS
139 Johnson, Mrs Louisa, hswf, 2625 Pasadena av, R
181 Jones, Mrs Edna L, nurse, 2619 Pasadena av, Pro
68 Jordan, Franklin, mlwrght, Temple st, R
66 Josleyn, Mrs Dora Leah, hswf, American av, D
65 Josleyn, William H, frmr, American av, R

K

141 Kimball, Mrs Mary, none, 2652 Pasadena av, D
183 King, Harry J, tmstr, Pepper dr, NS
69 King, Howard S, rnchng, Temple st, R
72 King, Mrs Mina S, hskpr, Temple st & Bixby rd, R
71 King, Mrs Mollie C, hswf, Temple st, R
140 King, Oscar J, frmng, Temple av, R
142 Klaproth, Henry L, pstl clrk, 245 Spring st, D
143 Knox, Albert W, rnchr, Palm st, R

L

80 Lamoreaux, Mrs Clara Belle, hswf, Roosevelt rd & Locust av, Pro

Index of Registered Voters. This 1916 index lists those registered to vote in the Cerritos precinct. Political party affiliation is listed for many residents. The majority are Republican or

TER OF VOTERS

recinct

ALIFORNIA, 1916

Key to Party Abbreviations
R—Republican
D—Democrat
P—Progressive
S—Socialist
Pro—Prohibition
NS—Not Stated

Name, Address, Occupation and Party

Lamoreaux, Robert M, prntr, Roosevelt st, Pro
Lasell, Samuel M, rtrd, Lincoln av, NS
Lasell, Mrs Edna R, hswf, Lincoln av, NS
Leavitt, Mrs Fannie, hswf, Elm av, NS
Leavitt, George C, lbr, Linden av & Columbia, NS
Lidell, Mrs Ella J, hswf, Temple st, D
Lidell, August H, rtrd, Temple st, D
Loper, Amos C, mchnc, 2658 Elm av, R
Loper, Mrs Blanch, hswf, 2658 Elm av, NS

M

Maltby, Benjamin F, dntst, 2660 Pasadena av, R
Maltby, Mrs Emily A, rtrd, 2658 Pasadena av, NS
Maltby, Miss Ruth E, lbrn, Pasadena av, NS
Maltby, Mrs Caroline A, hm mkr, 2660 Pasadena av, NS
Marsh, John W, cntrctr, American & Wardlow rd, R
Mattox, William A, slsmn, Long Beach blvd, NS
Meldrim, John H, trnsfr, Nieto av, R
Meldrim, Mrs Gertrude V, hswf, Nieto st, R
Miles, Mrs Margaret A, hswf, 2630 Linden av, R
Minter, Mrs Helen, hswf, American av, S
Minter, Mrs Kate J, hskpr, American av, S
Minter, Leo F, lthr, American av, S
Mitchell, Mrs Hattie, hskpr, Pacific av, R
Mitchell, Newel H, rtrd, Pacific & Roosevelt rd, R
Monroe, Miss Edna, stdnt, 3100 American av, D
Monroe, Mrs Etta, hswf, 3100 American av, D
Monroe, William T, crpntr, 3100 American av, D
Moulton, Miss Evelyn, stdnt, Perris rd, R
Moulton, W True, rnchr, Perris rd, R
Moulton, Mrs Margaret G, hswf, Perris rd, R

Mc

McAlister, Elonzo N, rl est, American av & Wardlow, P
McAlister, Mrs Delia C, hswf, Wardlow rd & American av, NS

N

Newman, Mrs Ida A, hswf, 2629 Pasadena av, D
Newman, Ai T, rtrd, 2629 Pasadena av, D

O

Oakford, Mrs Eddith H, hswf, Long Beach blvd & Brandon st, NS
Oakford, Richard S, drggst, L B blvd & Brandon st, R

P

Partridge, Elden H, rnchr, Perris rd, R
Patterson, Miss M Irene, schl tchr, Elm st, NS
Peach, Mrs Wildia, hswf, 2461 American av, NS
Pope, Henry, rtrd, 2236 American av, R

R

Richards, George A, drymn, Arabella st, NS
Richards, Miss Lillie J, hswf, 2700 Pasadena, NS
Richards, Mrs Mary, hswf, Linden av, NS
Richards, Mrs Mary E, hswf, 2700 Pasadena av, R
Richards, Milton, rtrd, Linden av, D
Rowett, Charles R, rl est, Nieto st, R

No. Name, Address, Occupation and Party

S

115 Schriver, Mrs Mary O, hskpr, Cota av, NS
150 Schriver, Fletcher F, ins, Cota av, R
195 Shaylor, Albert, frmr, Los Cerritos, R
119 Shoenberger, Engway, bkpr, Canton st, R
118 Shoenberger, George, hrnsmkr, 220 Canton, R
117 Shoenberger, Mrs Ida, hswf, Canton & American, NS
120 Sholes, Mrs Tennie C, hswf, San Antonio & Roosevelt dr, P
122 Shumard, Mrs Fannie S, hswf, Temple st, R
121 Shumard, Elmer A, rlrd mn, Temple st, R
109 Smith, David D, crpntr, 2650 Elm av, P
110 Smith, Mrs Eva L, hswf, 2650 Elm av, R
113 Snure, Mrs Augusta, hswf, Linden av, R
199 Stevens, Mrs Mabel F, hswf, Elm av, NS
198 Stevens, Robert, rnchr, Elm & Columbia, NS
201 Stewart, Irwin, rnchr, Perris rd, R
200 Stewart, Mrs Margaret A, hswf, Perris rd, NS
114 Sweningsen, Oliver, engnr, Cerritos School dist, R
197 Sweningsen, Mrs Edwine M, hmkpr, Nieto st, R
196 Swisher, John F, ret, Temple st, R

T

123 Taylor, Mrs Fleta H, hswf, Pacific av, P
202 Thompson, Eben, ret, Columbia & Elm av, D

V

151 Van Fossen, Francis K, ml car, 2615 Pasadena av, Pro
152 Van Fossen, Mrs Laura C, hswkr, 2615 Pasadena av, Pro
124 Vignes, Miss Marie K, tchr, Temple st, R
125 Vignes, Mrs Mary K, hskpr, Temple st, R
126 Vignes, Miss Louise A, stdnt, Temple st, R

W

209 Wabintz, Charles F, ret, American av, R
135 Walp, Bert J, mrchnt, Bixby rd & Cota av, R
129 Walp, Mrs Marguerite V, hswf, Cota av & Bixby rd, R
127 Warner, Miss Mary D, hm kpr, Cota av, R
133 Welker, Claude E, mrchnt, Arabella & American av, R
132 Welker, Mrs Winnifred, hswf, American & Arabella, R
156 Westcott, William A, tmstr, Locust & San Antonio, NS
128 Westcott, Mrs Myrtie C, hswf, Locust av, NS
155 Wheatly, Wilkins W, mtn petr prdcr, Lincoln av, D
206 Whitaker, Mrs Agnes H, hswf, Lincoln av, R
207 Whitaker, Forrest M, tchr, Lincoln av, R
203 Williams, Mrs Mary A, hswf, 2604 Pasadena av, NS
153 Wilson, Mrs Minnie E, hswf, Perris st, R
154 Wilson, Solomon D, frmr, Perris st, R
208 Wright, John, mchnst, 2644 Elm st, D
205 Wright, Mrs Kate, hswf, 5426 Elm av, D
130 Wohlwend, Otto A, clrk, 2277 American av, R
131 Wohlwend, Mrs Frieda, hswf, 2277 American av, R
204 Wuisemann, Frank W, crpntr, 538 Arabella st, D

Y

136 Youngker, Floyd L, sub frmn, 2611 Pasadena av, NS
137 Youngker, Mrs Irene L, hswf, 2611 Pasadena av, NS

Z

210 Zimmerman, Mrs Mattie, hswf, Elm av, NS

Democrat, with a few Progressives, Prohibitionists, or Socialists. Note that the Cerritos precinct is larger than today's neighborhood.

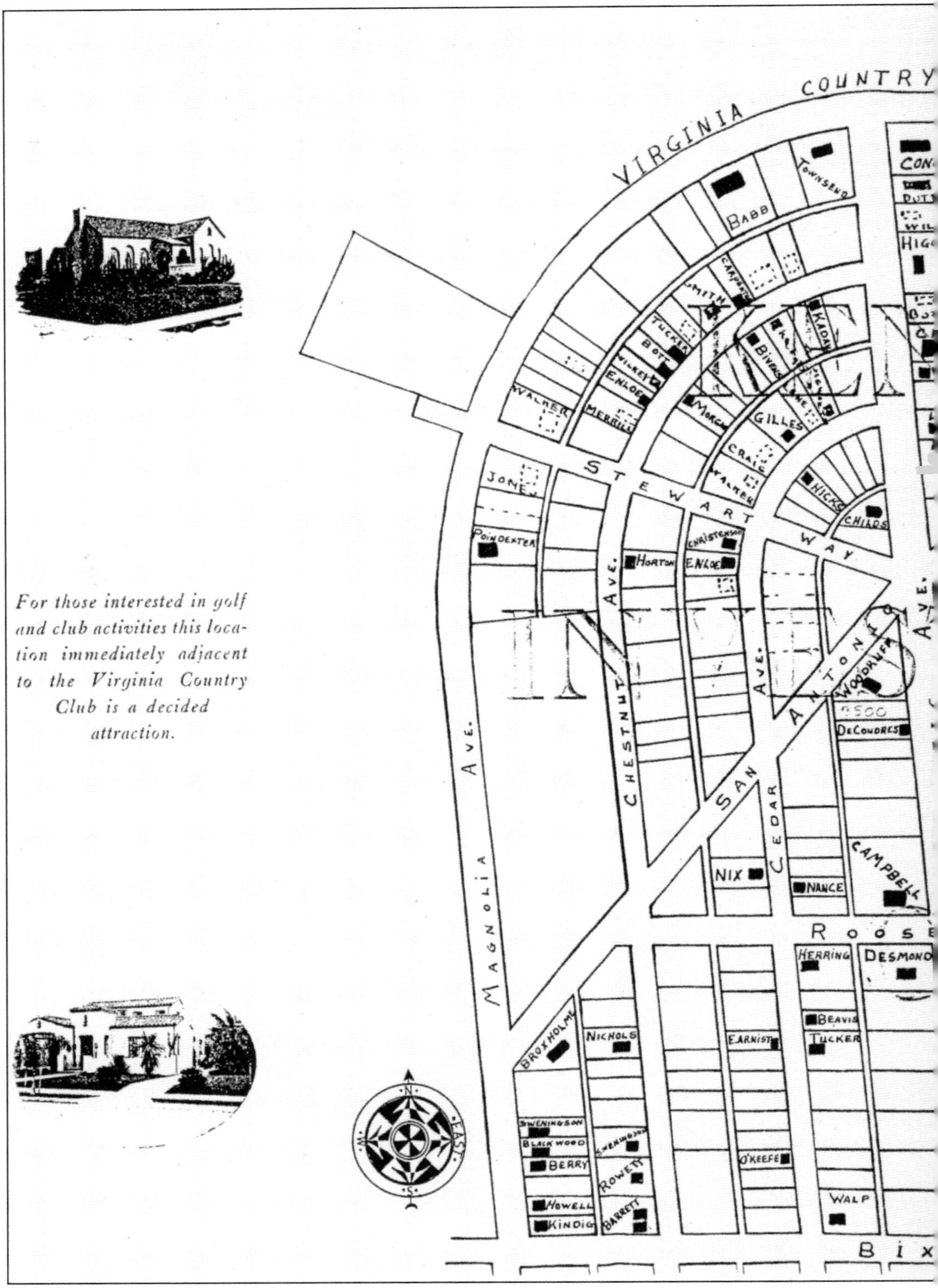

Map of Residents. This late-1920s map shows lot owners in a portion of the neighborhood. Made by the Krenek Investment Company, it was likely used to help sell real estate, as it promoted

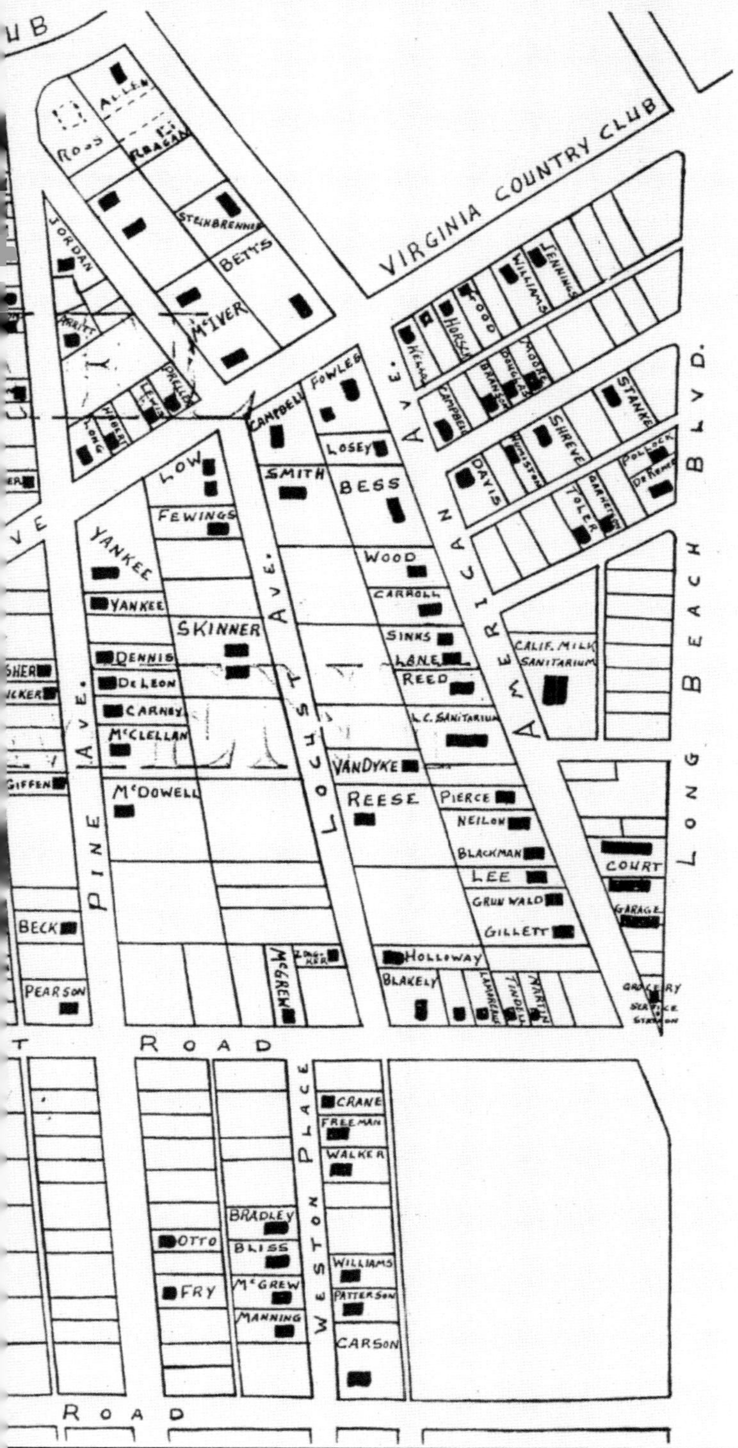

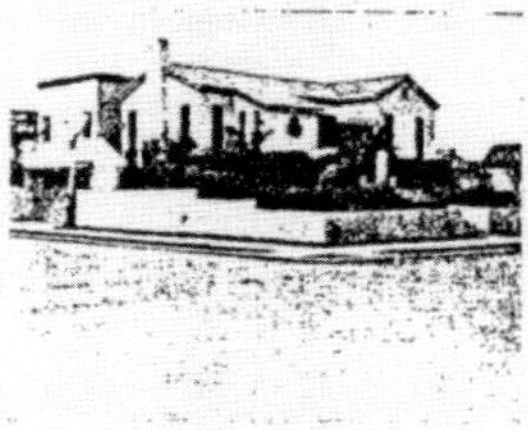

Los Cerritos is quite distinctive as a residential section because of the wide selection afforded in sizes and facings of building sites.

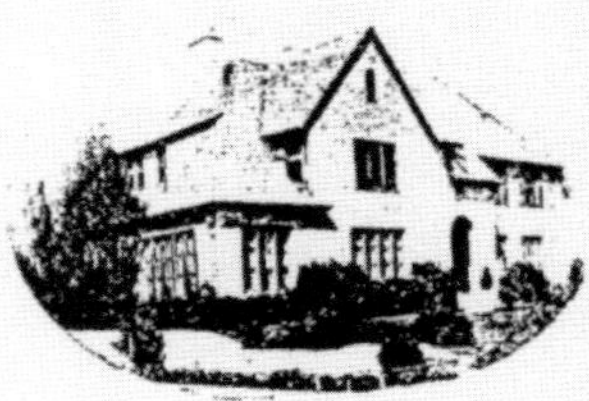

proximity to the country club and the diversity in size of lot and type of housing.

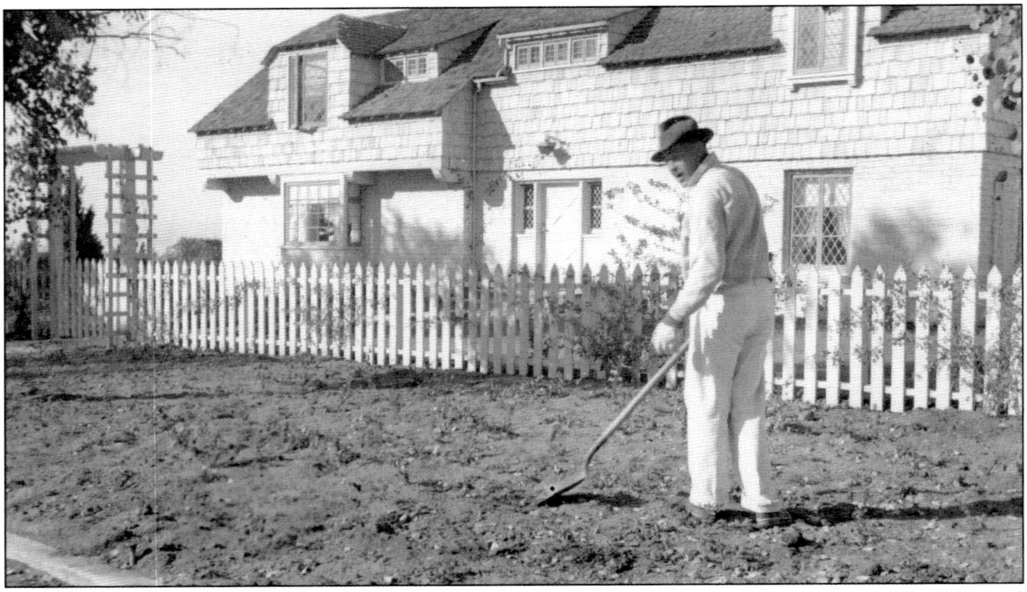

DR. JOHN R. JIMERSON. Jimerson was a well-traveled pediatrician with a love of nature. He delivered many of the babies born to residents of Los Cerritos. He contracted with noted architect Kirtland Cutter to build a cottage for he and his wife that would have plenty of niches for their collections. The home is at 4181 Country Club Drive. (Courtesy of Gary Holland.)

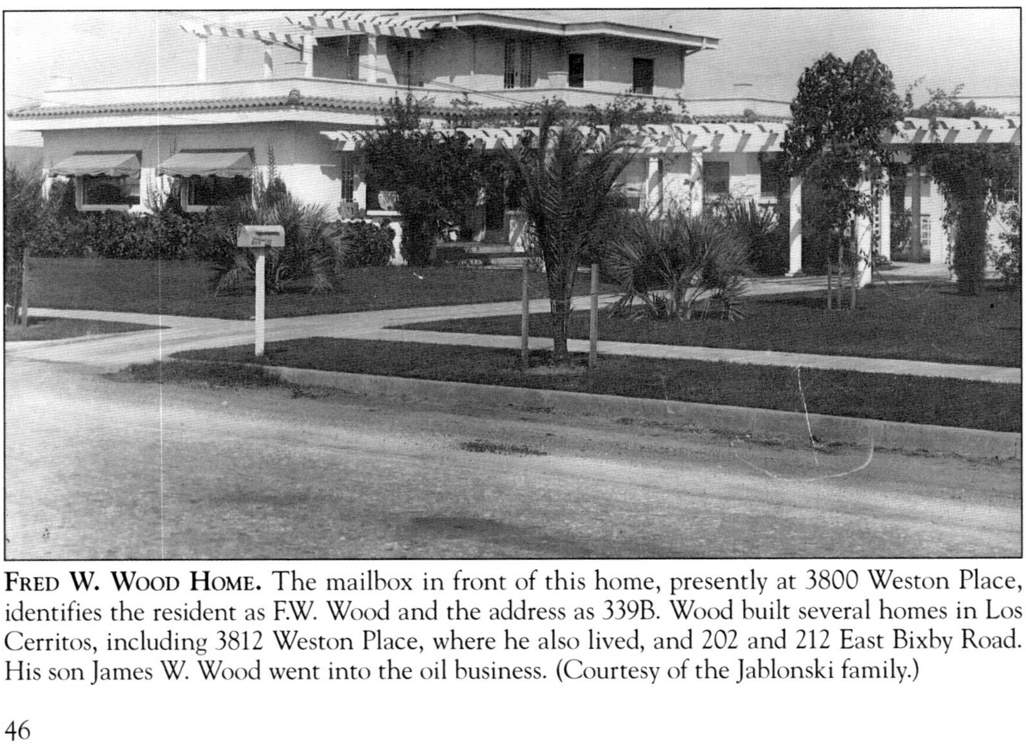

FRED W. WOOD HOME. The mailbox in front of this home, presently at 3800 Weston Place, identifies the resident as F.W. Wood and the address as 339B. Wood built several homes in Los Cerritos, including 3812 Weston Place, where he also lived, and 202 and 212 East Bixby Road. His son James W. Wood went into the oil business. (Courtesy of the Jablonski family.)

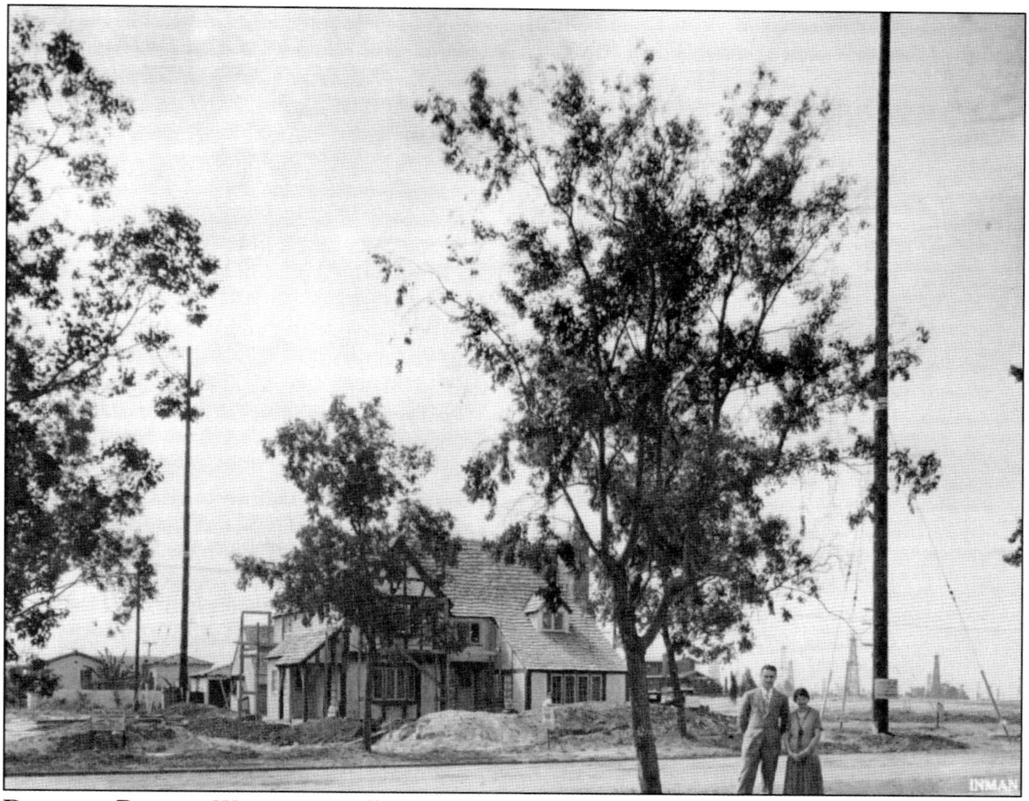

DON AND BERTHA WALLACE. Wallace was a world-renowned wireless radio operator. From his home in Los Cerritos, he kept Long Beach connected during the 1933 earthquake and made world news when he communicated with Admiral Byrd at the South Pole in 1930. (Courtesy of Jan David Perkins.)

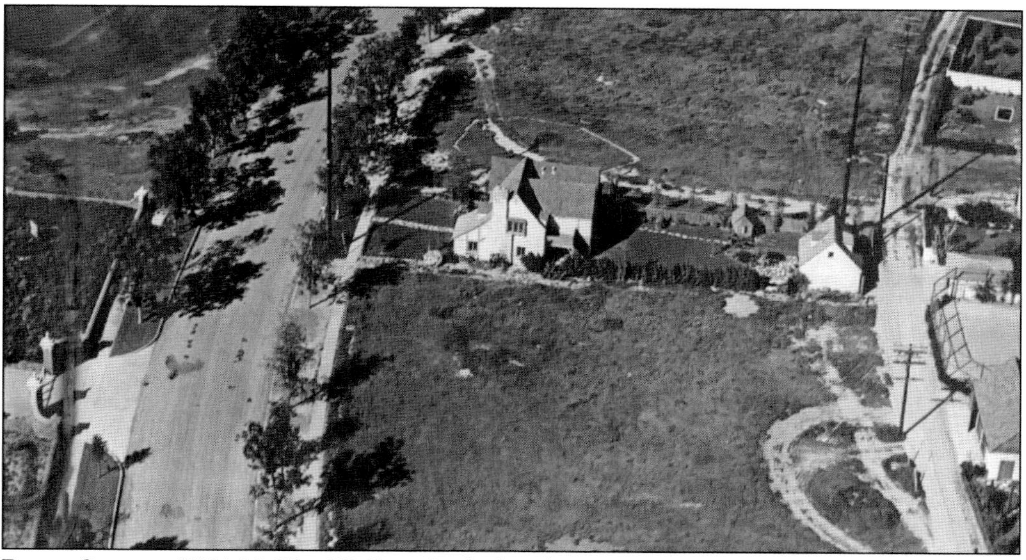

RADIO STATION W6AM. The Wallaces built their home in Los Cerritos in 1929 because of the open space for his radio antennas. The home is located at 4214 Country Club Drive. (VCC.)

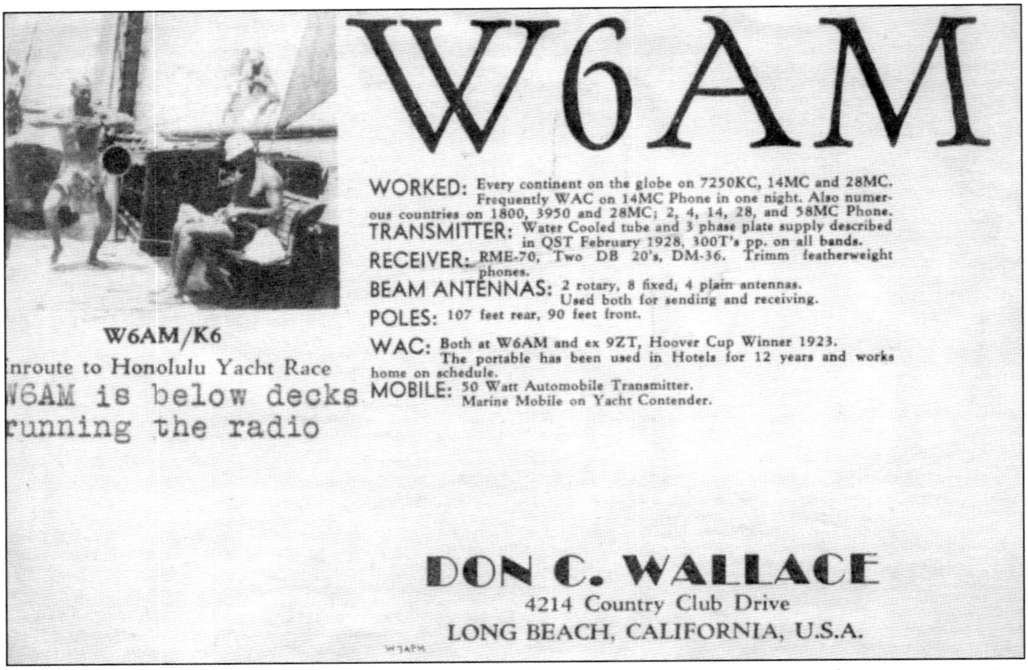

W6AM QSL Card. Amateur radio operators use QSL cards to confirm two-way radio communication between stations. Like postcards, they are sent through the mail. This QSL card from Don Wallace commemorates the 1933 Trans-Pacific Yacht Race, when Wallace operated W6AM from below decks on Capt. Richard Loynes's boat, the *Contender*. The *Contender* won the race.

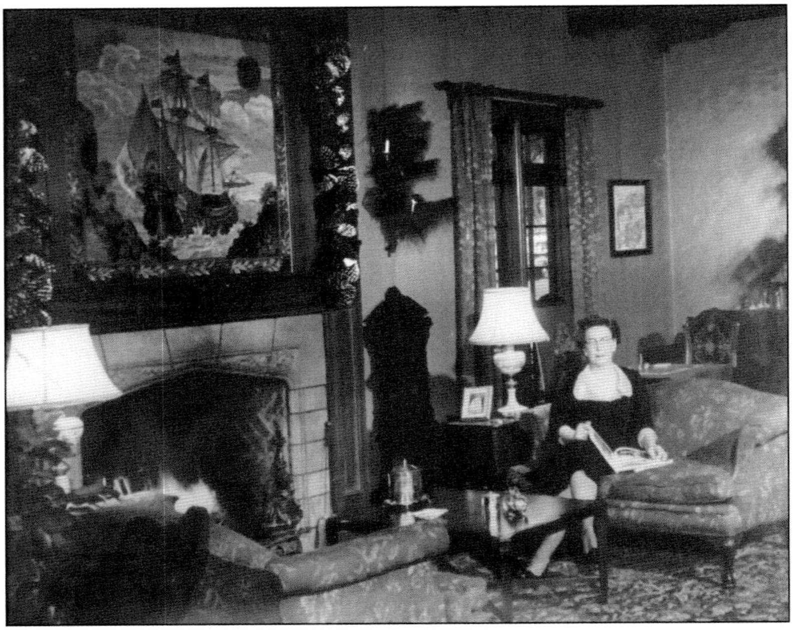

Ruth Craig Merrell. Merrell was the daughter of shipbuilder John F Craig. She married Thomas Merrell. She is shown in their home at 4201 Chestnut. She was an active club woman and a great organizer of events for the children of the neighborhood. The Merrells had three children: Edith, Marjorie, and John. (Courtesy of Janet Watt.)

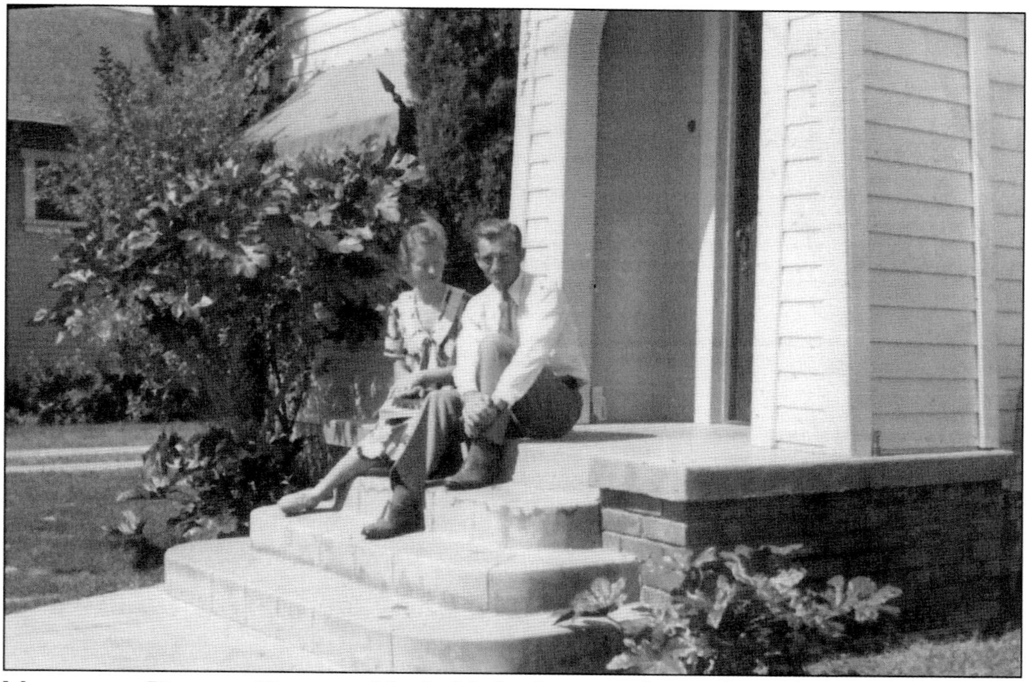

MANLEY AND DOROTHY NATLAND. Manley Natland was a geologist who worked for Shell and then the Atlantic Richfield Corporation (ARCO). He used fossilized rock found at the construction site of the ARCO Towers in Los Angeles to make tables and statuary. In 1981, in connection with the Los Angeles bicentennial, the fossilized rock Natlandite, named for Natland, became the official Los Angeles rock. The Natland home was at 4247 Pine Avenue.

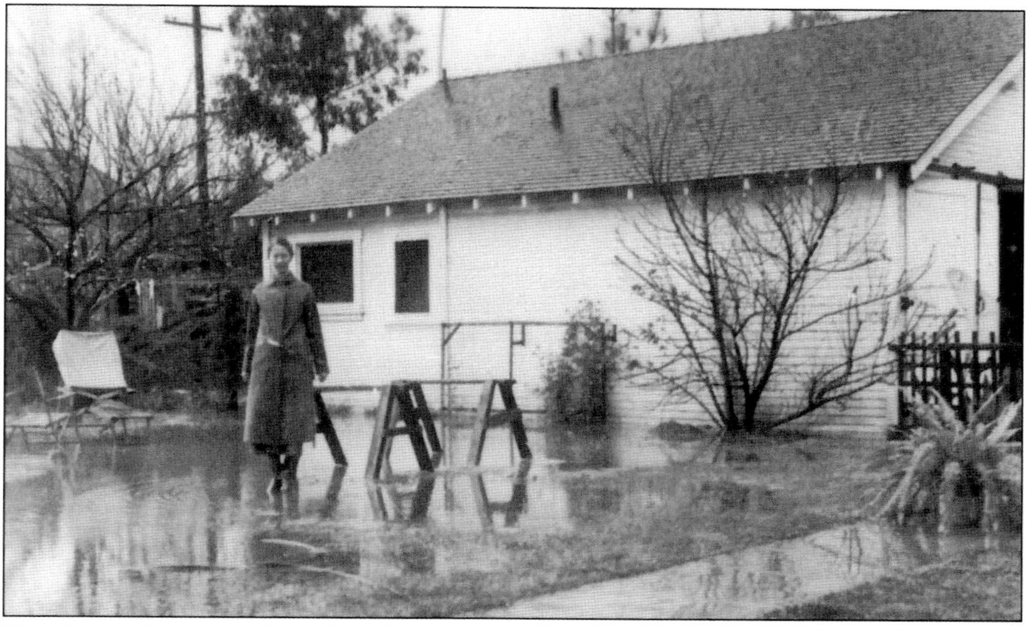

THE GREAT FLOOD OF 1938. On February 27, 1938, it began to rain. By March 4, the rain had dumped more than 11 inches on Los Angeles County. The Los Angeles River overflowed its banks, resulting in widespread flooding. Here, Dorothy Diehl Natland stands in her backyard at 4247 Pine Avenue during the flood.

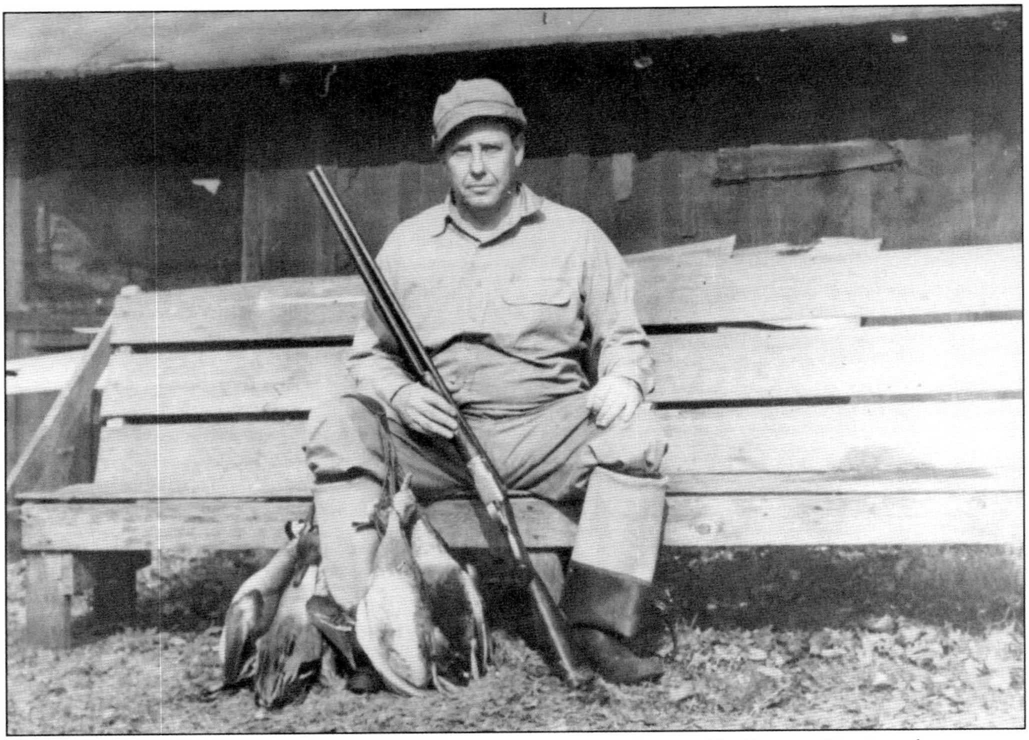

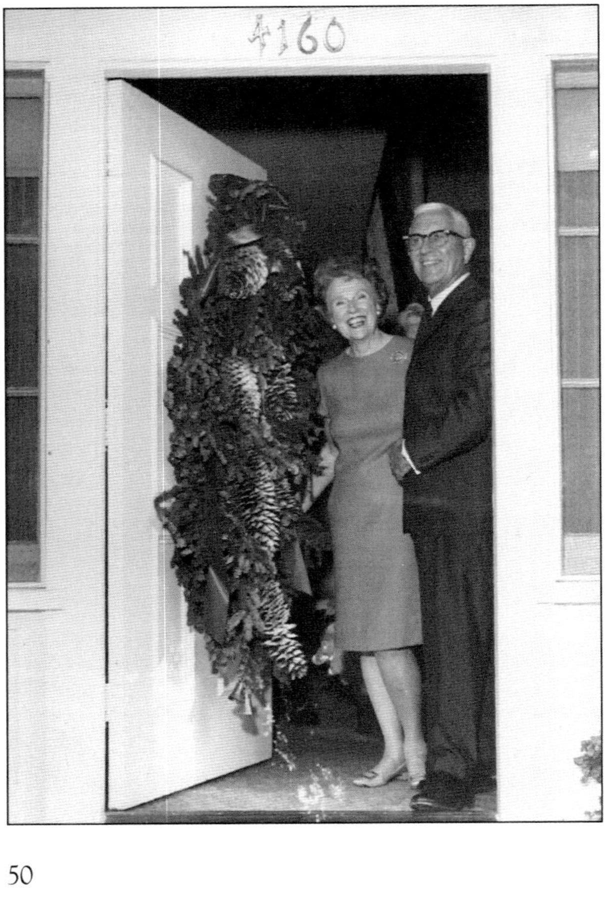

James G. Craig. During the early part of the 20th century, the wetlands of Los Angeles and Orange Counties were rich with ducks, and hunting was a common pastime of many Los Cerritos businessmen. Craig was an executive with the Craig Shipbuilding company and lived at 4242 Pacific Avenue with his wife, Evelyn, and family. He also was part owner of the Farmers Gun Club, located on a portion of former Rancho Los Alamitos land.

Mayor Burton Chase. Burton Chase and his wife, Polly Brown, lived at 4160 Country Club Drive. Chase was elected mayor of Long Beach in 1947 and was appointed by Earl Warren as a county supervisor in 1953. Burton Chase Park in Marina Del Rey is named for him. He is credited for the development of the Music Center in Los Angeles. (Courtesy of William Townsend.)

Three

Los Cerritos Schools

Families living in the Cerritos Colony petitioned the county for a school, and the first district was established in 1878. The Cerritos School District boundaries were Cherry Avenue on the west, the Los Angeles River on the east, the Dominquez School District on the north, and the ocean on the south. The Los Angeles County School District trustees were Mary Kent Vignes, William T. Cook, and Judge William True Moulton. The first school built by the county for the Cerritos District was located at 1415 West Willow Street, and it opened in 1881. After the subdivision of the Los Cerritos neighborhood, the trustees of the Cerritos School District at that time, George H. Bixby, Moulton, and Vignes, petitioned the county for another school. The petition was granted, and in 1912, the school district served the area north of Wardlow. The new school, located on San Antonio Drive at Pine Avenue, was called the "North" Cerritos School, to distinguish it from the old "South" Cerritos School on Willow Street. Opened in 1914, it was a one-room wood structure with a bell tower. The teacher, Marie Vignes, taught all grades to about 20 pupils.

As the population grew, a larger school was necessary. The school board purchased one acre of land for $3,000 near Los Cerritos Park, and Mrs. George H. Bixby donated the second. A new two-room schoolhouse of concrete and stucco was erected at San Antonio Drive and Del Mar Avenue. In 1921, the Long Beach School District attempted to annex the Cerritos School District. The South Cerritos School joined the Long Beach District, but 102 voters in Los Cerritos objected, so the North Los Cerritos school did not join the Long Beach District until 1924. In 1933, the Long Beach earthquake damaged the second Los Cerritos School. Children attended classes in bungalows and tents until the current school was erected. Los Cerritos School was not the only school in the neighborhood. In 1925, the Los Cerritos Military Academy was established in a homelike setting on American Avenue (now Virginia Road).

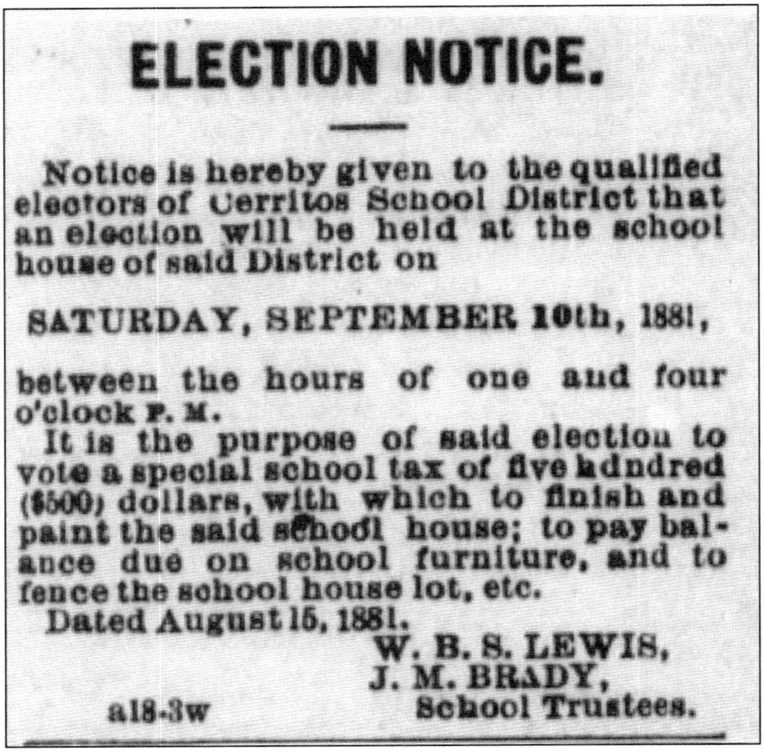

ELECTION NOTICE.

Notice is hereby given to the qualified electors of Cerritos School District that an election will be held at the school house of said District on

SATURDAY, SEPTEMBER 10th, 1881,

between the hours of one and four o'clock P. M.

It is the purpose of said election to vote a special school tax of five hundred ($500) dollars, with which to finish and paint the said school house; to pay balance due on school furniture, and to fence the school house lot, etc.

Dated August 15, 1881.

W. B. S. LEWIS,
J. M. BRADY,
School Trustees.

a18-3w

CERRITOS SCHOOL DISTRICT NOTICE. On July 7, 1881, colony resident Thomas B. Hayes sold the Cerritos School District one acre of land on Willow Street for $50 from the 40-acre parcel he purchased from the J. Bixby Company in July 1880. This August 15, 1881, notice is for an election for a $500 tax to finish the school. W.B.S. Lewis and J.M. Brady were listed as trustees. (LCS.)

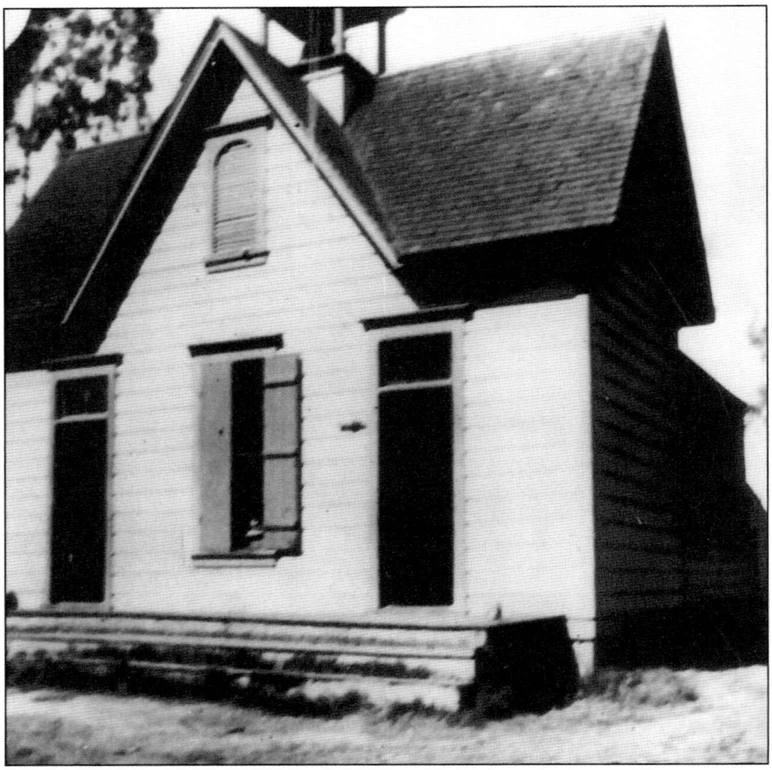

FIRST LOS CERRITOS SCHOOL. The classes at the first Cerritos School (later called the "South" Cerritos School) were held in a one-room building located at 1415 West Willow Street. The first teacher, a Mr. Cummings, taught all eight grades. Katherine Robinson Bushong, who grew up in the Cerritos Colony, attended the school from 1882 until 1887. She recalled her teachers were Mrs. Zumwalt, Mary McClain, Mrs. Remington, Nellie Fitzmier, and Walter Bailey. (LCS.)

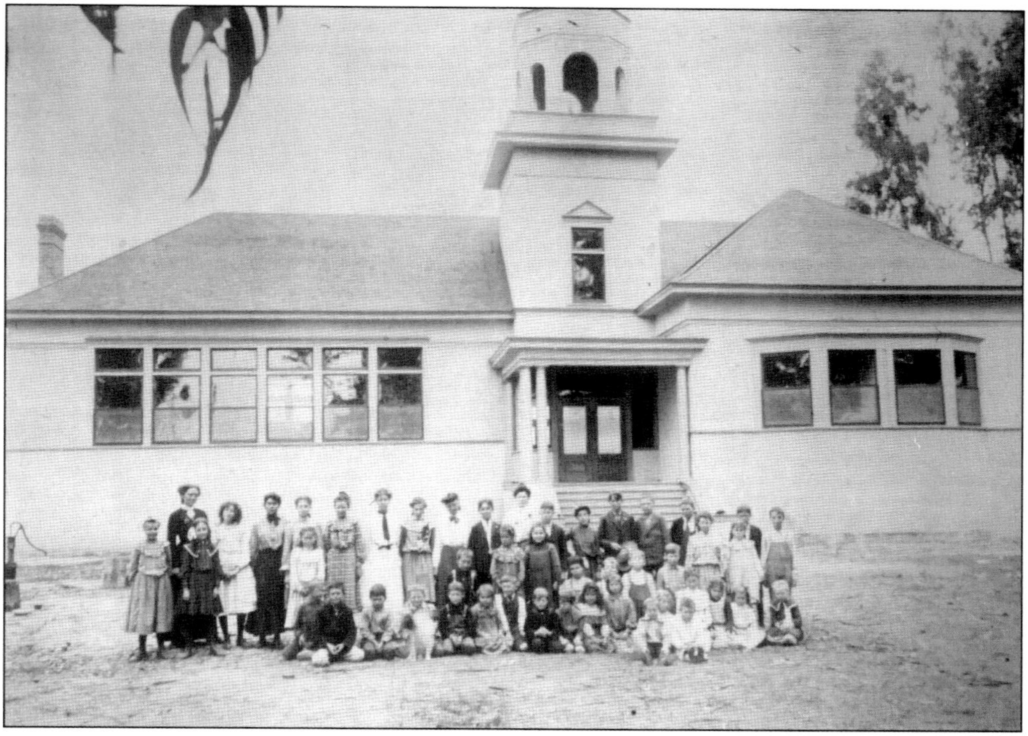

"SOUTH" LOS CERRITOS SCHOOL. By 1896, the Cerritos School District had 79 pupils. This is the second building, erected at 1445 West Willow Street, which served as Los Cerritos School in the Cerritos Colony. County records report this building having been erected in 1910, but other sources indicate approximately 1904. (HSLB.)

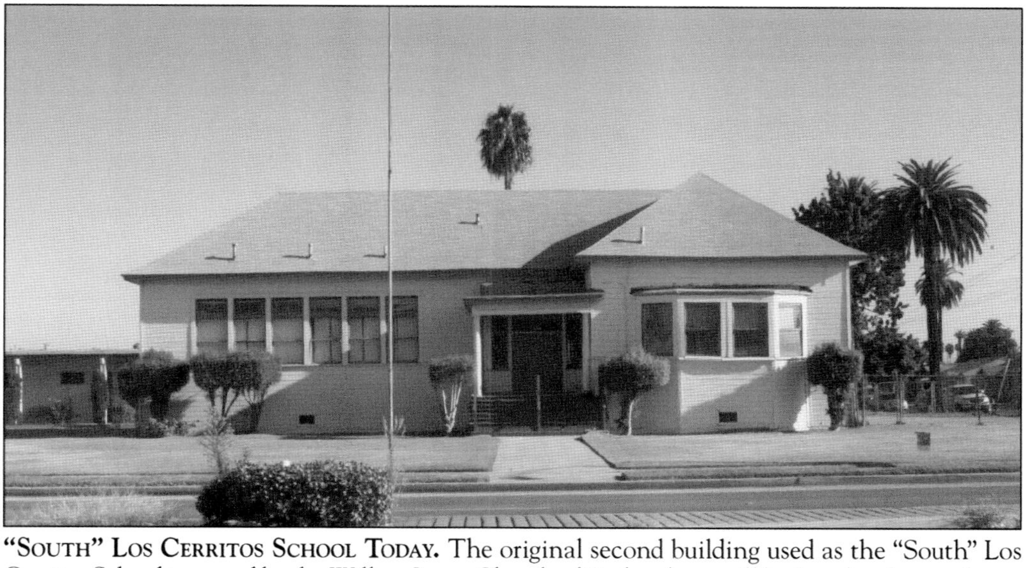

"SOUTH" LOS CERRITOS SCHOOL TODAY. The original second building used as the "South" Los Cerritos School is owned by the Willow Street Church of God and can still be found at the northwest corner of Willow Street and Delta Avenue in Long Beach. (Courtesy of John Mulvey.)

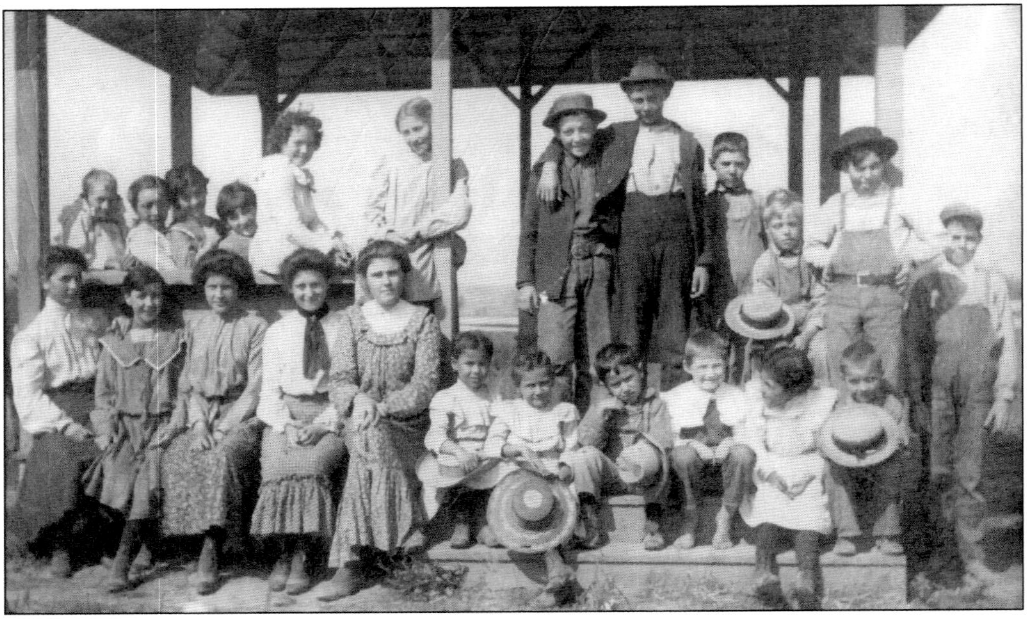

Lunch under the Arbor. After their family moved from Long Beach to a dairy on Watson property at Alameda Street and Wardlow Road, the Vignes girls attended the Dominguez School, next to the Dominguez adobe. Marguerite is leaning against the column on the left, her hand on the shoulder of sister Antoinette, who is left of sister Marie. In the back, Edwine is fourth from the left. Edwine graduated from this school in 1905. (LCS.)

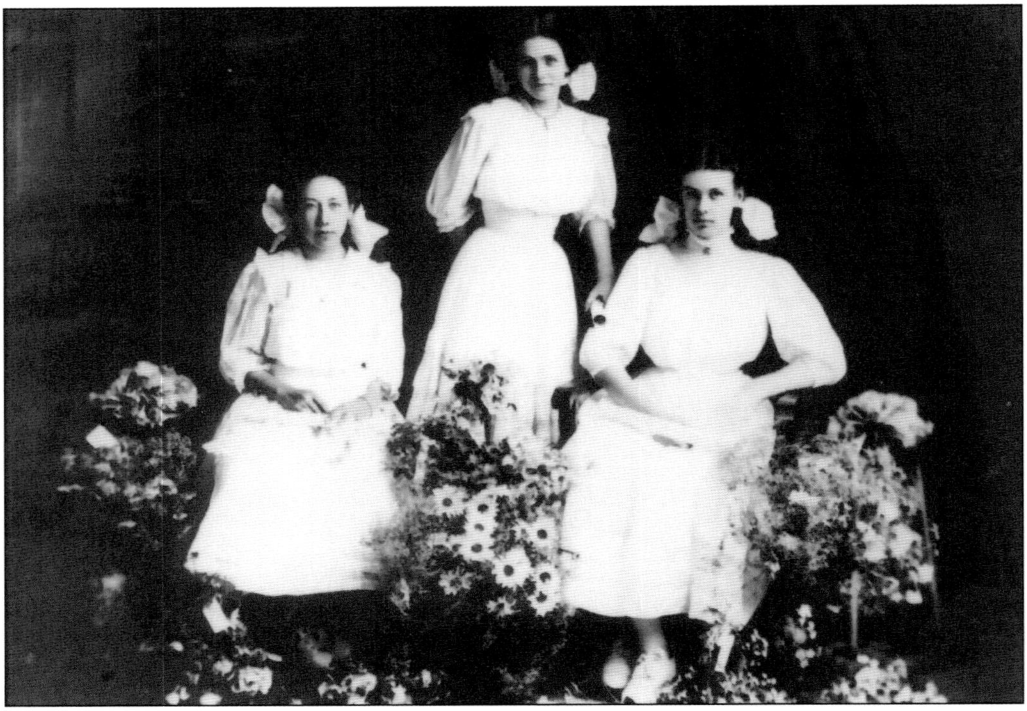

"South" Cerritos School Graduates. The 1908 graduates shown here are, from left to right, Ruth Wood, Antoinette Vignes, and Evelyn Moulton. Wood's and Moulton's families were living in the Los Cerritos Colony. (LCS.)

W. True Moulton. Judge W. True Moulton was a trustee for the Los Angeles County School District, along with Mary Vignes and William T. Cook. Moulton, along with Vignes and George H. Bixby, petitioned the board to establish the second school in the Los Cerritos area. The school was first known as the "North" Cerritos School but eventually took on the name Los Cerritos School. (LCS.)

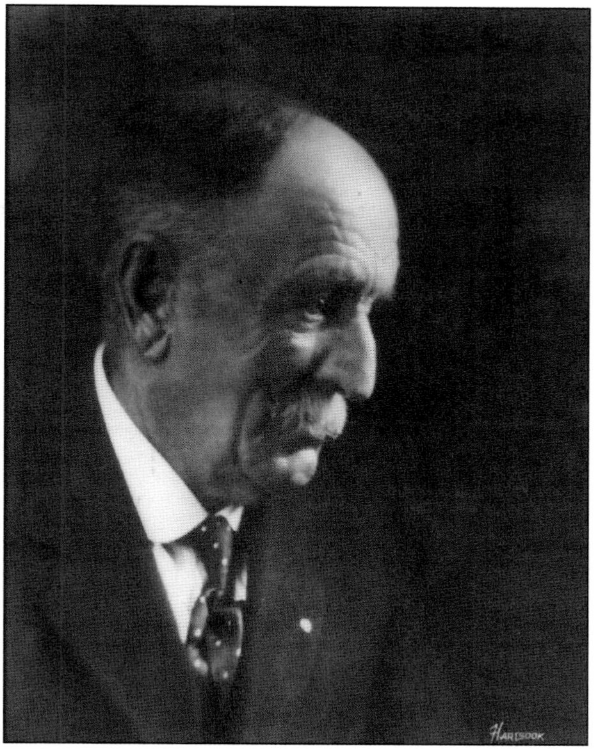

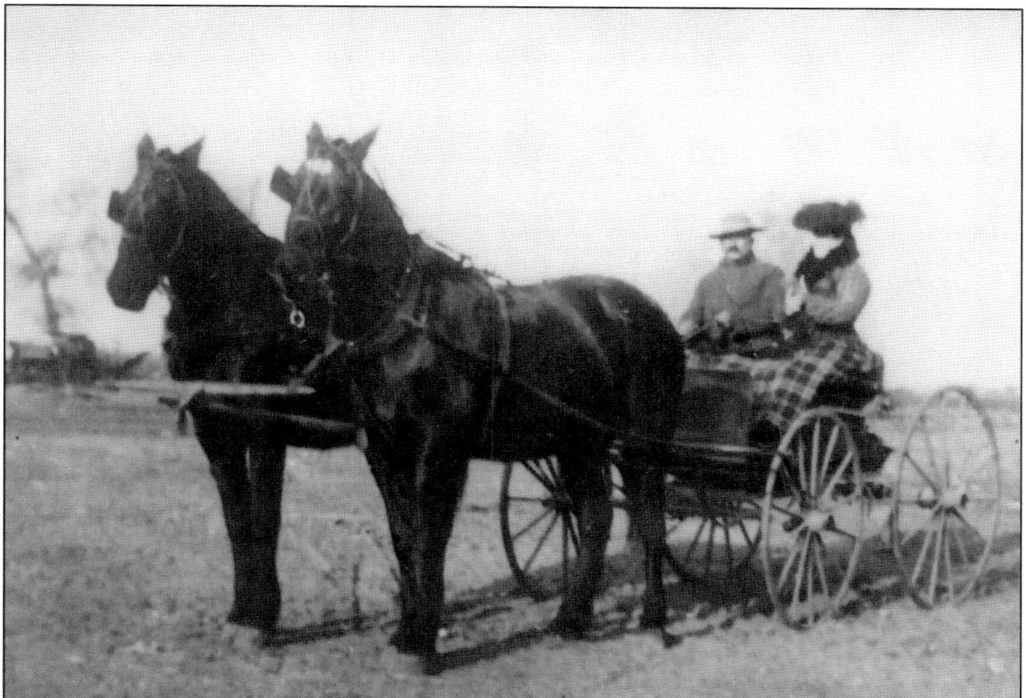

John Louis and Mary Kent Vignes. The Vigneses ensured that all their daughters were educated. Mary Vignes was instrumental in the founding of the Dominguez School and the original Los Cerritos "North" School, where her daughter became the first teacher. (LCS.)

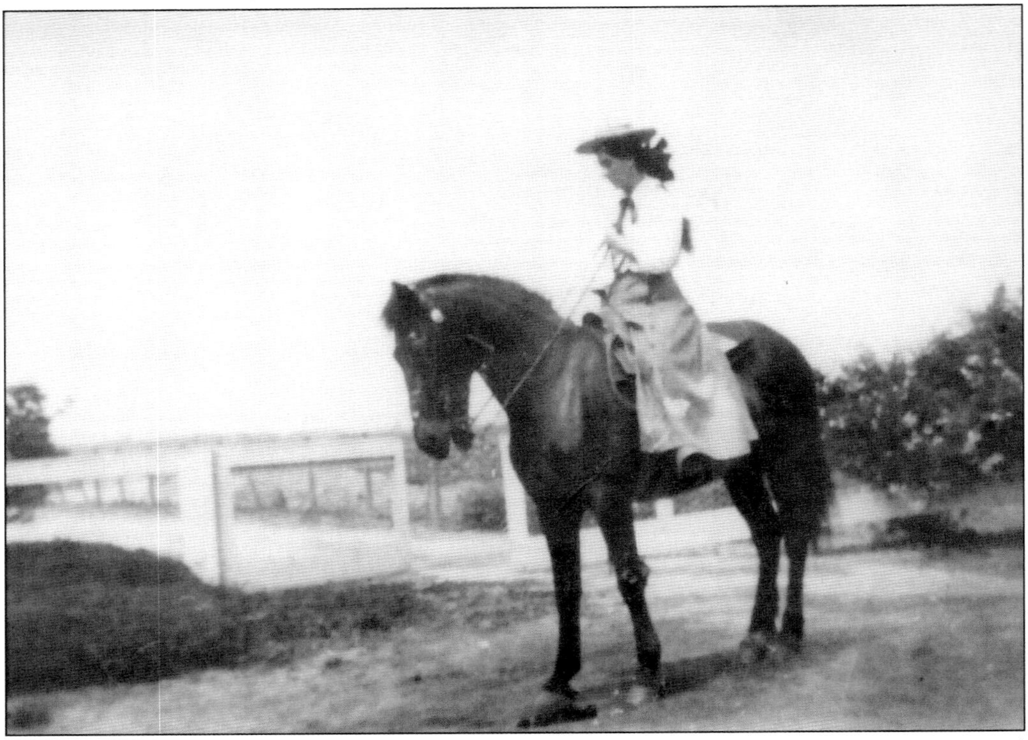

Marie Vignes. Marie Vignes, the daughter of John and Mary Vignes, was born in 1892 and attended the Los Angeles Normal School, graduating from the Professional School in June 1913. She was the only teacher at Cerritos "North" School, the one-room schoolhouse at the corner of Pine Avenue and San Antonio Drive. She is seen here riding to work. (LCS.)

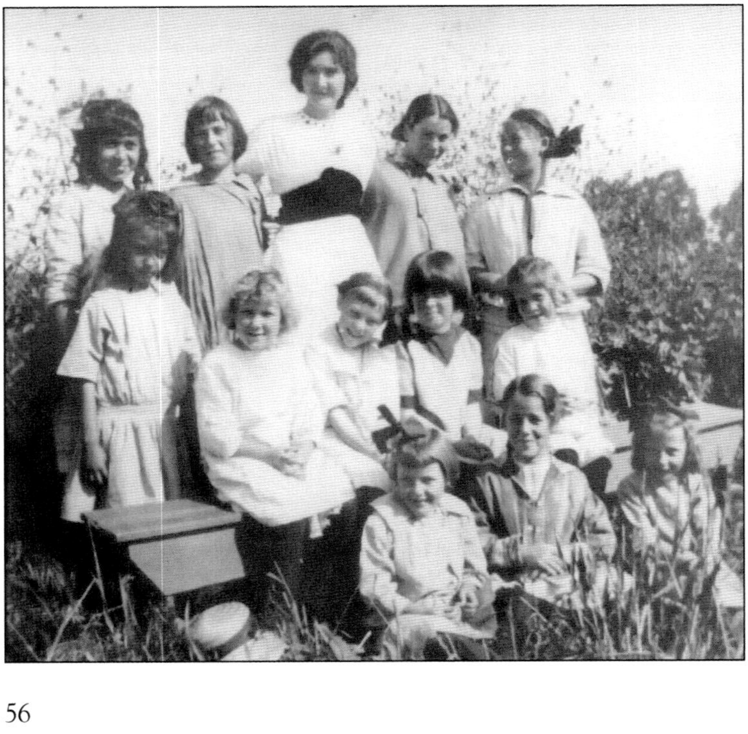

Marie Vignes's Girls. Marie Vignes taught all eight grades in one room during the years 1913 and 1914. She poses here with her female students. The girl sitting on the bench, second from the left, is Loretta Underkirchner, who became local historian Loretta Berner. (LCS.)

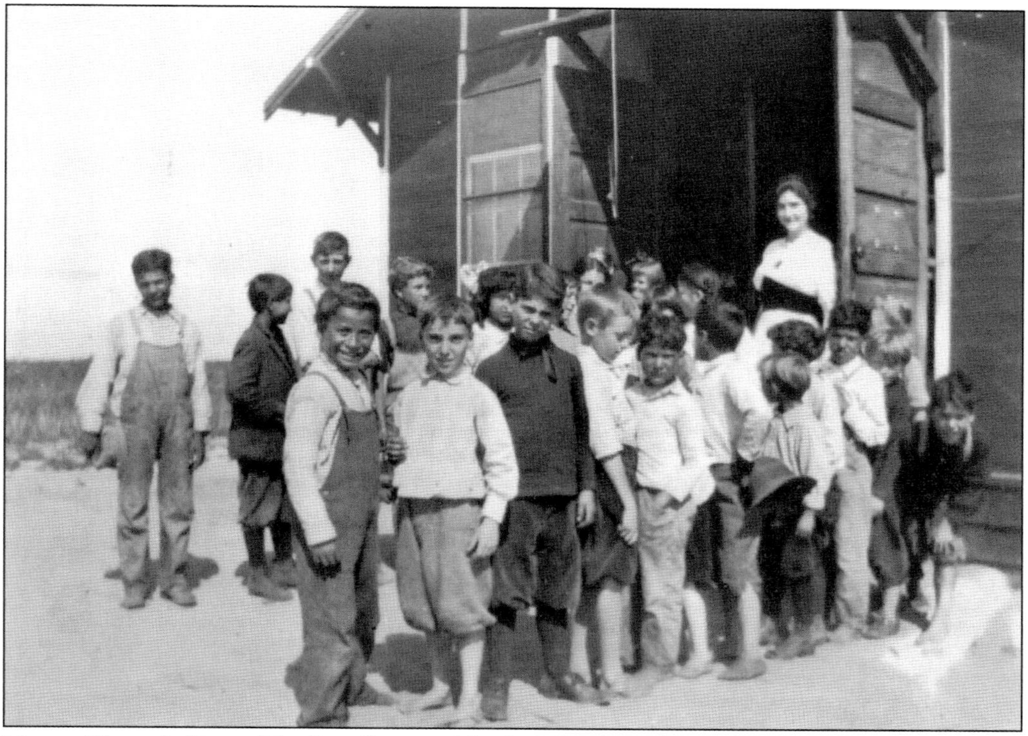

Marie Vignes's Boys. The Los Cerritos North School was located on Pine Avenue and San Antonio Drive. Teacher Marie Vignes lined boys on one side, girls on the other. In this 1914 photograph are, from left to right, (first row) Alfred Encinas, David Bixby, unidentified, Stephen Bixby, and the rest unidentified; (second row) two unidentified students, John Cumming, Paul Grisham, Elvera Encinas, Pauline King, and Amelia Vignes. (Courtesy of Ellen Collins.)

Los Cerritos Student Body. Teacher Marie Vignes stands with her class on April 29, 1915. Shown here are, from left to right, (first row) David Bixby, Stephen Bixby, Jewel King, Andrew Encinas, and Archie King; (second row) Marjorie King, Roberta Stewart, and three unidentified students; (third row) John Cumming, Alfred Encinas, unidentified, Rosalie Turner, Muriel Grisham, two unidentified students, and Marie Vignes; (fourth row) Don Christensen, two unidentified students, Pauline King, Elvera Encinas, and Amelia Vignes. (LCS.)

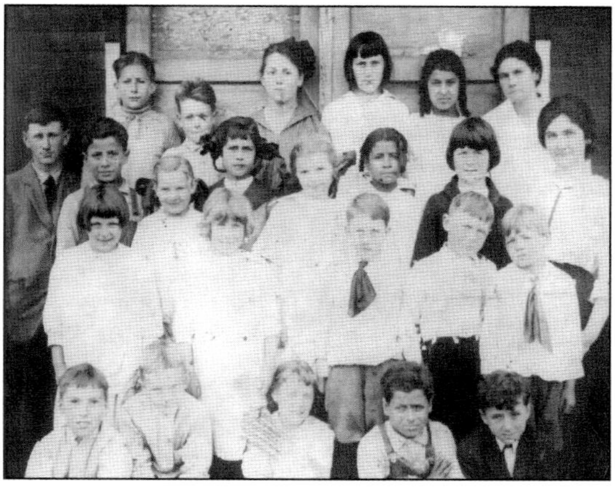

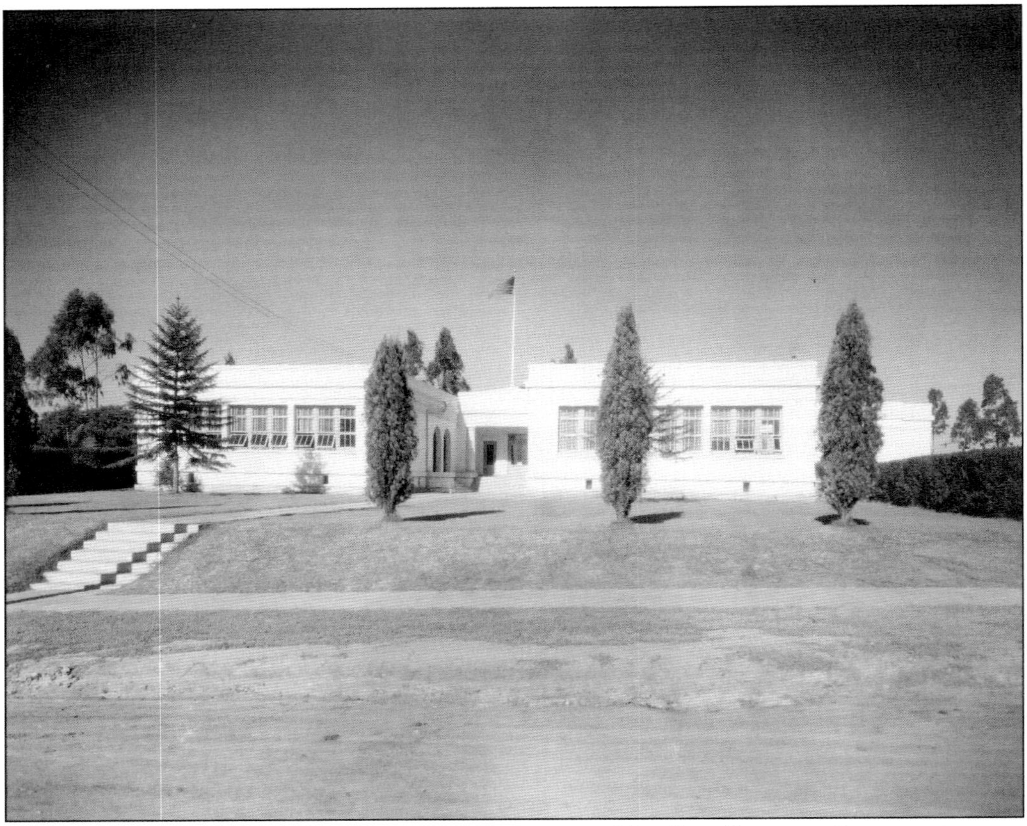

New Los Cerritos School. A school with two classrooms was built at 515 West San Antonio Drive. By 1920, two additional classrooms and a kindergarten were added. Joining the Long Beach School District in 1924, this was the last district school to maintain all eight grades, becoming an elementary school in December 1949. The school is seen here in 1915. (LCS.)

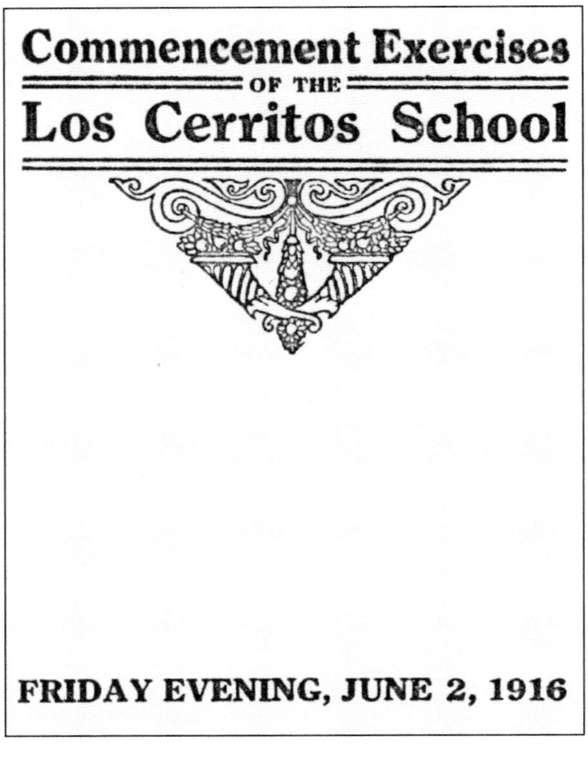

Commencement Exercises
OF THE
Los Cerritos School

FRIDAY EVENING, JUNE 2, 1916

Los Cerritos Commencement Program Cover. The 1916 graduates were Donald Christensen, Elvera Encinas, Amelia Vignes, Pauline King, and John Cumming. All lived in Los Cerritos except Encinas, whose father was a laborer on a beet farm until he bought the ranch across the river from the school, and Cumming, who lived in Compton.

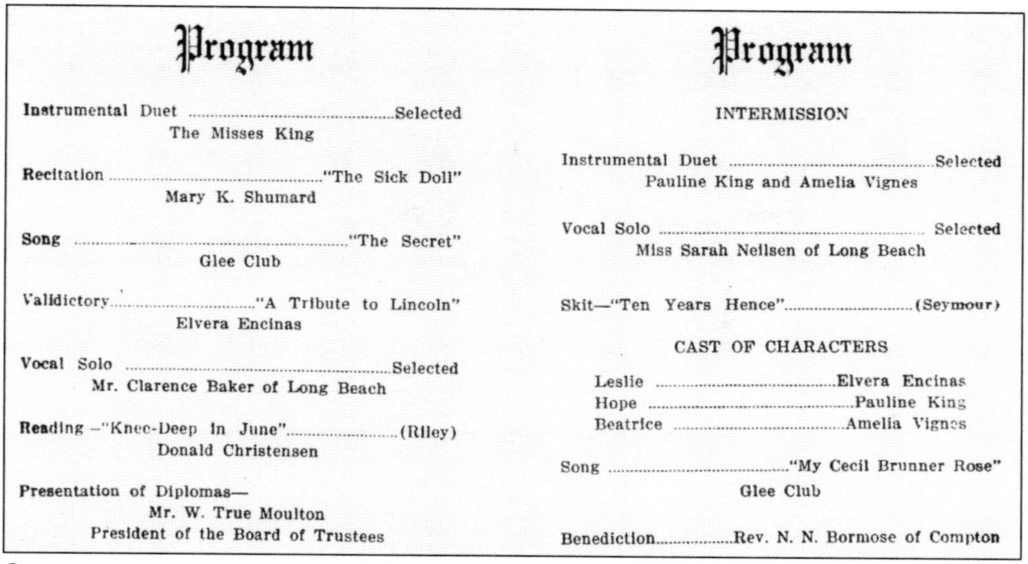

Program

Instrumental Duet .... Selected
The Misses King

Recitation .... "The Sick Doll"
Mary K. Shumard

Song .... "The Secret"
Glee Club

Validictory.. "A Tribute to Lincoln"
Elvera Encinas

Vocal Solo .... Selected
Mr. Clarence Baker of Long Beach

Reading –"Knee-Deep in June".. (Riley)
Donald Christensen

Presentation of Diplomas—
Mr. W. True Moulton
President of the Board of Trustees

Program

INTERMISSION

Instrumental Duet .... Selected
Pauline King and Amelia Vignes

Vocal Solo .... Selected
Miss Sarah Neilsen of Long Beach

Skit—"Ten Years Hence".. (Seymour)

CAST OF CHARACTERS

Leslie .... Elvera Encinas
Hope .... Pauline King
Beatrice .... Amelia Vignes

Song .... "My Cecil Brunner Rose"
Glee Club

Benediction.. Rev. N. N. Bormose of Compton

COMMENCEMENT SCHEDULE. The 1916 program indicates that students were instructed in music and instruments. Commencement ceremonies in those days typically included musical performances and skits. W. True Moulton, the president of the board of trustees, presented the diplomas.

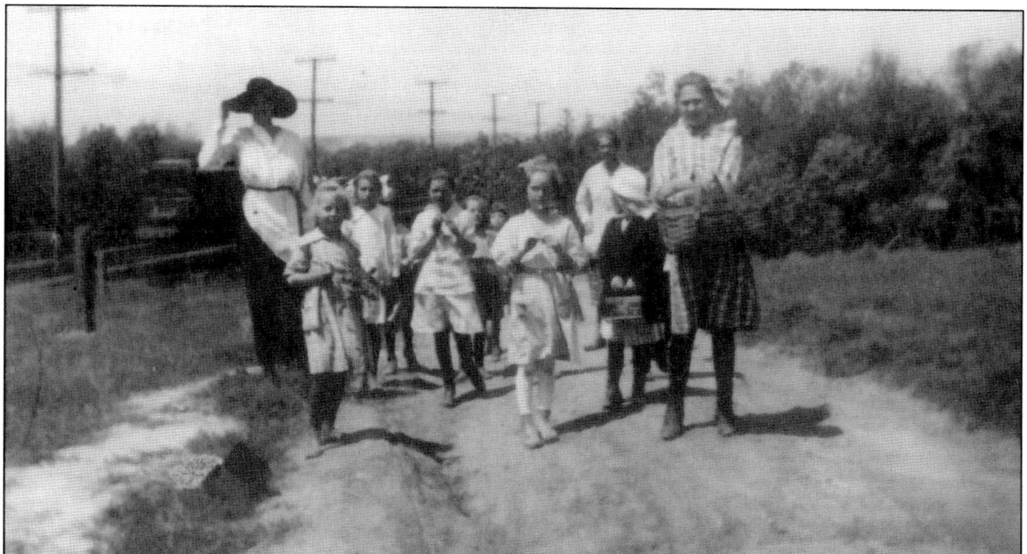

PICNIC DAY. Evelyn Moulton, a 1908 graduate of the original "South" Los Cerritos School, became a teacher at Los Cerritos School in 1917–1918 and served as principal in 1919 and 1920. Here, she takes her students on a picnic by the Los Angeles River. (LCS.)

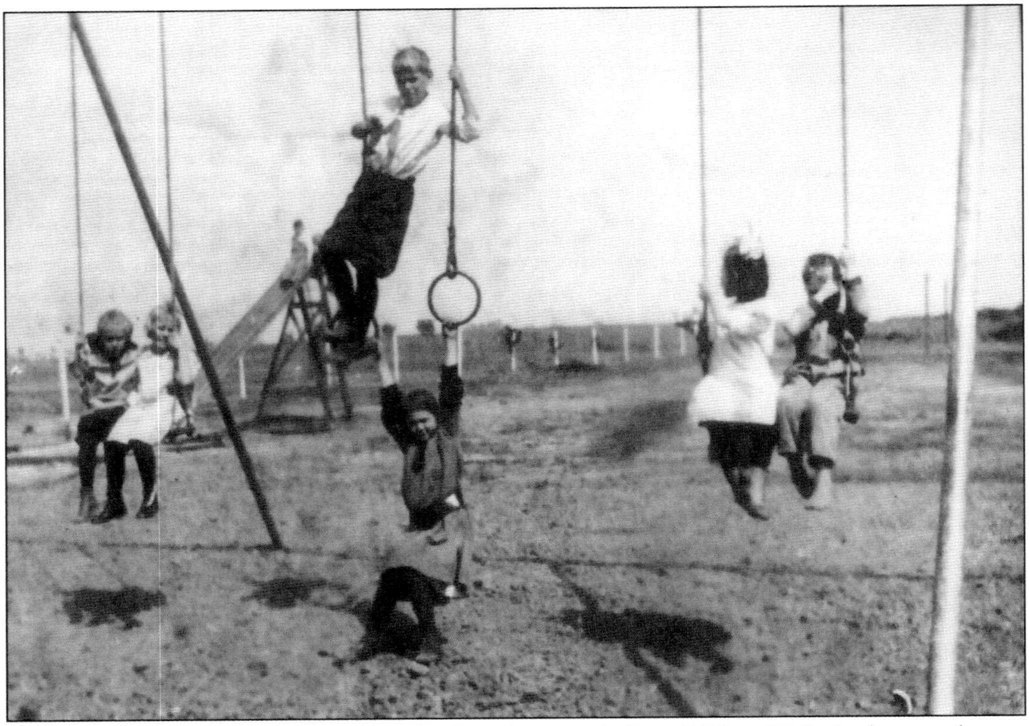

Los Cerritos School Playground. In this photograph from 1917 or 1918, the boy on the top ring is Frankie Jordan. Loretta Underkirchner is in the center, hanging on the rings. Also pictured are Eleanor Johansing, Margaret Johansing, and Simon McDonald. (LCS.)

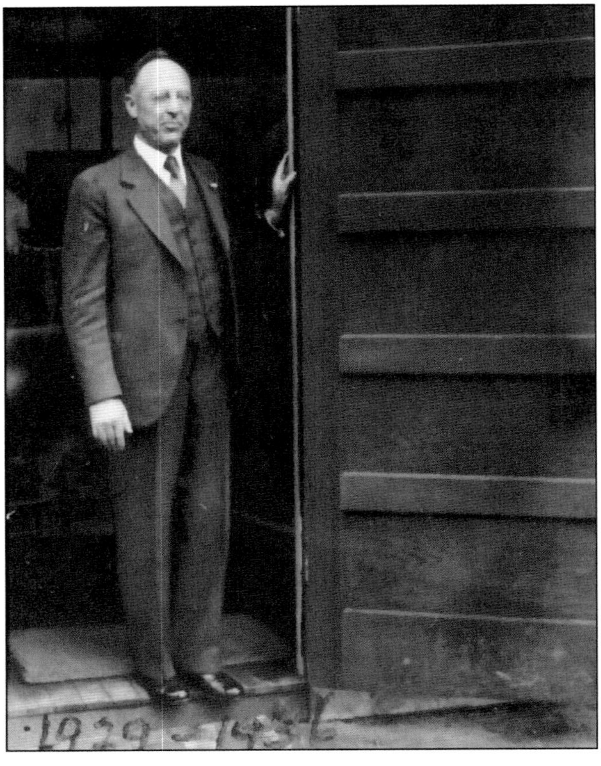

William Huff. Huff was principal of Los Cerritos School from 1929 to 1936. He made sure classes continued in tents after the 1933 Long Beach earthquake. (LCS.)

Marguerite Vignes, PTA Founder. Marguerite Vignes, wife of Bert Walp and daughter of John and Mary Vignes, was the founder of the Los Cerritos PTA in 1923. She served as president for two years, as well as acting as scholarship aid chairman and art and poster chairman. (LCS.)

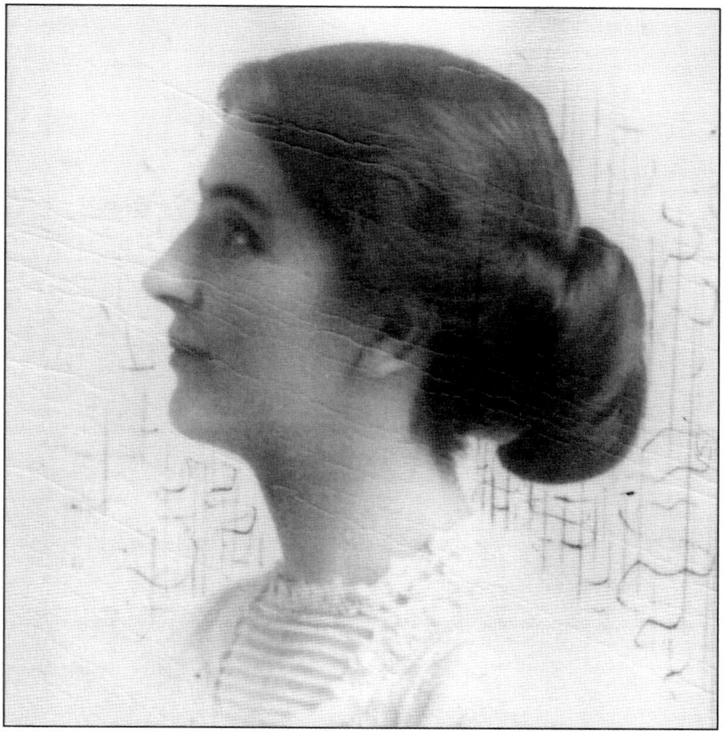

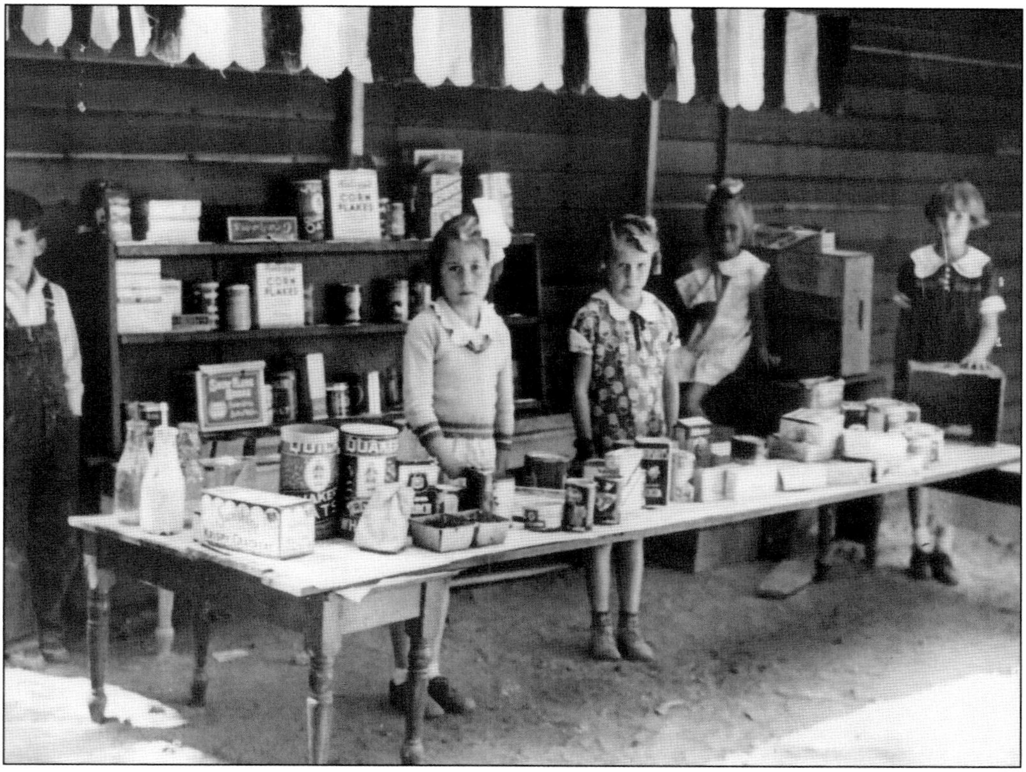

General Store at Los Cerritos School. This store was probably set up to teach math. The girl in the print dress is Edith Merrell. This photograph was taken in 1932. (LCS.)

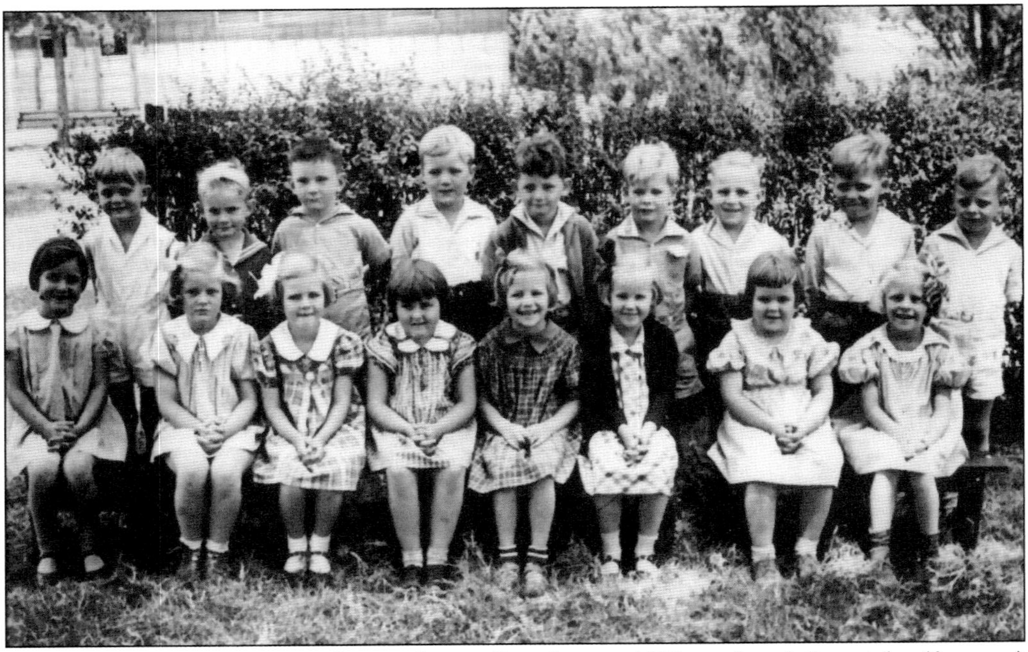

Los Cerritos School, First-Grade Class. Seen here in 1935 are, from left to right, (first row) Helen Newcomb, Barbara Enloe, Ronalie Smith, Rosemary Kelch, unidentified, Joan Updike, Mollie ?, and unidentified; (second row) Melvin Beckett, Dean Smith, Gene Hancock, Bobby McQueen, unidentified, Fred Ten Eyck, Dick Curtis, Bill Edwards, and unidentified. (LCS.)

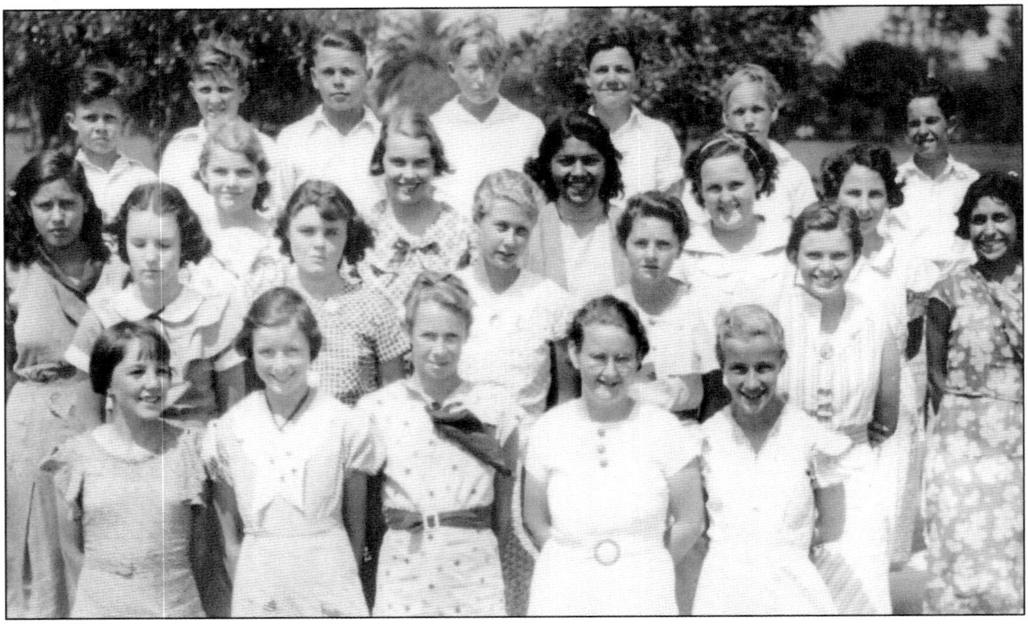

1934 Graduating Class. Shown here are, from left to right, (first row) Dorothy Hynes, Juanita Cozart, Nebra Boardwell, Charlotte Kennedy, and Helen Caron; (second row) Doris Cole, Marialice DeCoudres, Edith Merrell, Norma Campbell, and Emma Lou Robertson; (third row) Natalie Aquilar, Melissa Munn, Janet Sigworth, Virginia Coronado, Dixie Nobel, Marian Duncan, and Louise Aquilar; (fourth row) Hal Heckman, Chuck Walker, Bill Becker, Dick Buffum, Rod Rothgeb, Bob Broxholme, and Joe Deeble. (LCS.)

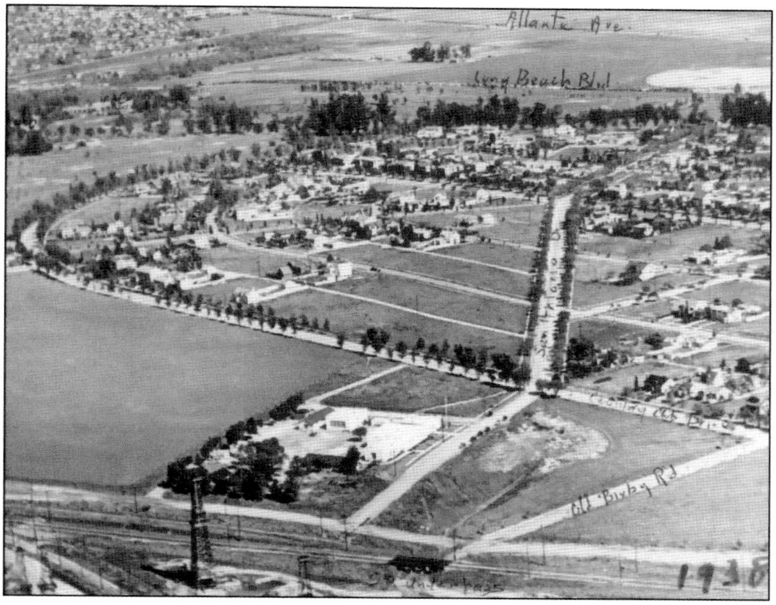

LOS CERRITOS SCHOOL AFTER EARTHQUAKE. This aerial photograph, dated March 4, 193?, shows the Los Cerritos School constructed after the 1933 Long Beach earthquake. The architect was H. Alfred Anderson. The school was first occupied in 1935.

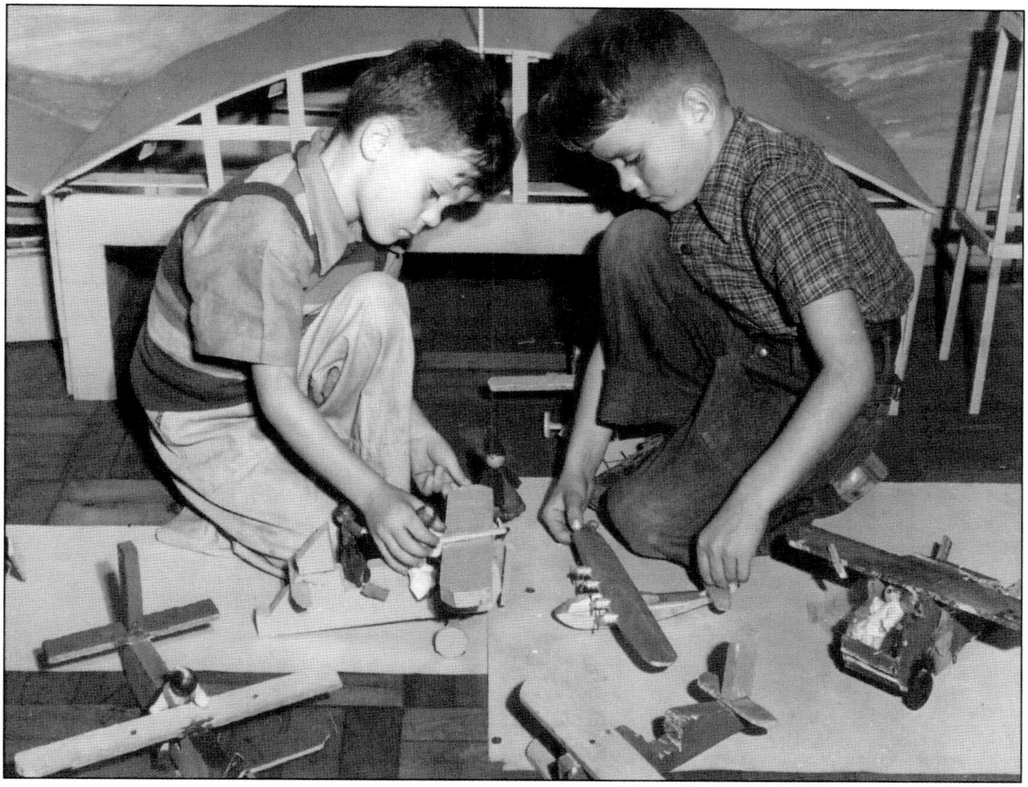

LOS CERRITOS SCHOOL WOOD SHOP, C. 1940. The one-room schoolhouse located at San Antonio Drive and Pine Avenue was moved behind the new Los Cerritos School on San Antonio Drive and Del Mar Avenue. The bungalow was then used for wood shop classes, where students learned to make their own planes. (LCS.)

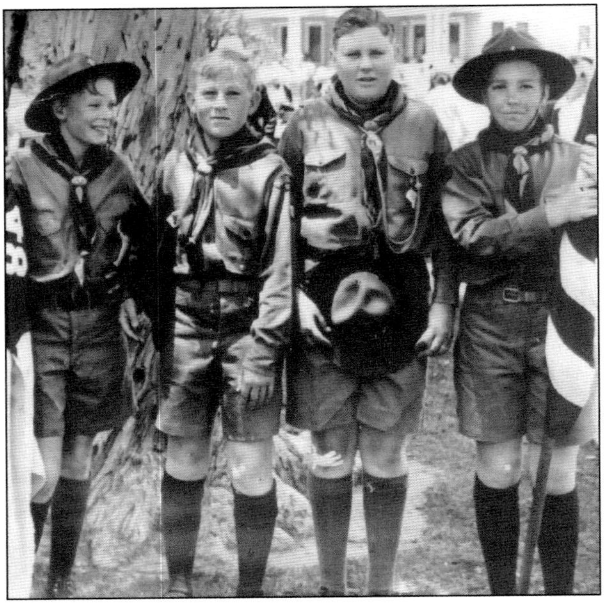

Boy Scouts. This 1940 photograph shows a Scouts color guard from Los Cerritos School. From left to right are Fred Ten Eyck, Lester Callahan, Pete Updike, and Bill Edwards. (LCS.)

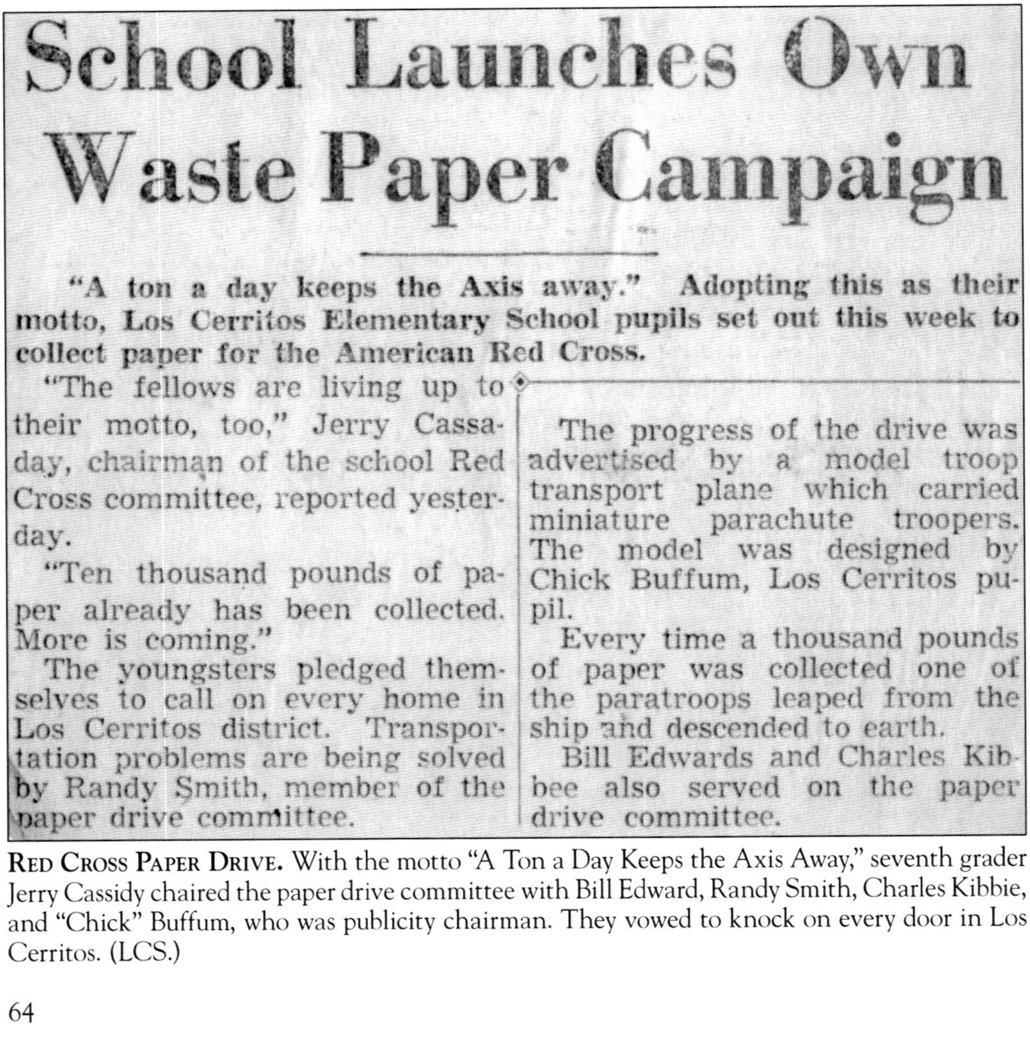

School Launches Own Waste Paper Campaign

"A ton a day keeps the Axis away." Adopting this as their motto, Los Cerritos Elementary School pupils set out this week to collect paper for the American Red Cross.

"The fellows are living up to their motto, too," Jerry Cassaday, chairman of the school Red Cross committee, reported yesterday.

"Ten thousand pounds of paper already has been collected. More is coming."

The youngsters pledged themselves to call on every home in Los Cerritos district. Transportation problems are being solved by Randy Smith, member of the paper drive committee.

The progress of the drive was advertised by a model troop transport plane which carried miniature parachute troopers. The model was designed by Chick Buffum, Los Cerritos pupil.

Every time a thousand pounds of paper was collected one of the paratroops leaped from the ship and descended to earth.

Bill Edwards and Charles Kibbee also served on the paper drive committee.

Red Cross Paper Drive. With the motto "A Ton a Day Keeps the Axis Away," seventh grader Jerry Cassidy chaired the paper drive committee with Bill Edward, Randy Smith, Charles Kibbie, and "Chick" Buffum, who was publicity chairman. They vowed to knock on every door in Los Cerritos. (LCS.)

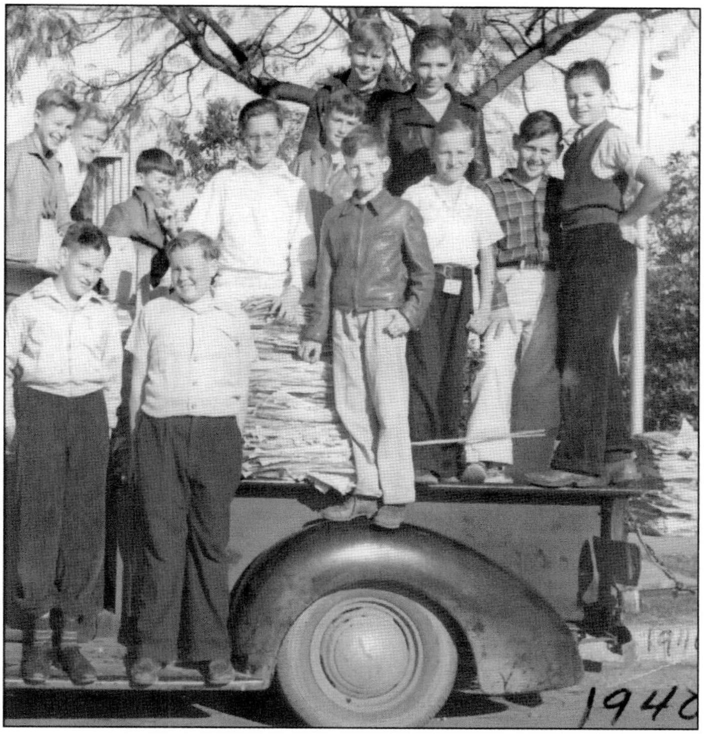

PAPER DRIVE WORKERS. This 1940 photograph shows the results of the multiday effort undertaken by the paper drive committee to help the Red Cross. Every time 10,000 pounds was collected, paratroops leaped from a model transport plane designed by "Chick" Buffum and floated down to earth, advertising the campaign success. (LCS.)

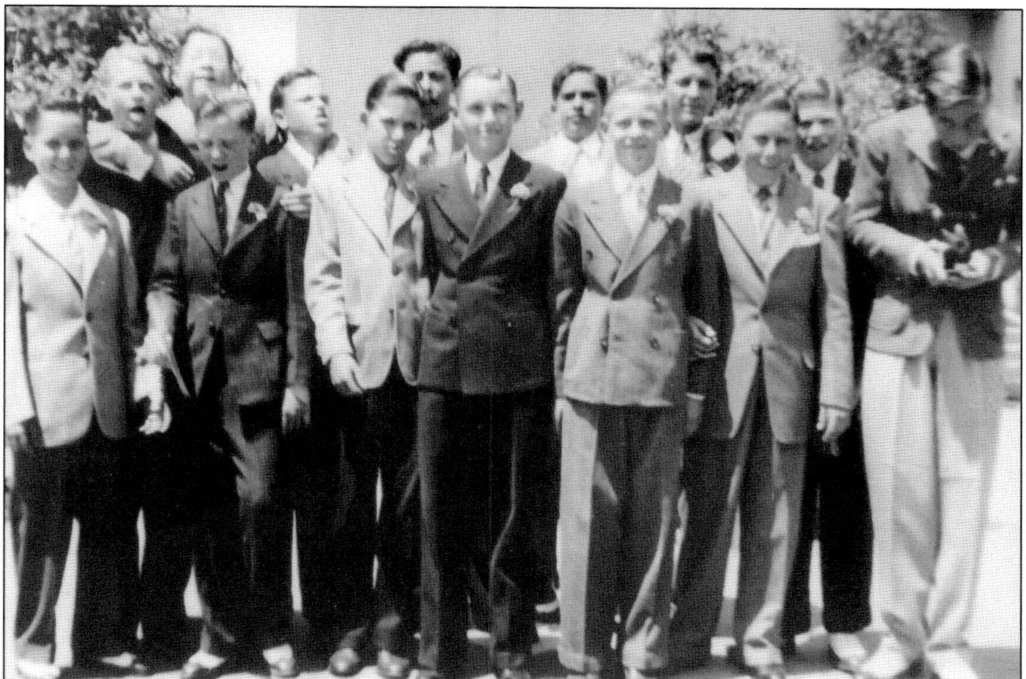

THE BOYS OF 1941. The Los Cerritos eighth-grade graduating class of 1941 included 14 boys. They are, from left to right, Llewelyn Mahieu, Bill Bussie, Jack Miller, Bill Brinkman, Roscoe Wilkie, Cedric White, Louis Gonzales, Harry Ames, Bob Bristol, Kenny Walker, John Wallace, Wayne Wells, Gil Walker, and Edger Bourne. (LCS.)

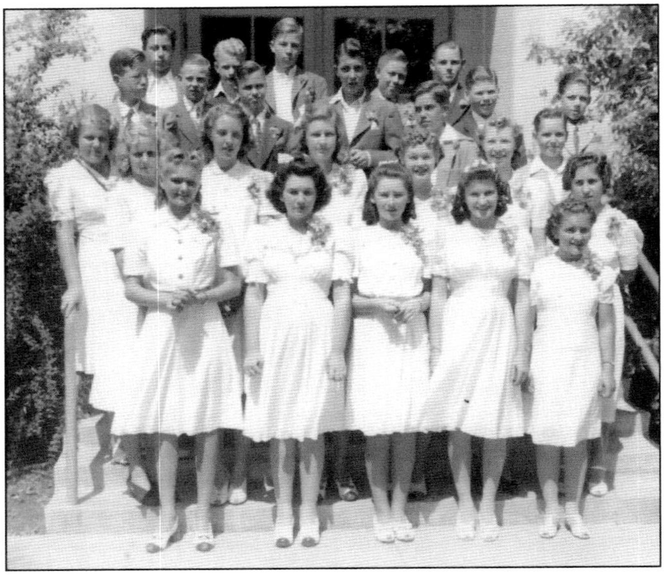

EIGHTH-GRADE CLASS. The 1941 graduates shown here are, from left to right, (first row) Betty Cree, Lorene Simmons, Barbara Inman, Phyllis McPheeters, and Cora Barker; (second row) Jewell Mars, Marjorie Merrell, Margaret Wilkinson, Carolyn Clock, Renee Mae Nagy, Gloria Moore, Llewelyn Mahieu, and Tillie Galaz; (third row) Jack Miller, Kenny Walker, Roscoe Wilkie, John Wallace, Bob Bristol, Gil Walker, and Cedric White; (fourth row) Louis Galaz, Bill Bussee, Edgar Boune, Wayne Wells, and Harry Aine. (LCS.)

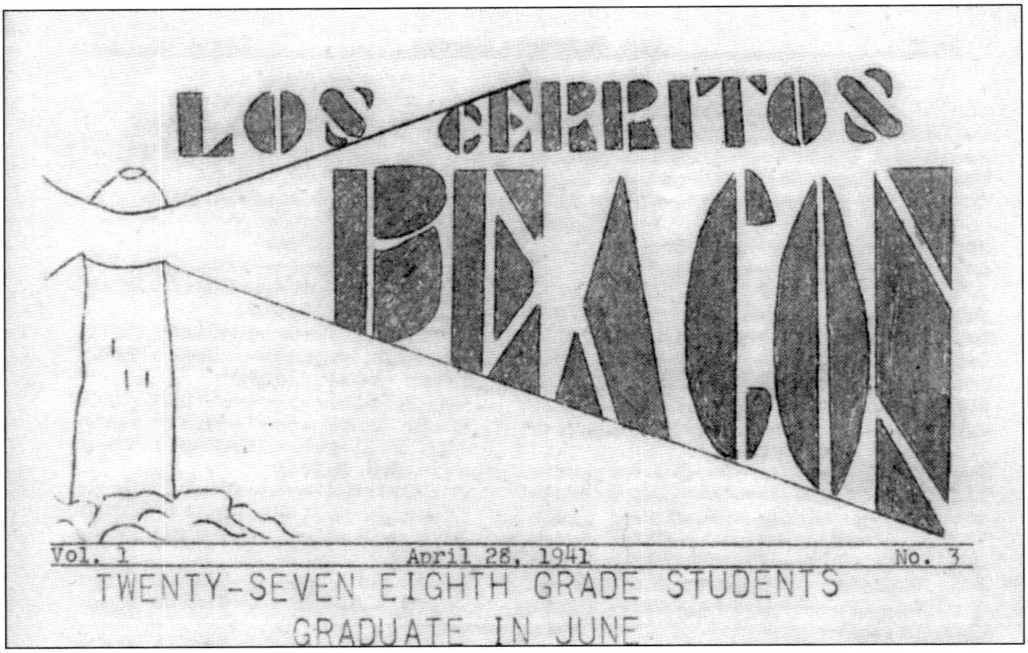

LOS CERRITOS STUDENT NEWSPAPER. The students of Los Cerritos produced their own newspaper, the *Beacon*. In prior years, the newspaper was called the *Los Cerritos Star*. The eighth-grade class started the newspaper when they were fifth graders. The 18-page-long paper included the honor roll, class activities, sports, book reviews, and several pages of large type for the lower grades. (Courtesy of Margaret Wilkinson Mahannah.)

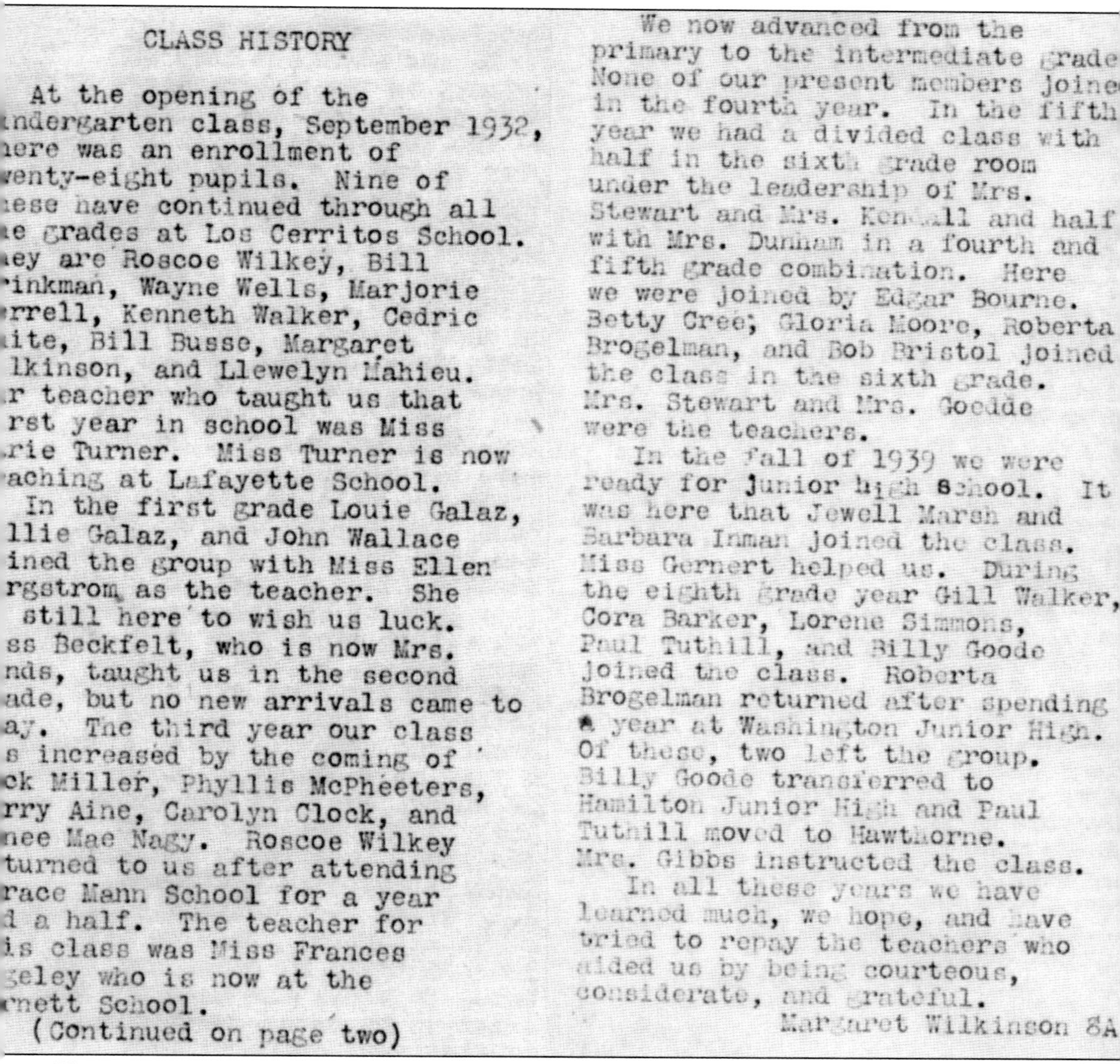

CLASS HISTORY

At the opening of the ındergarten class, September 1932, ıere was an enrollment of venty-eight pupils. Nine of ıese have continued through all ıe grades at Los Cerritos School. ıey are Roscoe Wilkey, Bill 'inkman, Wayne Wells, Marjorie rrell, Kenneth Walker, Cedric ıite, Bill Busse, Margaret lkinson, and Llewelyn Mahieu. ır teacher who taught us that rst year in school was Miss ırie Turner. Miss Turner is now aching at Lafayette School.

In the first grade Louie Galaz, llie Galaz, and John Wallace ined the group with Miss Ellen rgstrom as the teacher. She still here to wish us luck. ss Beckfelt, who is now Mrs. nds, taught us in the second ade, but no new arrivals came to ay. The third year our class s increased by the coming of ck Miller, Phyllis McPheeters, rry Aine, Carolyn Clock, and nee Mae Nagy. Roscoe Wilkey turned to us after attending race Mann School for a year d a half. The teacher for is class was Miss Frances ;eley who is now at the rnett School.

(Continued on page two)

We now advanced from the primary to the intermediate grade None of our present members joine in the fourth year. In the fifth year we had a divided class with half in the sixth grade room under the leadership of Mrs. Stewart and Mrs. Kendall and half with Mrs. Dunham in a fourth and fifth grade combination. Here we were joined by Edgar Bourne. Betty Cree, Gloria Moore, Roberta Brogelman, and Bob Bristol joined the class in the sixth grade. Mrs. Stewart and Mrs. Goedde were the teachers.

In the fall of 1939 we were ready for Junior high school. It was here that Jewell Marsh and Barbara Inman joined the class. Miss Gernert helped us. During the eighth grade year Gill Walker, Cora Barker, Lorene Simmons, Paul Tuthill, and Billy Goode joined the class. Roberta Brogelman returned after spending a year at Washington Junior High. Of these, two left the group. Billy Goode transferred to Hamilton Junior High and Paul Tuthill moved to Hawthorne. Mrs. Gibbs instructed the class.

In all these years we have learned much, we hope, and have tried to repay the teachers who aided us by being courteous, considerate, and grateful.

Margaret Wilkinson 8A

History of the 1941 Class. The April 28, 1941, edition of the Los Cerritos student newspaper traces the school history of the graduating class, from their kindergarten year of 1932. Margaret Wilkinson was the editor-in-chief in 1941 and wrote this column. (Courtesy of Margaret Wilkinson Mahannah.)

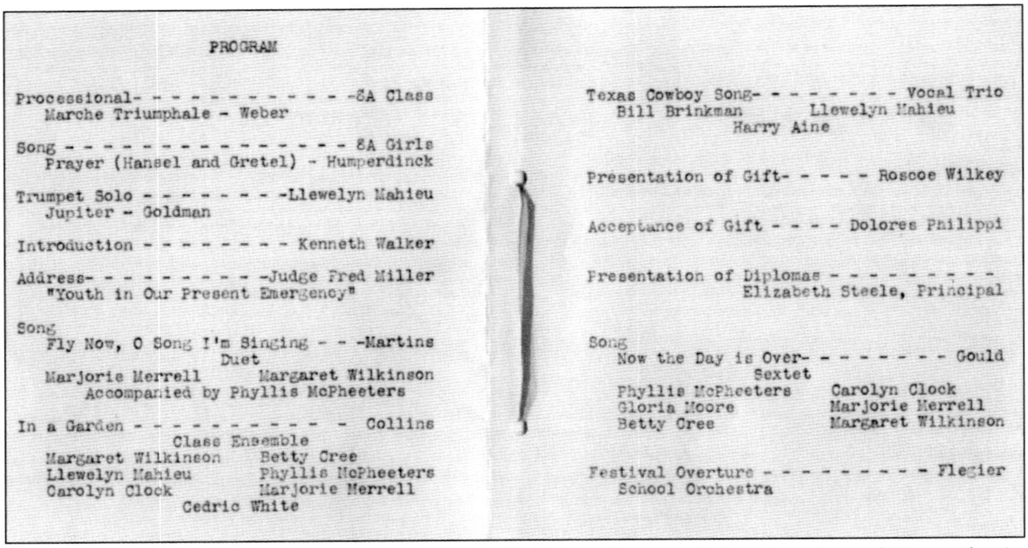

PROGRAM

Processional- - - - - - - - - - - - -8A Class
Marche Triumphale - Weber

Song - - - - - - - - - - - - - - - - 8A Girls
Prayer (Hansel and Gretel) - Humperdinck

Trumpet Solo - - - - - - - -Llewelyn Mahieu
Jupiter - Goldman

Introduction - - - - - - - - Kenneth Walker

Address- - - - - - - - - -Judge Fred Miller
"Youth in Our Present Emergency"

Song
Fly Now, O Song I'm Singing - - -Martins
Duet
Marjorie Merrell Margaret Wilkinson
Accompanied by Phyllis McPheeters

In a Garden - - - - - - - - - - - Collins
Class Ensemble
Margaret Wilkinson Betty Cree
Llewelyn Mahieu Phyllis McPheeters
Carolyn Clock Marjorie Merrell
Cedric White

Texas Cowboy Song- - - - - - - - Vocal Trio
Bill Brinkman Llewelyn Mahieu
Harry Aine

Presentation of Gift- - - - - Roscoe Wilkey

Acceptance of Gift - - - - Dolores Philippi

Presentation of Diplomas - - - - - - - - -
Elizabeth Steele, Principal

Song
Now the Day is Over- - - - - - - - Gould
Sextet
Phyllis McPheeters Carolyn Clock
Gloria Moore Marjorie Merrell
Betty Cree Margaret Wilkinson

Festival Overture - - - - - - - - - Flegier
School Orchestra

1941 COMMENCEMENT PROGRAM. On June 14, 1941, Los Cerritos School graduated 27 pupils. At that time, Elizabeth Steele was the principal. Several members of this graduating class still live in or near Los Cerritos, and many are still in Long Beach. (LCS.)

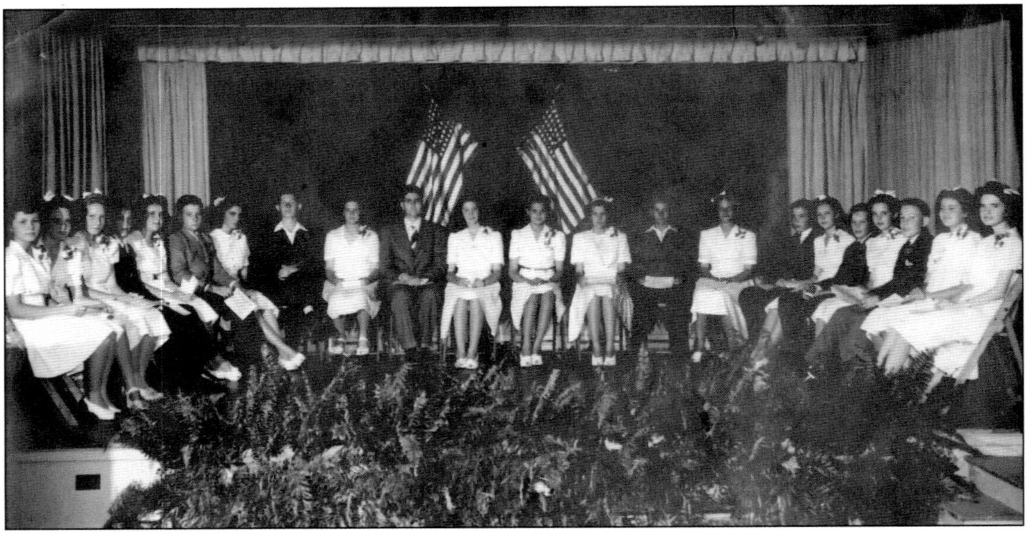

GRADUATING CLASS OF 1942. The eighth graders shown here are, from left to right, Fonita Lane, Lucille Murphy, Edwina Olsen, unidentified, Rosemary Kelch, Gene Hancock, Barbara Decker, Roger Freeman, unidentified, George Winslow, Patricia Bishop, Helene Erickson, Ronalee Smith, Ronald Freeman, Barbara Enloe, Bill Edwards, Joan Updike, Fred Ten Eyck, Patricia Spencer, Dick Curtis, unidentified, and Nancy Kirkwood. (LCS.)

ORIGINAL SCHOOL BELL MONUMENT. On the left is Evelyn Moulton Coigdarripe, the second teacher at the "North" Los Cerritos School. With her is Long Beach historian Loretta Underkirchner Berner, who attended school in the one-room schoolhouse in 1914. They are shown at the dedication of the original school bell monument in 1958. (LCS.)

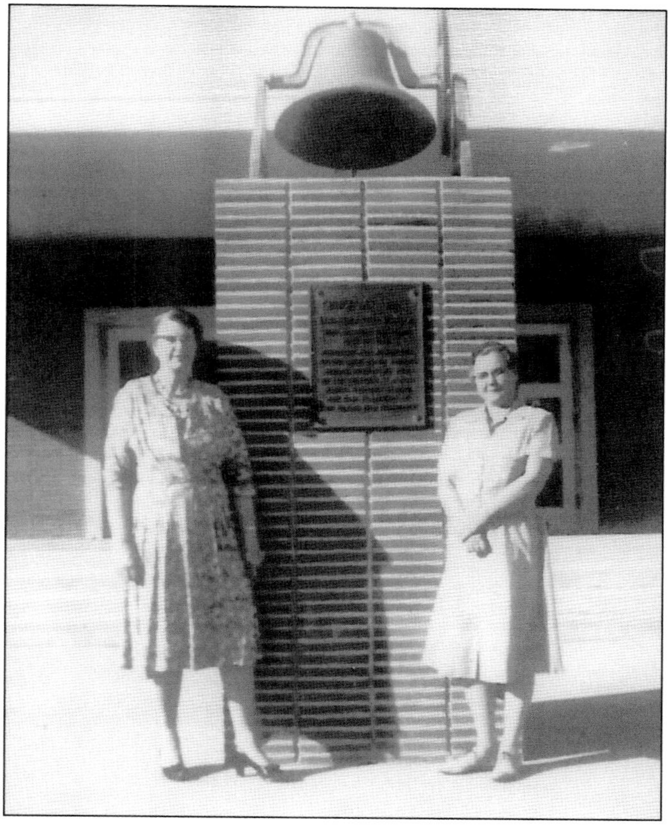

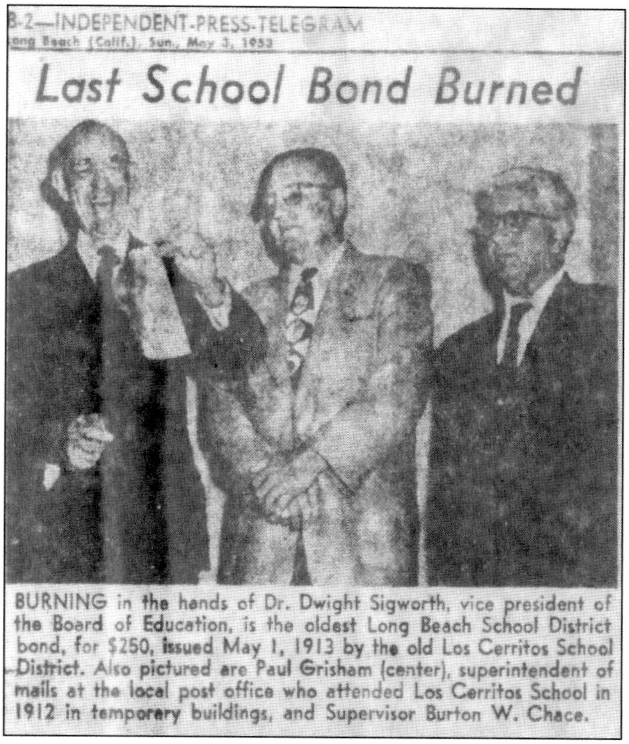

B-2—INDEPENDENT-PRESS-TELEGRAM
Long Beach (Calif.), Sun., May 3, 1953

Last School Bond Burned

BURNING in the hands of Dr. Dwight Sigworth, vice president of the Board of Education, is the oldest Long Beach School District bond, for $250, issued May 1, 1913 by the old Los Cerritos School District. Also pictured are Paul Grisham (center), superintendent of mails at the local post office who attended Los Cerritos School in 1912 in temporary buildings, and Supervisor Burton W. Chace.

LAST SCHOOL BOND. The bond to construct the first one-room Los Cerritos North School was issued on May 1, 1913. This newspaper photograph depicts officials burning the final bond in May 1953. Pictured from left to right are Dr. Dwight Sigworth, vice-president of the board of education, holding the bond; Paul Grisham, superintendent of mails at the local post office, who attended the one-room school; and supervisor Burton Chace.

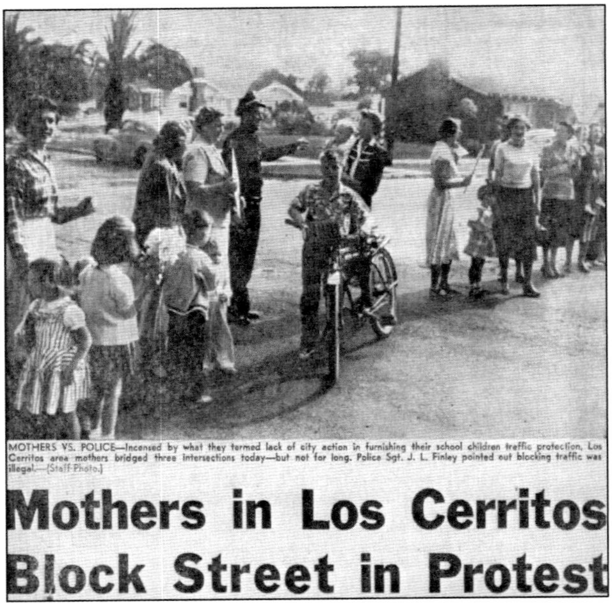

MOTHERS VS. POLICE—Incensed by what they termed lack of city action in furnishing their school children traffic protection, Los Cerritos area mothers bridged three intersections today—but not for long. Police Sgt. J. L. Finley pointed out blocking traffic was illegal.—(Staff Photo.)

Mothers in Los Cerritos Block Street in Protest

MOTHERS PROTEST. Calling themselves "crossing guard gangs," mothers blocked traffic on Pacific Avenue in 1953 to "awaken the City Council" to their children's safety. For three years, the Los Cerritos Improvement Association had appealed to the city for traffic relief. Resident Ruth Craig Merrell told the press, "it's action we want and it's action we'll get, no matter how long we have to keep this up."

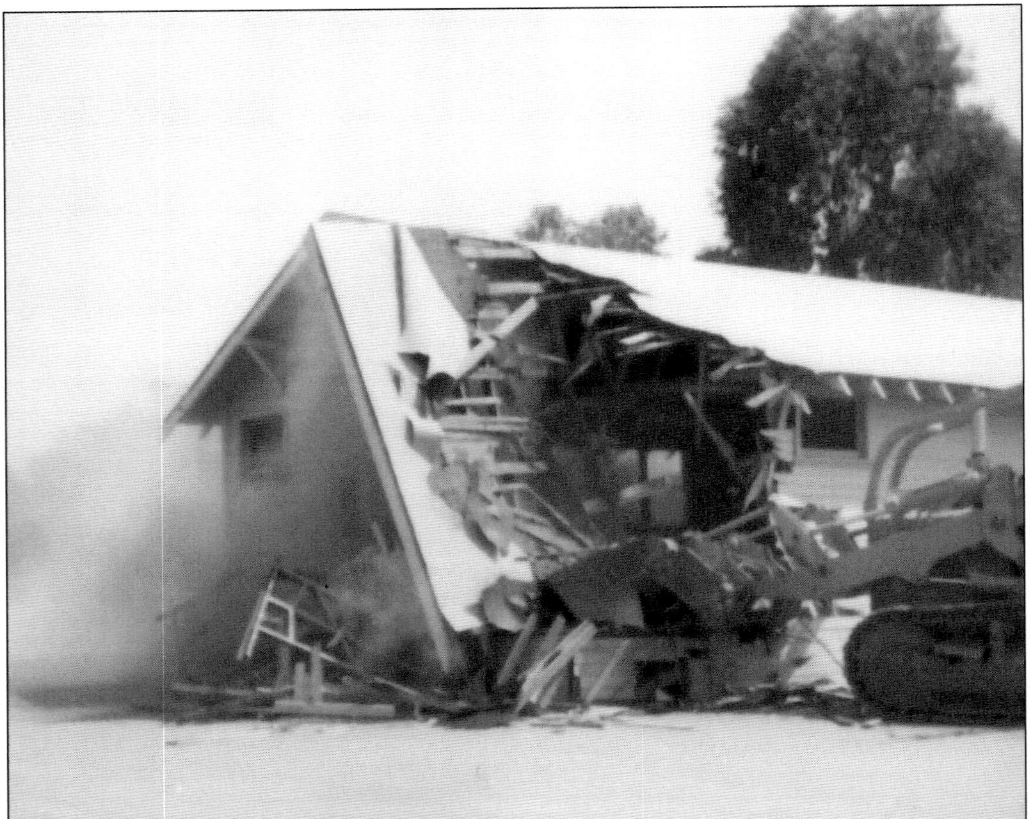

DEMOLITION OF ORIGINAL SCHOOLHOUSE. The original one-room schoolhouse building was moved to the current school site when the second "North" Los Cerritos School was built in 1915. The bungalow served as a woodshop and caretaker's quarters until it was demolished in June 1970. (LCS.)

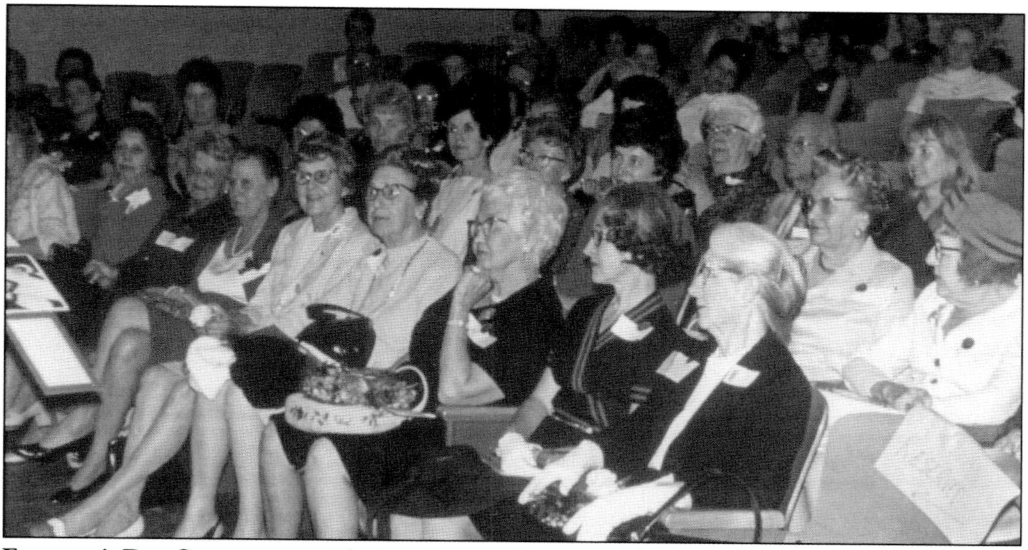

FOUNDER'S DAY CELEBRATION. The Los Cerritos Parent Teacher Association celebrated Founder's Day in February 1971. Honored guests were Mrs. Bert Walp (founder and president from 1923 to 1924), Mrs. P.C. Nix, Mrs. B.S. Parson, Mrs. I.S. Clarke, Mrs. Robert Broxholme, Mrs. Frank Parr, Mrs. Charles Decoders, Mrs. Ray K. Person, Mrs. Gerald Beck, Mrs. Dwight S. Sigworth, Mrs. Ruth Hall Mills, Mrs. Marion Lower, Mrs. Don C. Wallace, Mrs. Charles Z. Walker, Mrs. Ruth Craig Merrell, Mrs. Milton McGrew, Mrs. Gus A. Walker, Mrs. Leland T. Edwards, Mrs. Douglas A. Newcomb, and Mrs. Warren Ten Eyck. Shown here in the front row are, from left to right, Encinas, DeCoudres, Ten Eyck, Gernert, Edwards, Stacey, Burrell, and Walp. (LCS.)

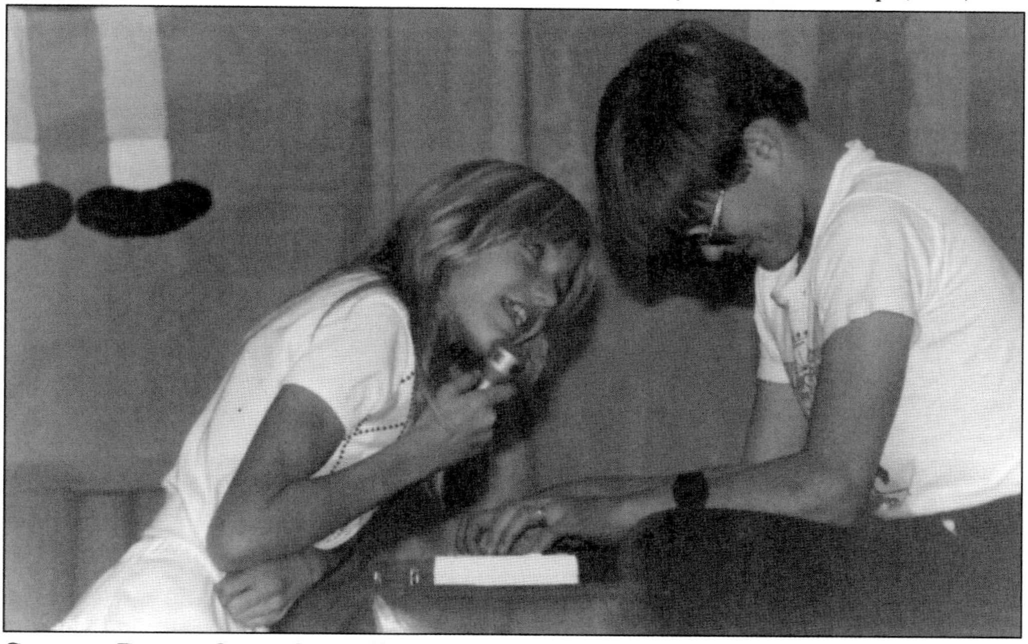

CAMERON DIAZ IN SIXTH-GRADE PRODUCTION. The sixth-grade class performance of *You're a Good Man, Charlie Brown* in March 1984 included student Cameron Diaz. Diaz grew up in Long Beach and attended Los Cerritos and Long Beach Poly High School. She rose to prominence in the 1990s with leading roles in films such as *My Best Friend's Wedding* and *There's Something About Mary*. (LCS.)

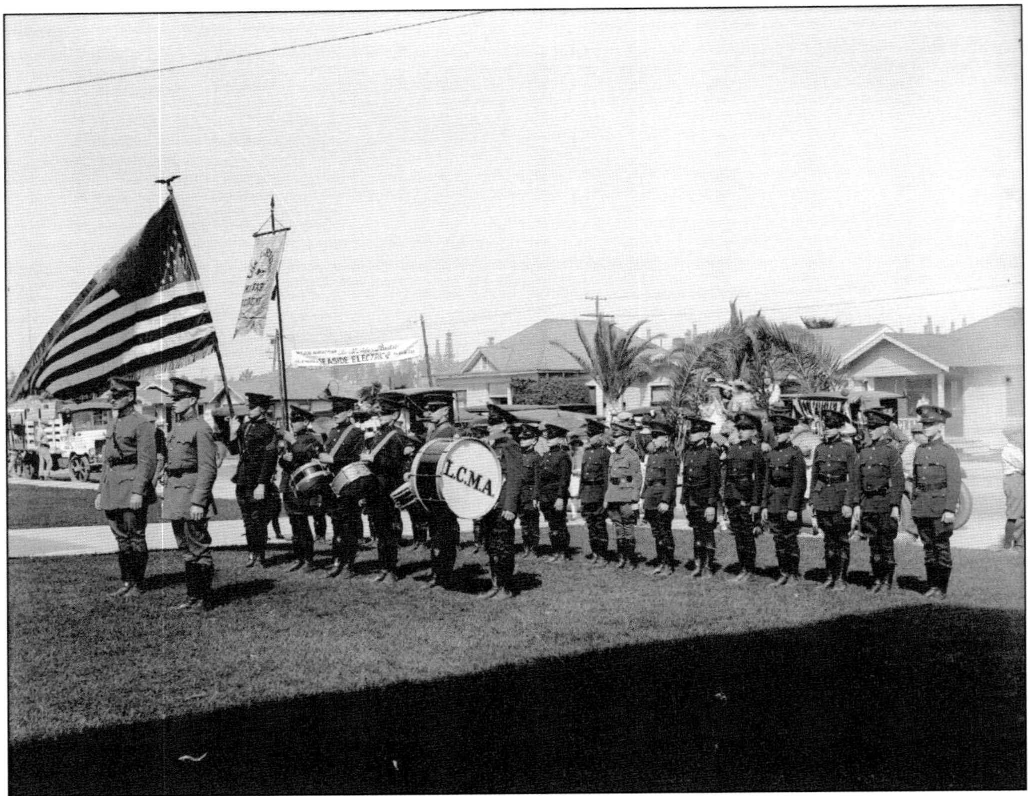

Los Cerritos Military Academy, 1926. The Los Cerritos Military Academy opened on September 8, 1925. The president was T.M. Welch, and board members were John H. Betts, president of B.H. Transportation; C.A. Buffum, president of Buffum's Department Store; E. J. Wightman, president of Marine Trust & Savings Bank; E.J. Colbert, physician; and R.H. Fowles, capitalist. Maj. Wilbur Watkins was headmaster. (HSLB.)

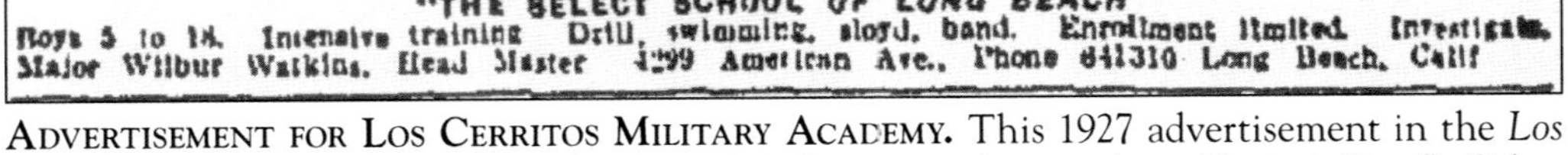

LOS CERRITOS MILITARY ACADEMY

"THE SELECT SCHOOL OF LONG BEACH"

Boys 5 to 18. Intensive training. Drill, swimming, sloyd, band. Enrollment limited. Investigate. Major Wilbur Watkins, Head Master 4299 American Ave., Phone 641310 Long Beach, Calif

Advertisement for Los Cerritos Military Academy. This 1927 advertisement in the *Los Angeles Times* indicated the school was at 4299 American Avenue (now Virginia Road). Other sources indicate the location as 4141 American Avenue. Norma Campbell Craig said the school was across from her house at 235 Claiborne Place. School board members owned both 4141 and 4201 American Avenue. In August 1927, the school announced the addition of its third unit to its building program, so it likely occupied homes at 4141, 4123, and 4125 American Avenue.

Four

The Bixby Homes and La Linda

In 1890, George H. Bixby and his family moved into a new home constructed on 10 acres given to him by his father, Jotham. The firm of Coxhead and Coxhead designed the structure, and the younger Coxhead lived on-site for the three years that the house was under construction. The 17-room, 6,996-square-foot home was remodeled in 1901 under Coxhead's direction. Some of its Victorian features were retained but with the hallmarks of the Shingle style, including hipped and gabled dormers and a gambrel roof. Due to failing health, Bixby retired in 1919 and sold the home in 1920 to Thomas Gilchrist, an Oklahoma oilman, for $10,000. The Bixby family moved across Bixby Road to live with George's brother Richard. After George H. Bixby died, Amelia Bixby further subdivided the neighborhood, including the property surrounding the Richard Bixby home. That home was a victim of encroaching oil and was relocated to 638 East Sunrise Drive, where it stands today. Amelia Bixby lived there for several decades with her servants.

In 1924, Gilchrist subdivided the property into 33 residential lots, known as the Country Club Heights Tract, now La Linda Drive. The lot owners met in 1926 and voted unanimously to forego their dreams of a residential community and to lease the tract for oil drilling. A few homes were built in the development before this vote (addresses 25, 32, and 54 La Linda Drive were built in 1924, 26 La Linda in 1925, and 7 La Linda in 1927), but most were built after oil-drilling operations stopped in the late 1920s. The Bixby home was vacant during this period, and in the late 1940s, the home was purchased by Revan and Lillian Kamaroff. In 1989, owners Sam Picone and Nancy Good contracted with historical builder Peter Devereaux to restore the house, including rebuilding all the chimneys and the foundations. In 1995, the home was purchased by Gary Smith and Duane Rose. Rose has been faithfully restoring the gardens and lily ponds to their original design.

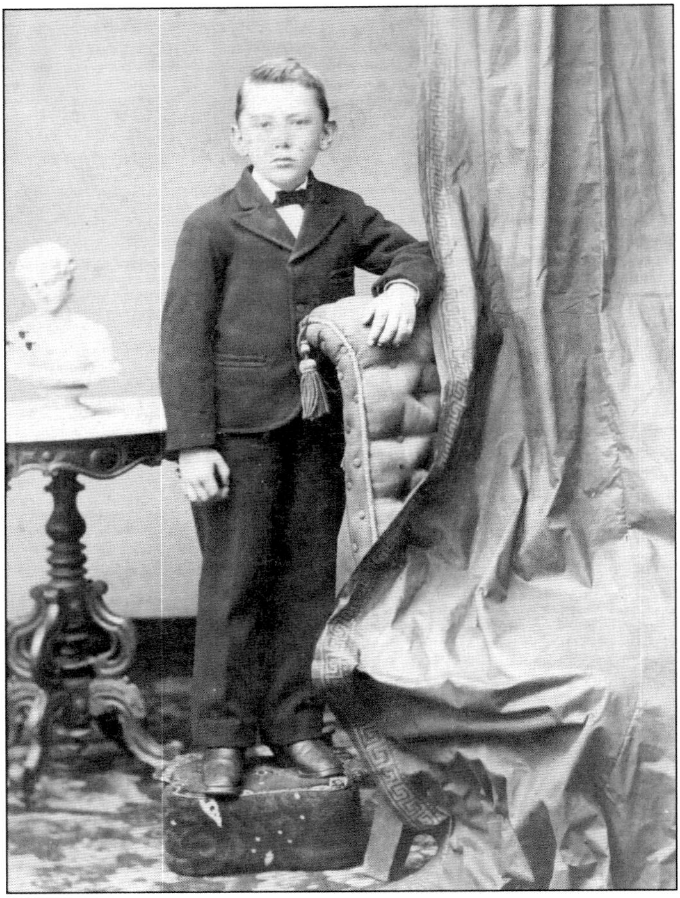

George Hathaway Bixby. Jotham Bixby and Margaret Hathaway were married in 1862 and moved to the rancho adobe in 1866 after it was purchased by the Flint Bixby and Company. Jotham and Margaret had seven children; the oldest, George Hathaway, was born in 1864. This image shows George at age 9 or 10. George married Amelia Mary Elizabeth Andrews in 1887. (RLC.)

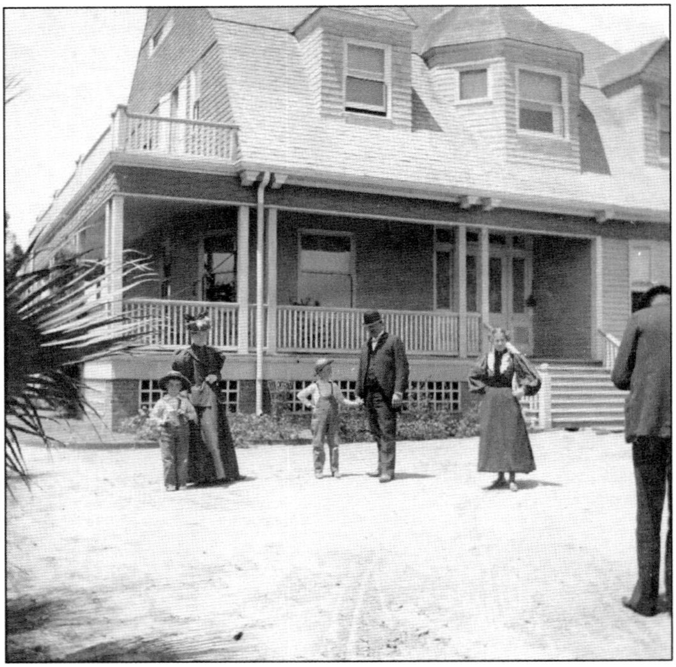

Bixby Family. This photograph, taken in 1899 or 1900, shows George Bixby's wife, Amelia, next to her son Philip L. George H. Bixby is holding son Richard's hand. The family is gathered in front of the Bixby home. (RLC.)

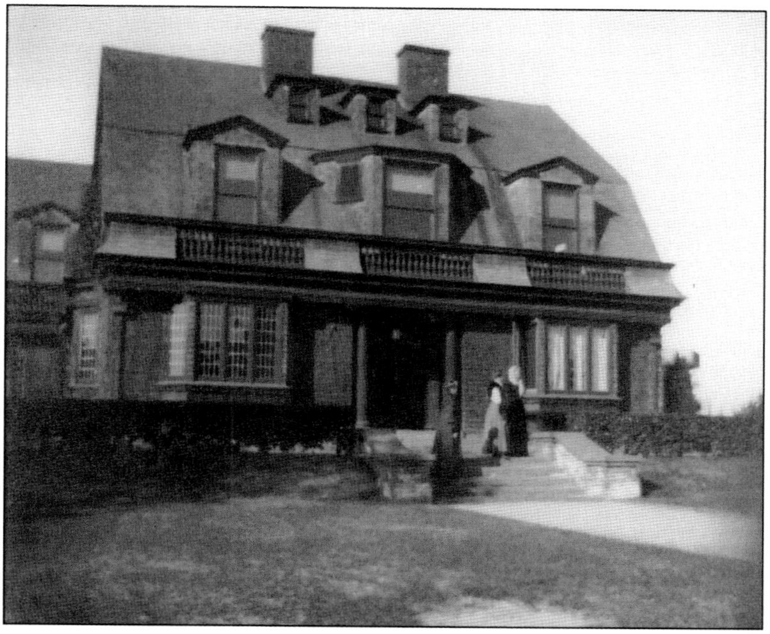

George H. Bixby House. The George H. Bixby home, seen here around 1918, was remodeled by Coxhead and Coxhead Architects around 1901. Bixby operated the rancho business interests from this home after his father Jotham's death in 1917. However, his health began to decline, and he retired in 1919. His wife, Amelia, took over many of the responsibilities. (Courtesy of Duane Rose).

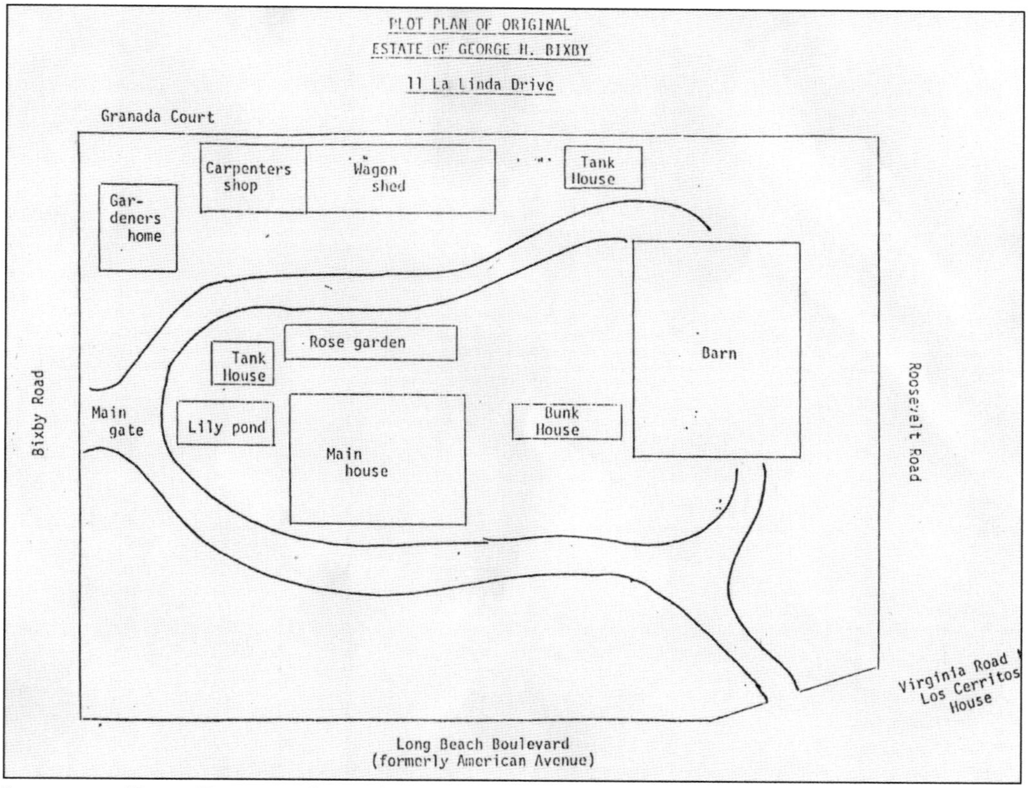

Layout of Bixby Estate. The Bixby property had a bunkhouse, barn, shops, and a water-tank house. There was an English gardener, Fred Moore, and two Japanese gardeners who lived in a small house on the southwest corner of the property. Moore and Thor Polson, the chauffeur, shared quarters in the tank house and then the barn. The bunkhouse was demolished around 1910, when automobiles became popular. (Courtesy of Duane Rose.)

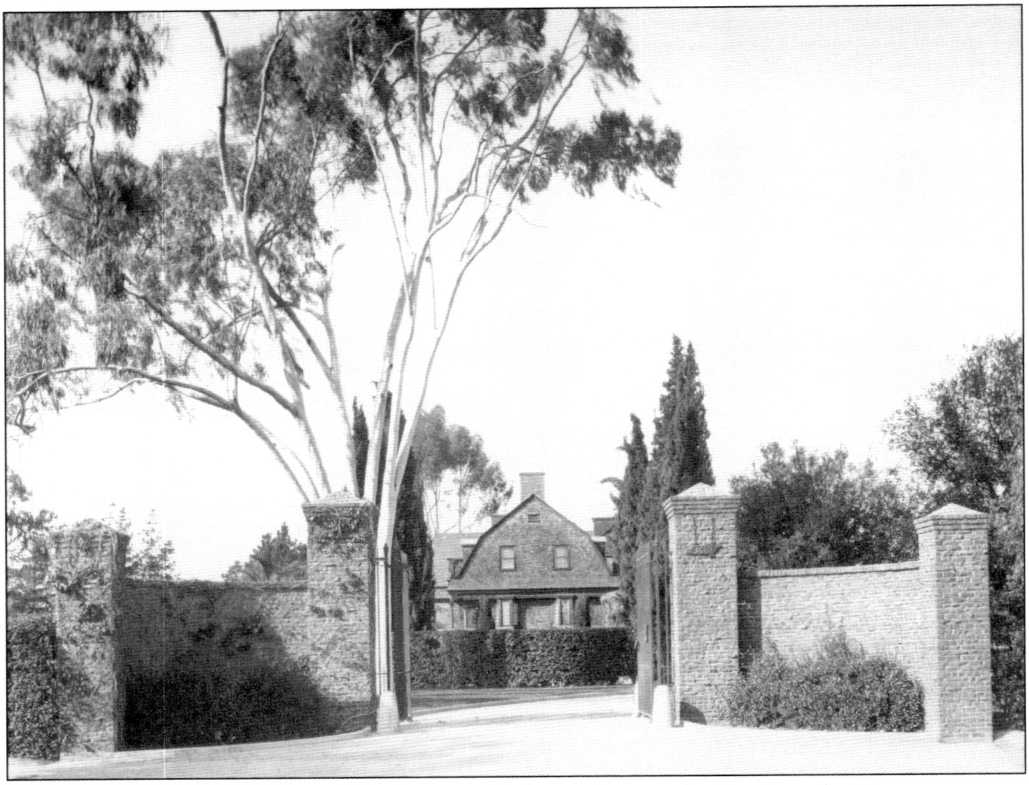

Gates to Bixby House. This 1920s photograph shows the gates leading into the 10-acre property off of Bixby Road. (RLC.)

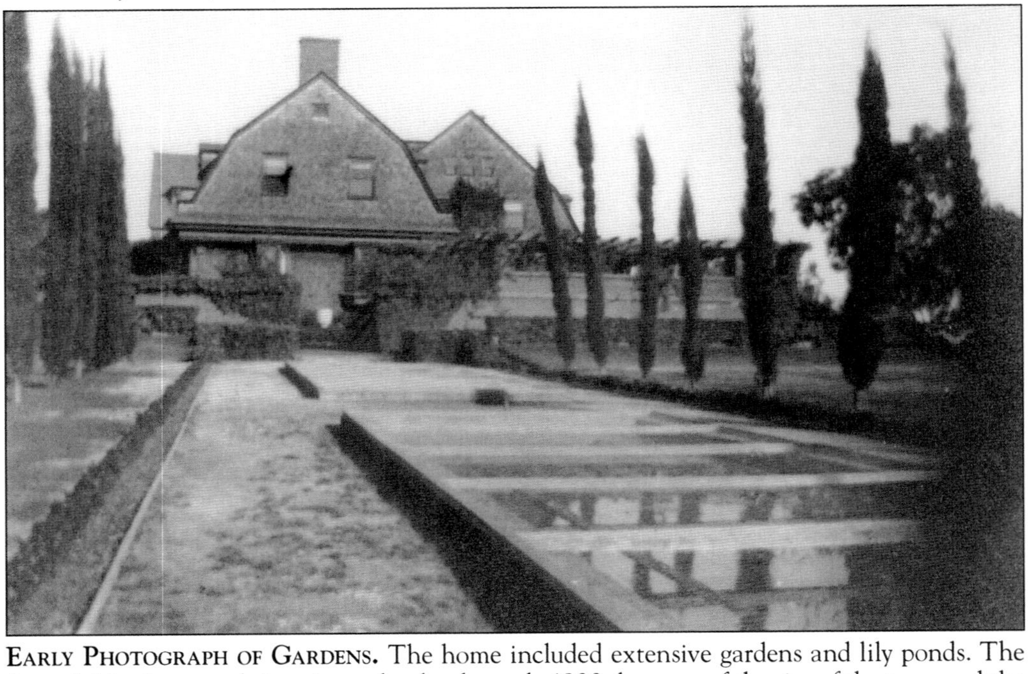

Early Photograph of Gardens. The home included extensive gardens and lily ponds. The date of this photograph is estimated to be the early 1900s because of the size of the trees and the growth of the plant material in the garden and lily ponds. (Courtesy of Duane Rose.)

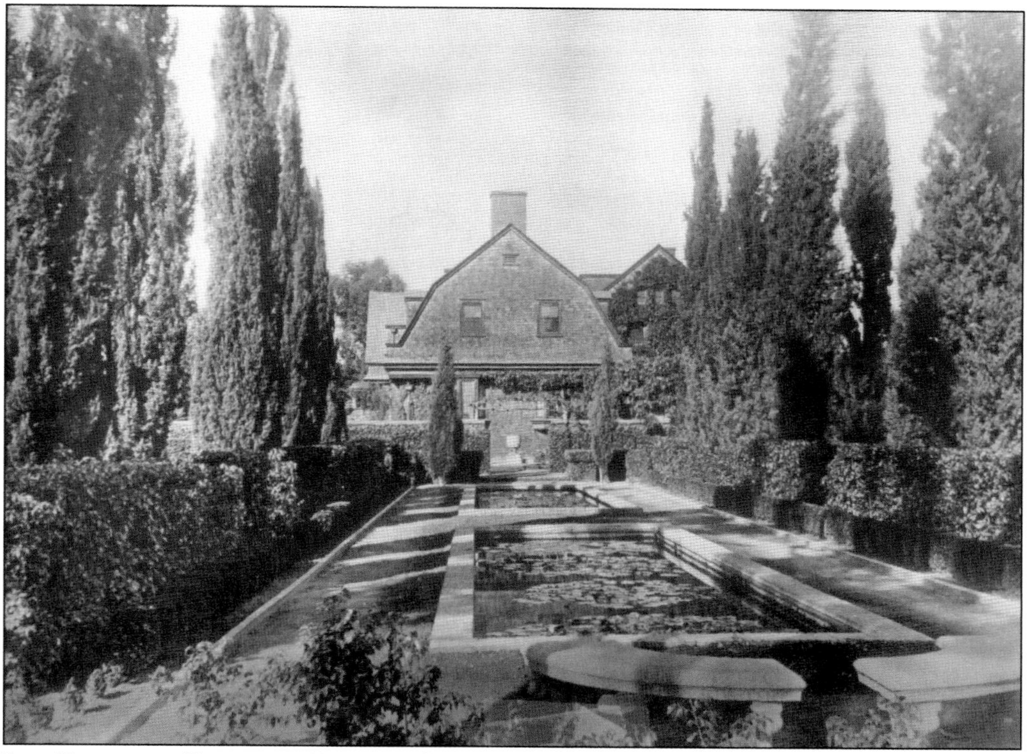

Lily Pond and Fountain. By 1920, the trees, roses, and lily-pond vegetation is in a mature state. This photograph served as the inspiration for the recent re-creation of the lily ponds by current owner Duane Rose. The original round white fountain is still in place and is in working condition. (Courtesy of Duane Rose.)

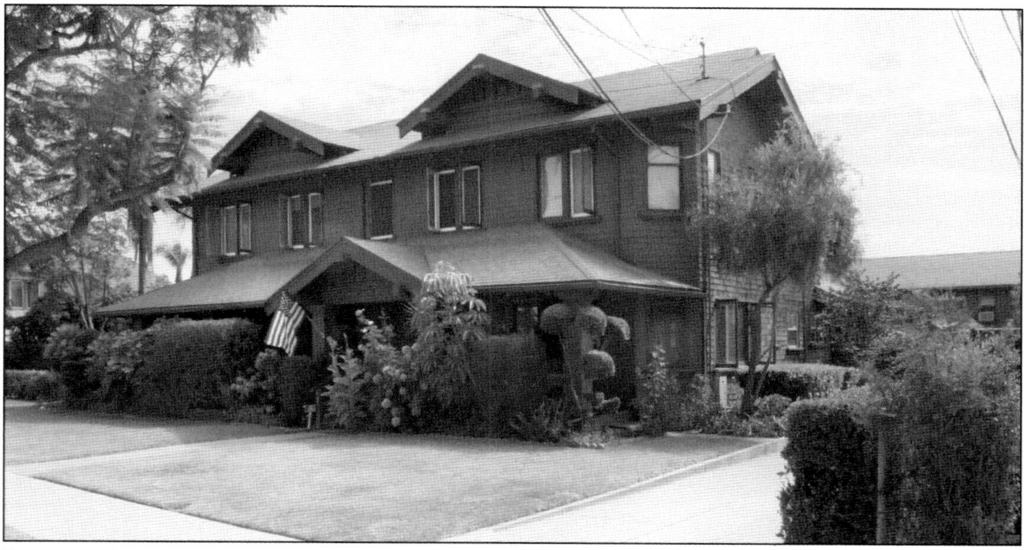

Richard Bixby Home. Amelia Bixby moved to her son Richard's home just across Bixby Road in 1920. The Craftsman home had six bedrooms and 5,460 square feet. Richard's home was built by C.T. McGrew and Sons in 1913 on 20 acres reserved for the family from the 1906 subdivision. The house was moved to 638 East Sunrise Boulevard in the 1920s due to oil operations. (Courtesy of John Mulvey).

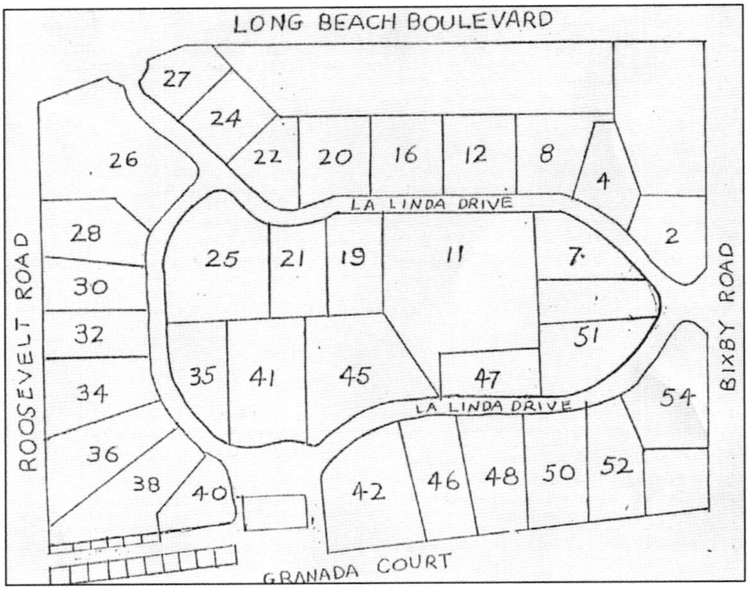

Creating La Linda. Thomas Gilchrist, who purchased the home from George H. Bixby, subdivided the 10 acres into 33 lots in 1922. The first home was built in 1924, although many lot owners held off construction until after they first exploited the site for oil operations. La Linda means "the pretty" in Spanish. By 1938, about half of the lots were built on. (Courtesy of Duane Rose.)

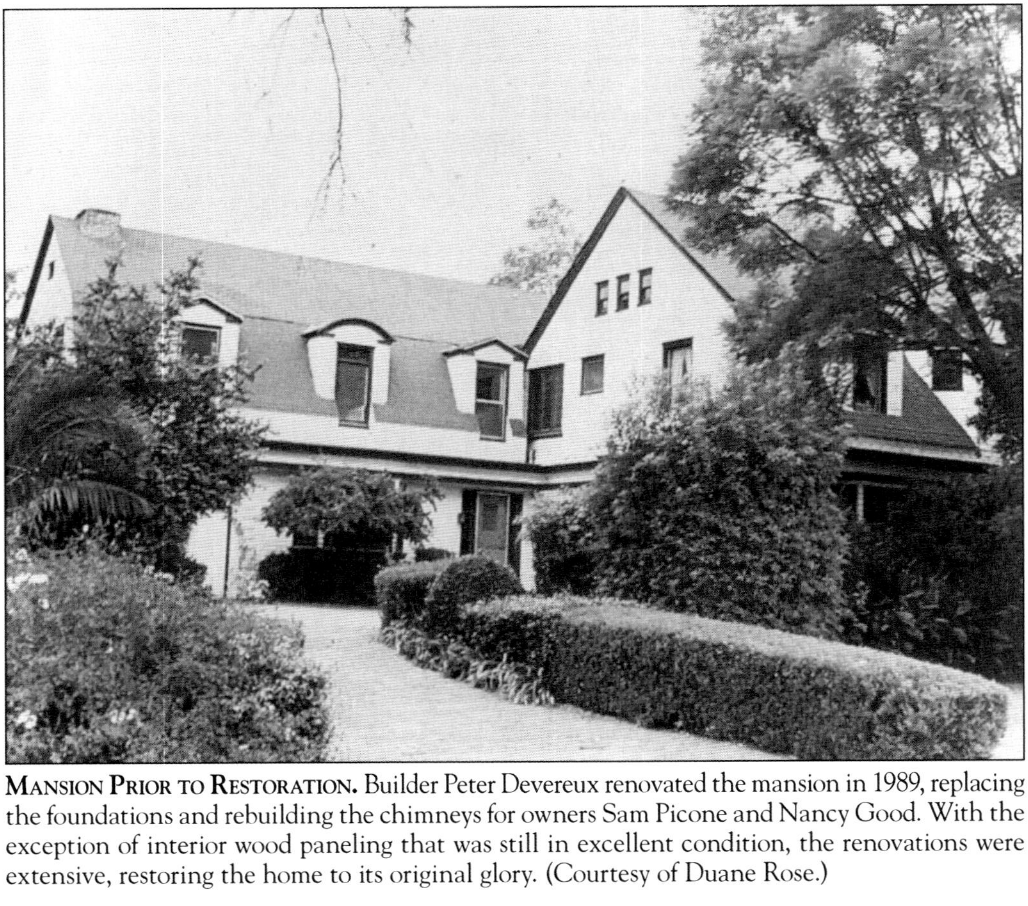

Mansion Prior to Restoration. Builder Peter Devereux renovated the mansion in 1989, replacing the foundations and rebuilding the chimneys for owners Sam Picone and Nancy Good. With the exception of interior wood paneling that was still in excellent condition, the renovations were extensive, restoring the home to its original glory. (Courtesy of Duane Rose.)

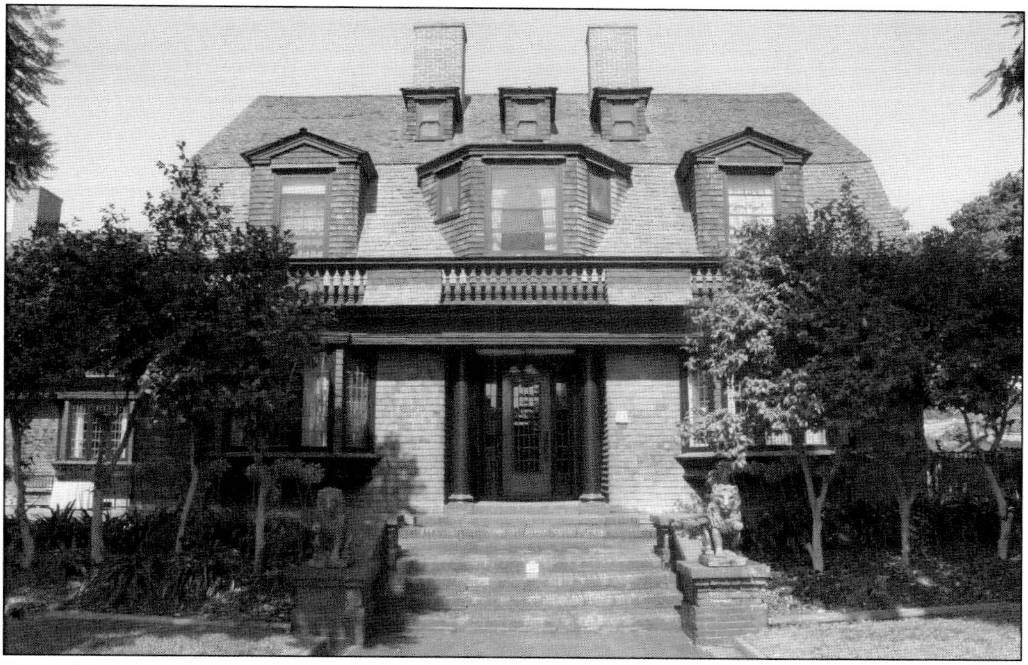

Bixby Mansion Today. The Bixby mansion stands as a representation of the ranching days of Los Cerritos. Current owner Duane Rose not only has been maintaining the home to reflect its historical significance, but he graciously allows others to share in its magnificence. (Courtesy of John Mulvey.)

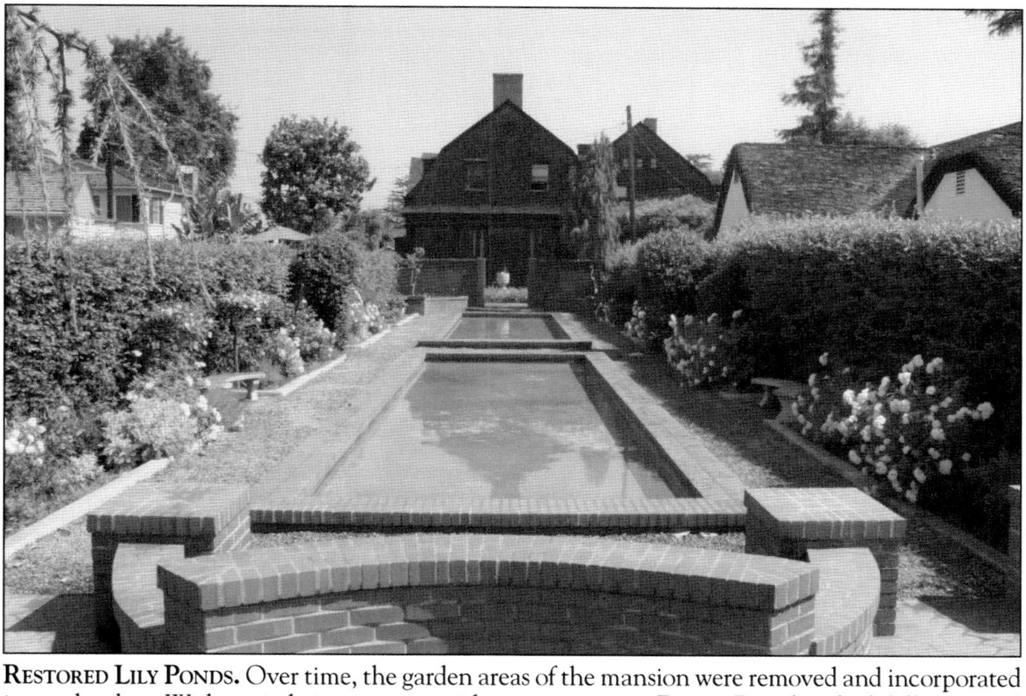

Restored Lily Ponds. Over time, the garden areas of the mansion were removed and incorporated into other lots. With period pictures as a guide, current owner Duane Rose has faithfully restored the lily ponds and the fountain to their original condition and revised the subdivision map to ensure the period gardens would be retained as part of the mansion lot. (Courtesy of John Mulvey.)

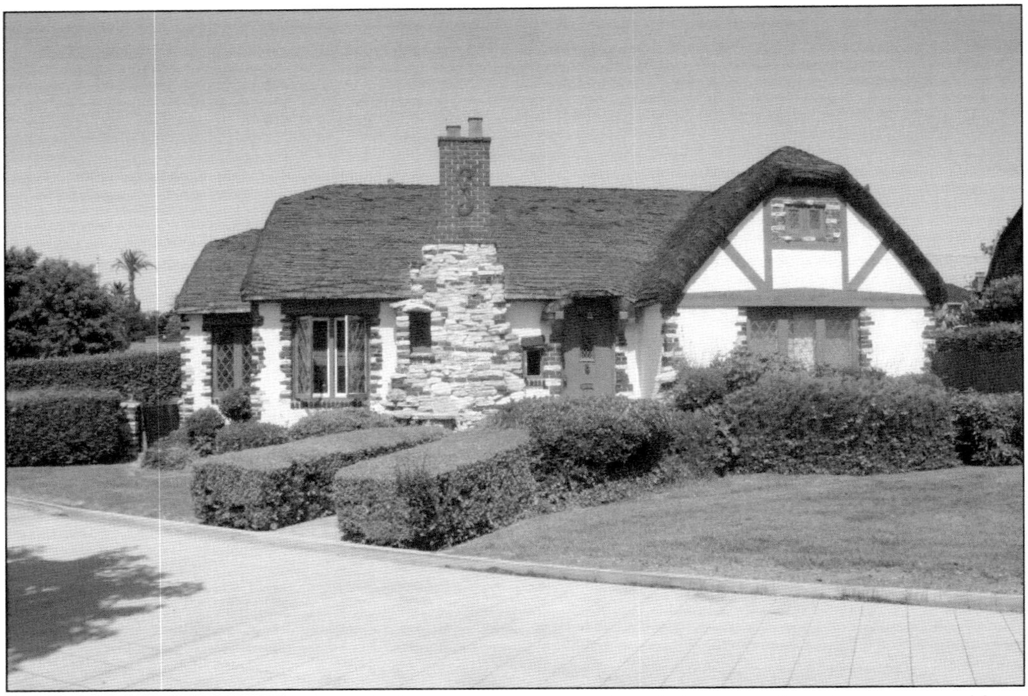

"Three Bears Cottage." This delightful cottage at 7 La Linda Drive evokes the cottages of fairy tales. Some children referred to this as "the three bears cottage." The rolled roof edges, along with the rough brickwork, leaded glass windows, and half-timbering, lend this home its "fairy tale" aura. (Courtesy of John Mulvey.)

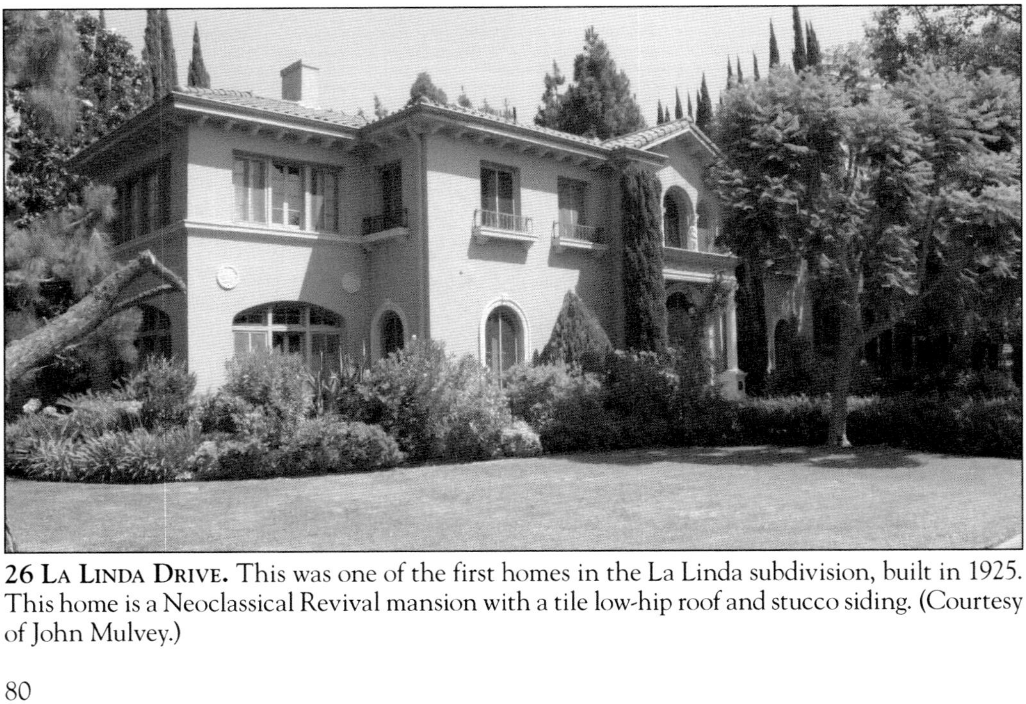

26 La Linda Drive. This was one of the first homes in the La Linda subdivision, built in 1925. This home is a Neoclassical Revival mansion with a tile low-hip roof and stucco siding. (Courtesy of John Mulvey.)

Five

Oil Operations and the Battle over Annexation

The discovery of oil in Signal Hill in June 1921 and the subsequent invasion of oil drilling operations into the Los Cerritos neighborhood became the critical factor in determining whether Los Cerritos would agree to annexation by Long Beach. Los Cerritos residents voted down annexation in 1922 by a vote of 187 to 110, which was a win for the oil companies. Phillip L. Bixby entered into a lease with the United Oil Company for drilling on 30 acres between Cota Avenue, the Pacific Electric right-of-way, Wardlow Road, and Bixby Road. Nearly every lot on Pine Avenue, Weston Place, Pacific Avenue, and Chestnut Avenue south of Bixby Road had an oil well on it. Between the fires and noise, many residents chose to abandon the neighborhood. Some took their houses with them, and a nightly "parade of houses" began. On January 14, 1926, a gas blowout occurred on the southwest corner of Bixby Road and Pacific Avenue. On February 23, E.E. Combs Well No. 5, at the northeast corner of Pacific Avenue and Bixby Road, caught fire, injuring many, including the fire chief, who collapsed from smoke inhalation. Children could not walk home from school unescorted because of the fires. The wells were initially productive. Getty No. 13, on Weston Place, drilled to 4,400 feet, brought in 700 barrels a day. Of the 42 drilling permits issued by the state in March 1926, 15 were for Los Cerritos. In 1927, the field declined and the oil flow collapsed. By then, the neighborhood was devastated.

The city sought initially to appease those favoring drilling to secure annexation, even proposing to allow each citizen to decide on drilling on their lots. Ultimately, the city was pressured into banning oil operations in residential neighborhoods, including Los Cerritos. Los Cerritos was annexed to Long Beach in 1924 after a contested election in December 1923 was upheld. The Los Cerritos Improvement Association, under the leadership of its first president, Charles R. Rowett, worked to return the area to its former beauty. In 1951, a portion of Los Cerritos Park was renamed for Rowett.

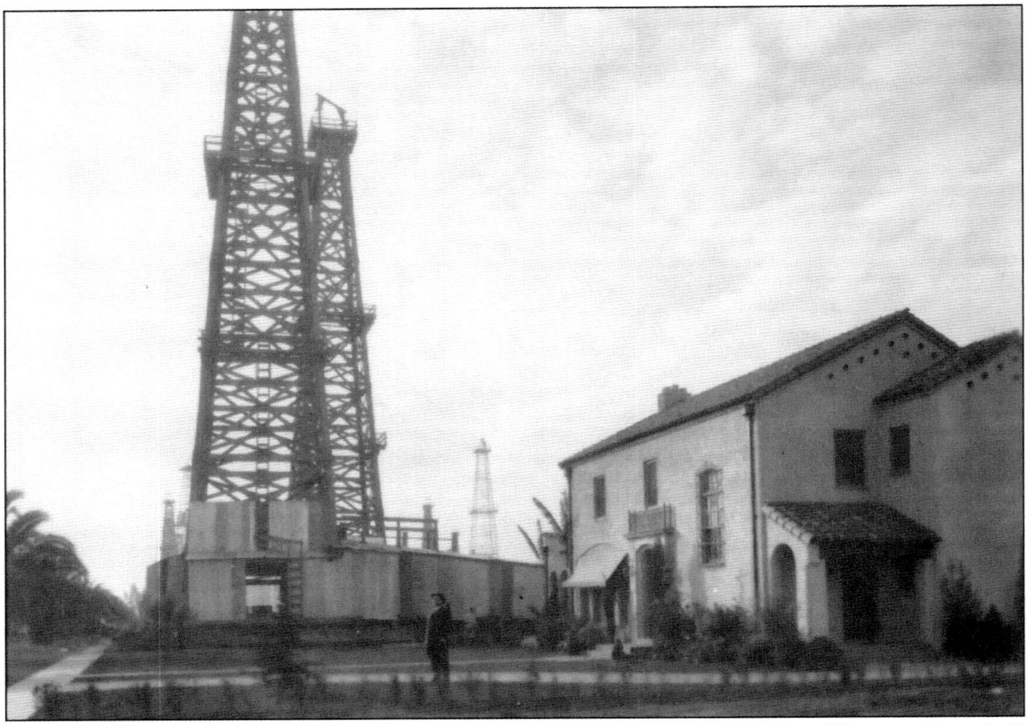

Campbell Home and Oil Well. Reginald Campbell, a plumber and father of Norma Campbell Craig, stands in his backyard at 3841 Pacific Avenue in 1926. The Campbells moved the house to 235 East Claiborne Place to escape oil drilling. (Courtesy of Hyra and David Goldberg.)

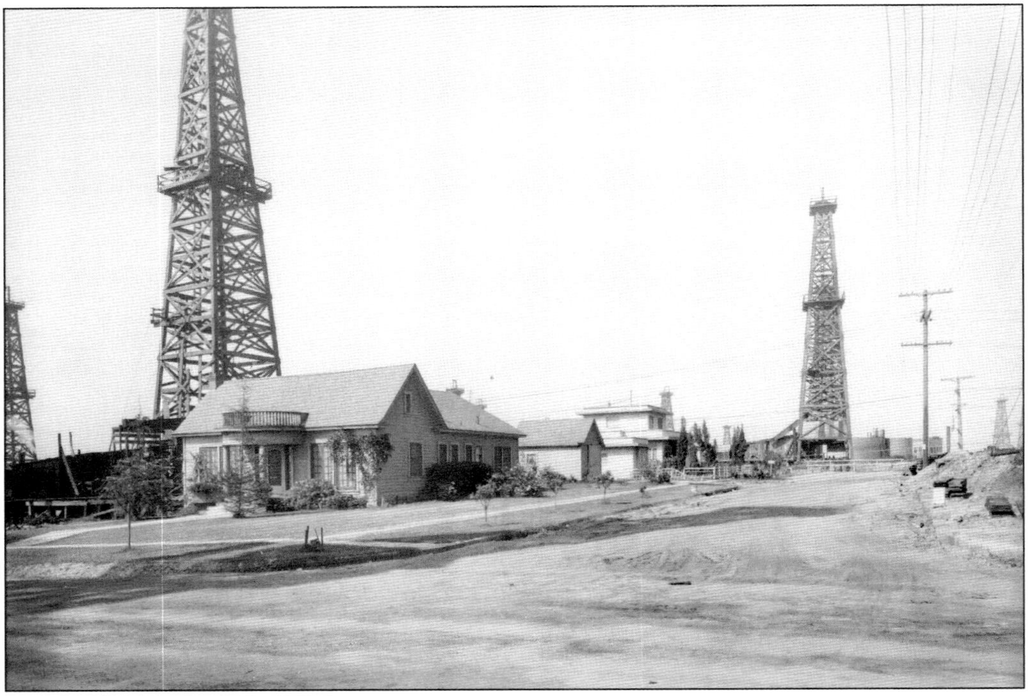

Derricks in Los Cerritos. This mid-1920s photograph shows how oil wells were positioned very close to homes. (LBHS.)

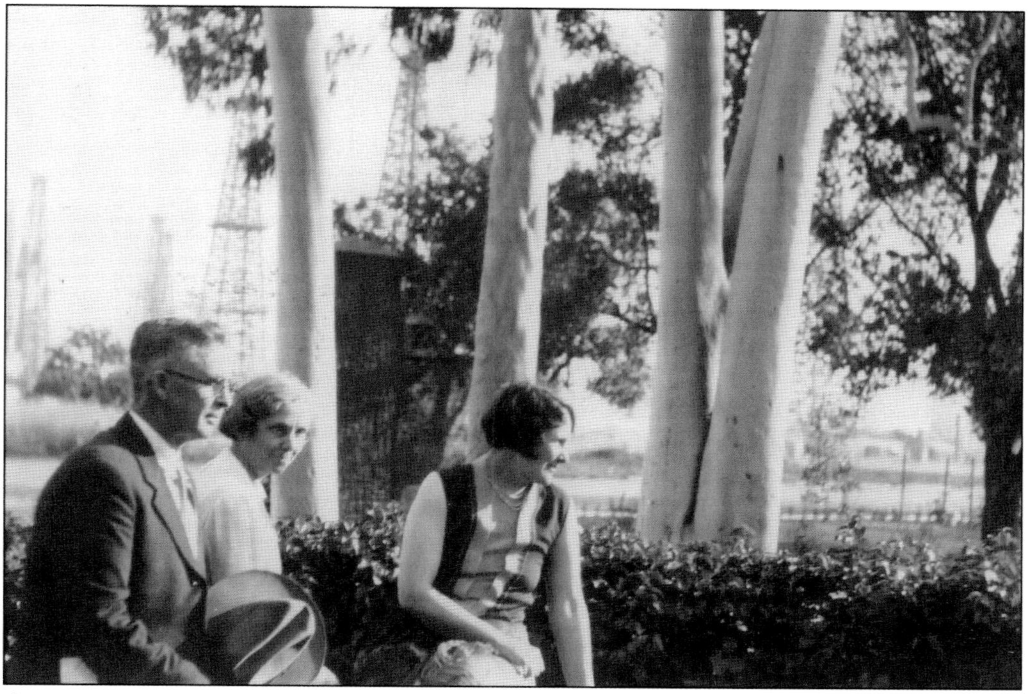

Outside Yard of Bixby Mansion during Oil Drilling. Thomas Gilchrist, who purchased the Bixby mansion in the 1920s, was an Oklahoma oilman. Arriving in California at an opportune time, his house positioned him to experience the oil-drilling operations firsthand, but it remained vacant during peak drilling periods. At one point, even this home was thought to be threatened by oil operations. (Courtesy of Duane Rose.)

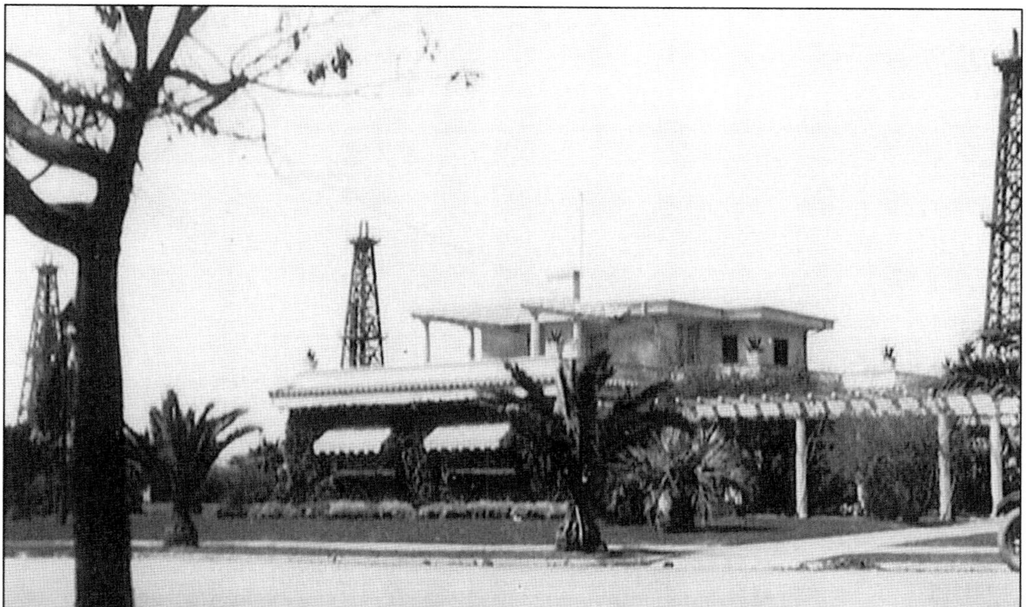

Oil Wells in La Linda. This photograph of 3800 Weston Place shows the oil derricks in La Linda after many residents who bought the lots decided in 1926 to delay home construction to drill for oil. (Courtesy of the Jablonski family.)

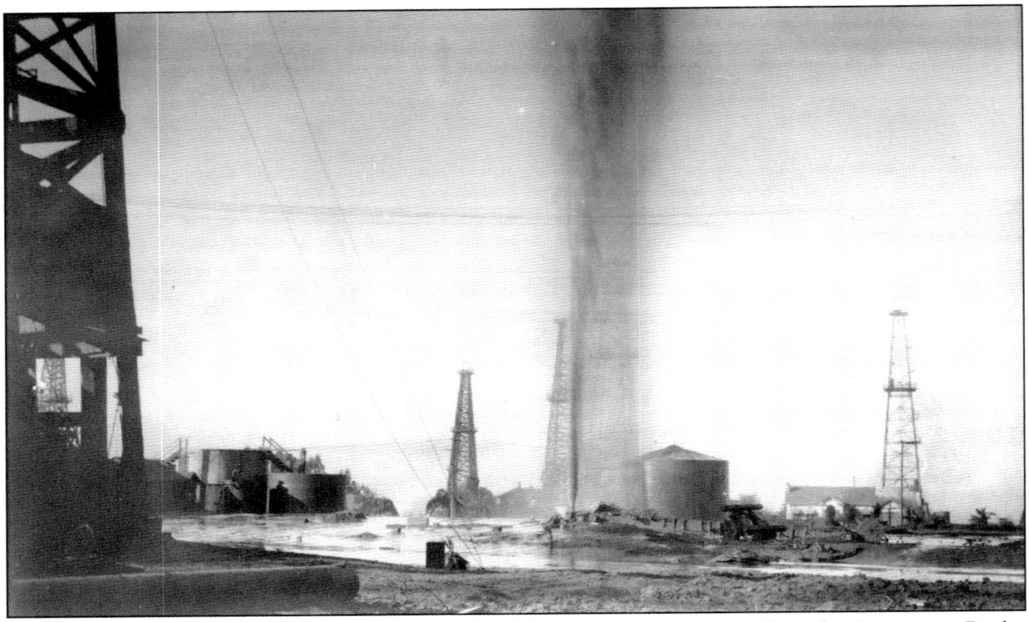

Oil Well Blowout. This blowout occurred on the southwest corner of Pacific Avenue at Bixby Road on January 14, 1926. The George Johnson No. 4 well blew, raining water and oil onto the neighborhood. Many residents recall being escorted by their parents back and forth to Los Cerritos School because of oil fires. (RLC.)

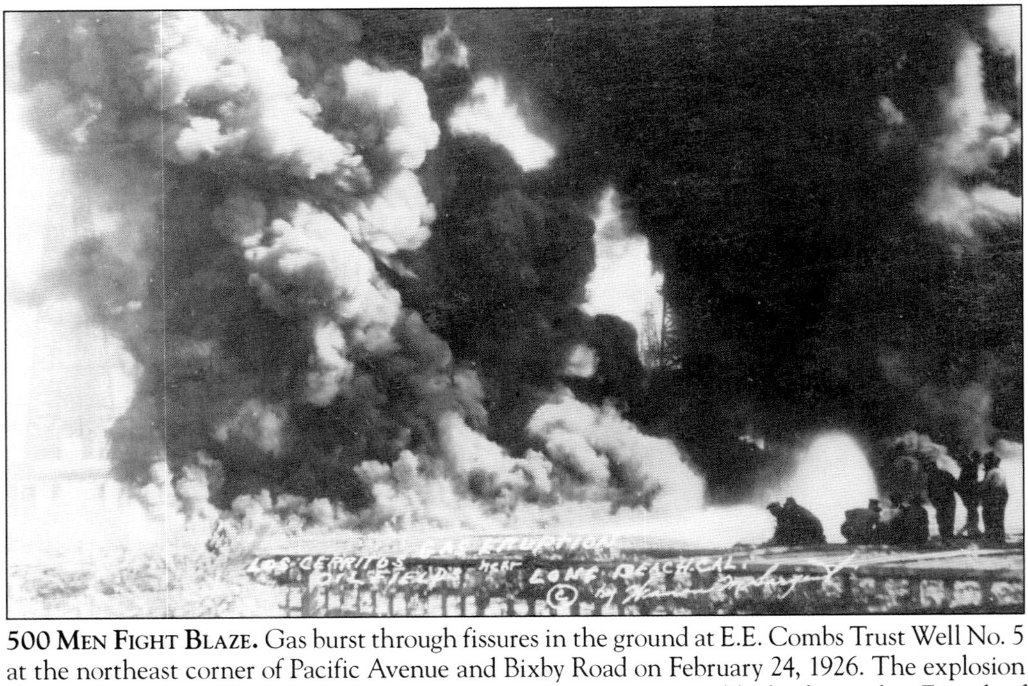

500 Men Fight Blaze. Gas burst through fissures in the ground at E.E. Combs Trust Well No. 5 at the northeast corner of Pacific Avenue and Bixby Road on February 24, 1926. The explosion caused the George Johnson No. 5 well to blow. The fire was visible for five miles. Fire chief William Minter collapsed from exhaustion and smoke inhalation, and six men were injured. Welch Stanberry's house was significantly damaged. (Courtesy of CSU Dominguez Hills Archives.)

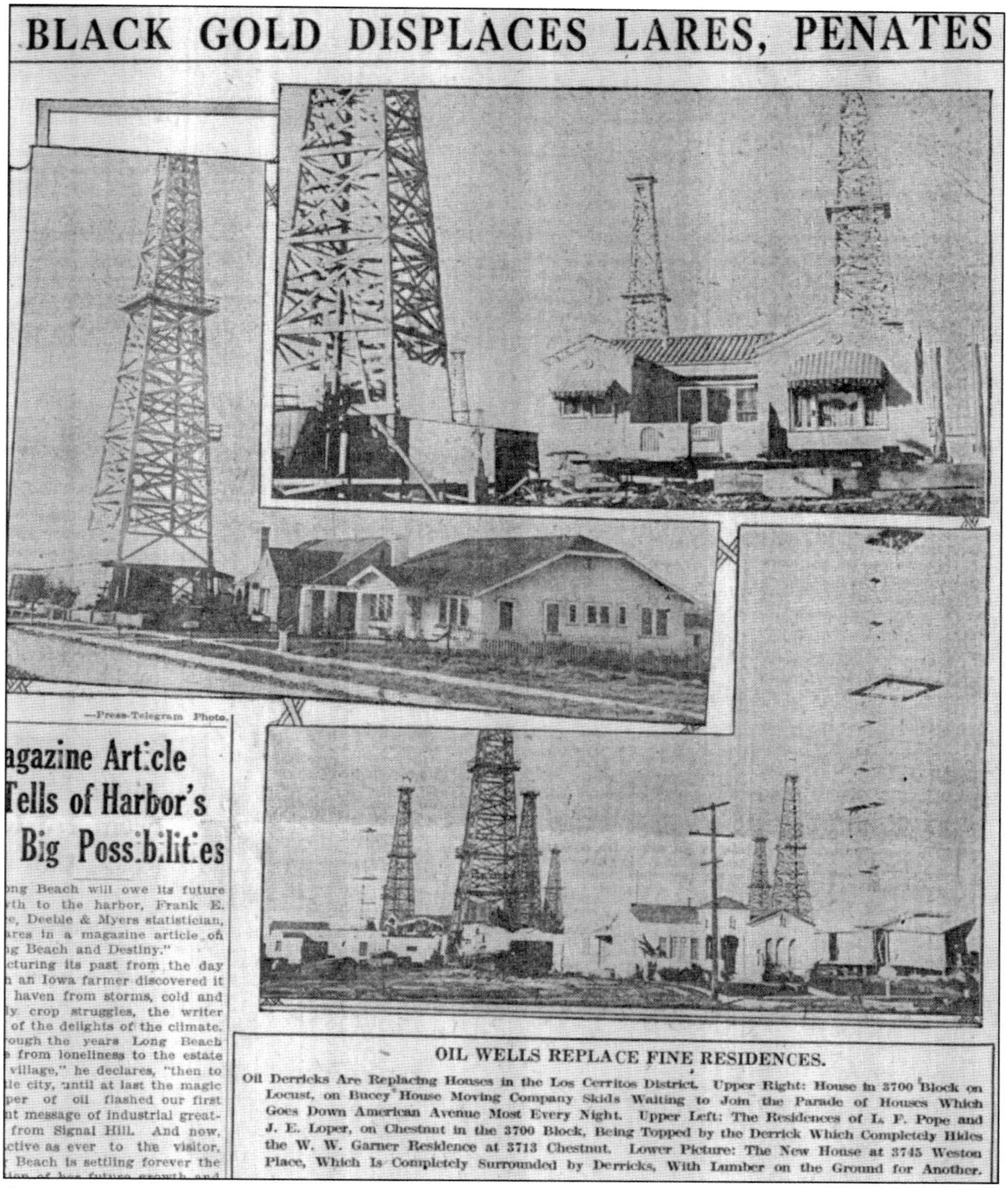

BLACK GOLD DISPLACES LARES, PENATES

—Press-Telegram Photo.

agazine Article Tells of Harbor's Big Possibilities

ong Beach will owe its future wth to the harbor, Frank E. e, Deeble & Myers statistician, ares in a magazine article on g Beach and Destiny."

cturing its past from the day h an Iowa farmer discovered it haven from storms, cold and ly crop struggles, the writer of the delights of the climate. ough the years Long Beach from loneliness to the estate village," he declares, "then to le city, until at last the magic per of oil flashed our first nt message of industrial great- from Signal Hill. And now, ctive as ever to the visitor, Beach is settling forever the

OIL WELLS REPLACE FINE RESIDENCES.

Oil Derricks Are Replacing Houses in the Los Cerritos District. Upper Right: House in 3700 Block on Locust, on Bucey House Moving Company Skids Waiting to Join the Parade of Houses Which Goes Down American Avenue Most Every Night. Upper Left: The Residences of L. F. Pope and J. E. Loper, on Chestnut in the 3700 Block, Being Topped by the Derrick Which Completely Hides the W. W. Garner Residence at 3713 Chestnut. Lower Picture: The New House at 3745 Weston Place, Which Is Completely Surrounded by Derricks, With Lumber on the Ground for Another.

OIL WELLS REPLACE HOMES. This clipping from the December 27, 1925, *Press Telegram* notes a parade of houses moving down American Avenue (now Long Beach Boulevard) nearly every night as residents escape the oil-drilling operations. In the center photograph, rigs tower over the homes of L.F. Pope, J.E. Loper, and W.W. Gardiner. In the bottom photograph, the home at 3745 Weston Place is completely surrounded by drilling rigs.

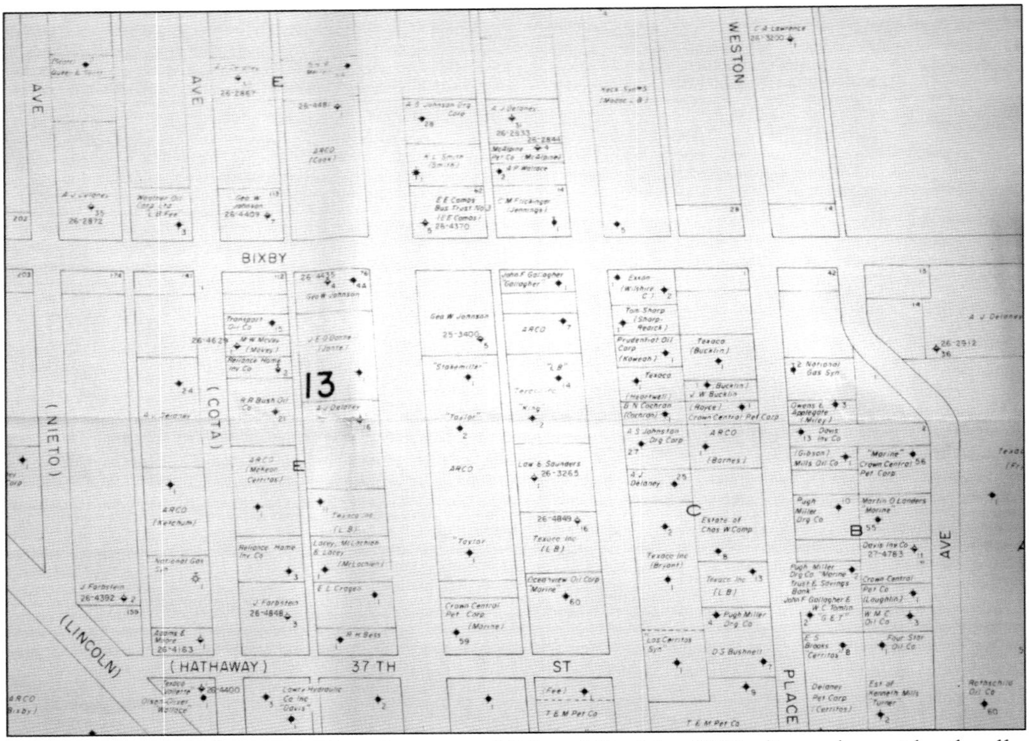

Oil Wells in Los Cerritos. State Division of Oil and Gas Map 137 indicates lots with oil wells. By the end of 1926, 236 wells had been drilled in Los Cerritos, with 158 producing oil. Only 25 percent of these would recoup their investment, and most would not last another year. The map identifies the individual oil wells and owners.

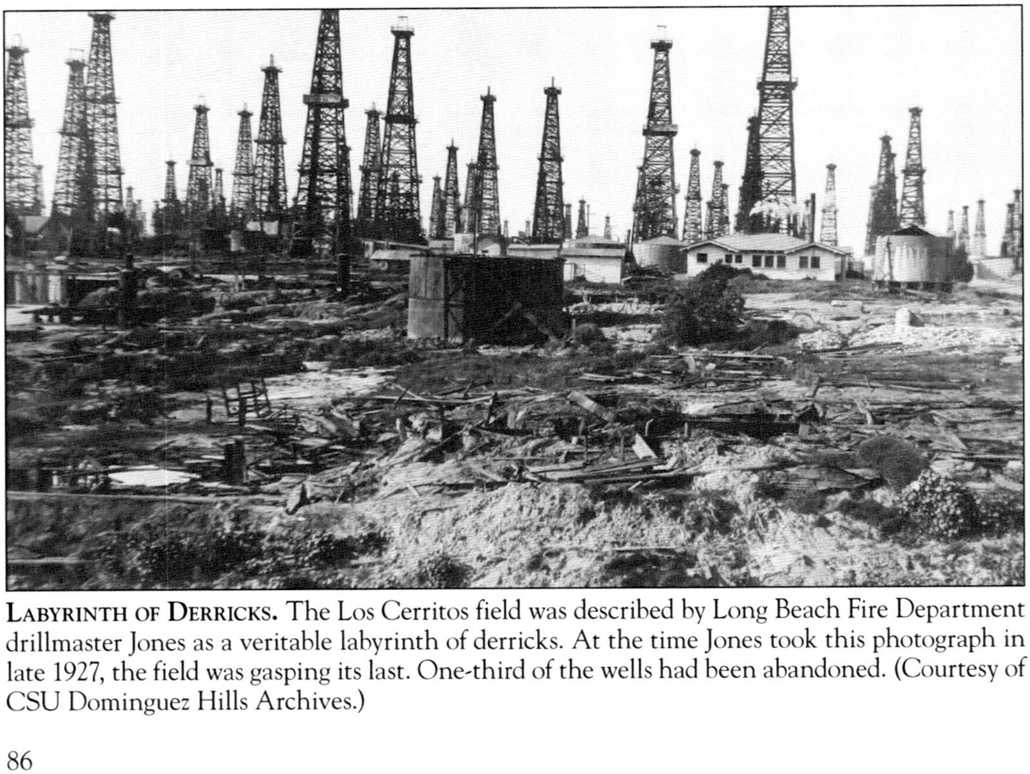

Labyrinth of Derricks. The Los Cerritos field was described by Long Beach Fire Department drillmaster Jones as a veritable labyrinth of derricks. At the time Jones took this photograph in late 1927, the field was gasping its last. One-third of the wells had been abandoned. (Courtesy of CSU Dominguez Hills Archives.)

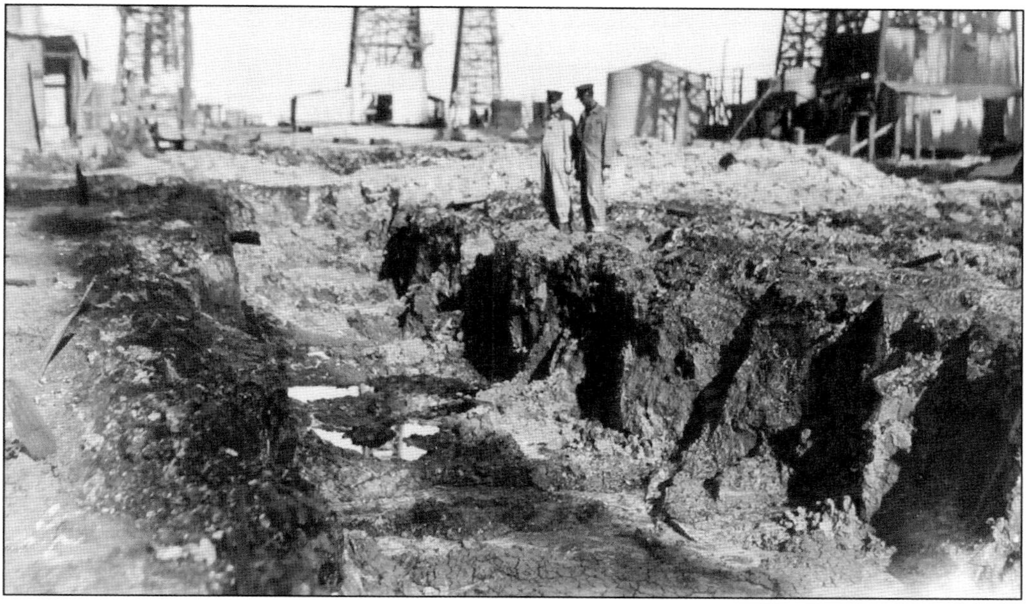

Oil Well Abandonment Process. Drillmaster Jones of the Long Beach Fire Department documented through photographs the abandonment of wells in Los Cerritos. Here, after the rotary mud has been removed from the sump, the excavation must be filled in and the surface of the lot graded before the property owner would accept a quit claim deed. (Courtesy of the CSU Dominguez Hills Archives.)

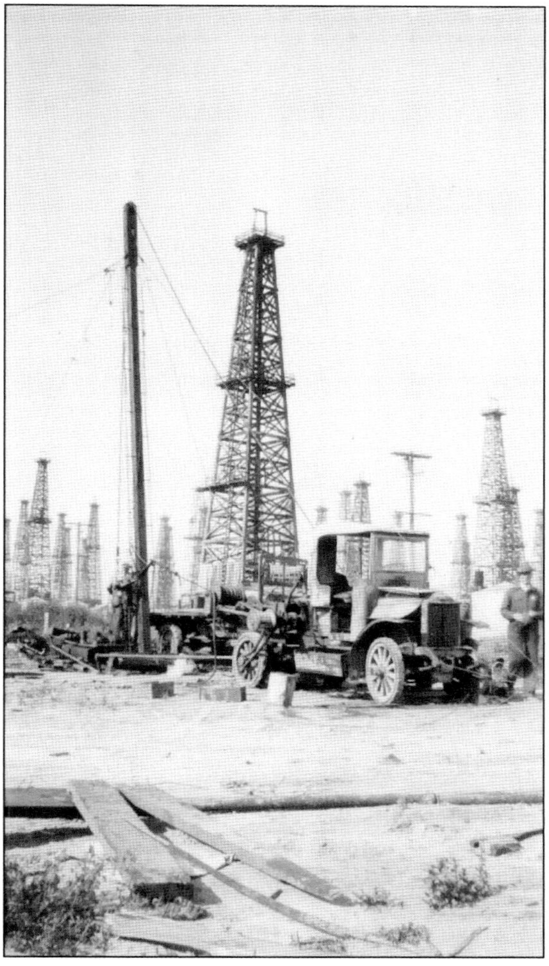

Oil Well Casing Removal. After the well has been abandoned to the satisfaction of the California State Mining Bureau, a certain percentage of the casing may be salvaged. The casing is dynamited loose at a proper level, and raised out of the hole by means of hydraulic jacks. (Courtesy of CSU Dominguez Hills Archives.)

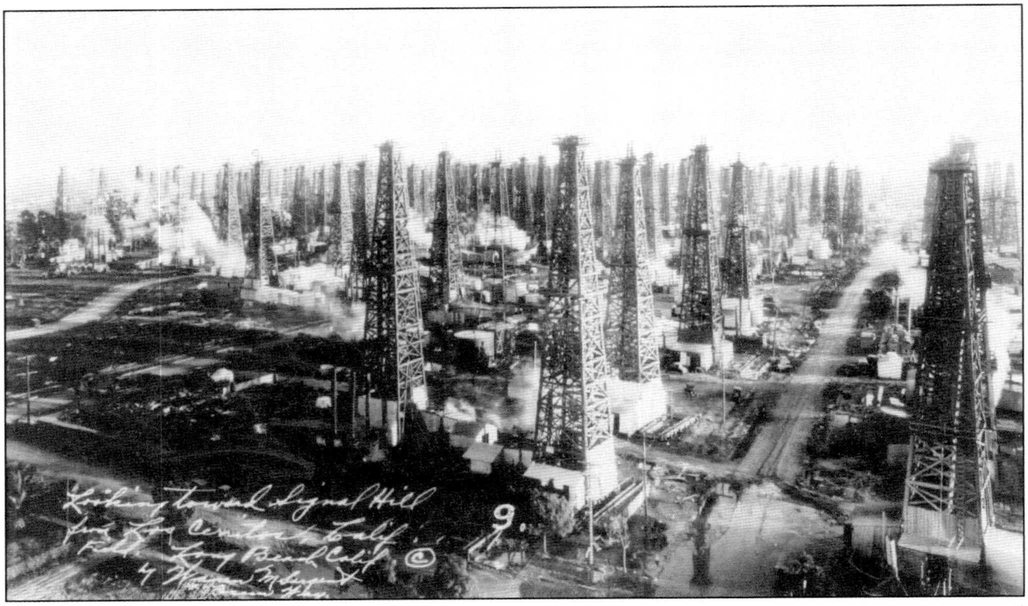

VIEW FROM LOS CERRITOS. Even after drilling ceased in Los Cerritos, this was the view toward Signal Hill that greeted residents from the edge of their neighborhood.

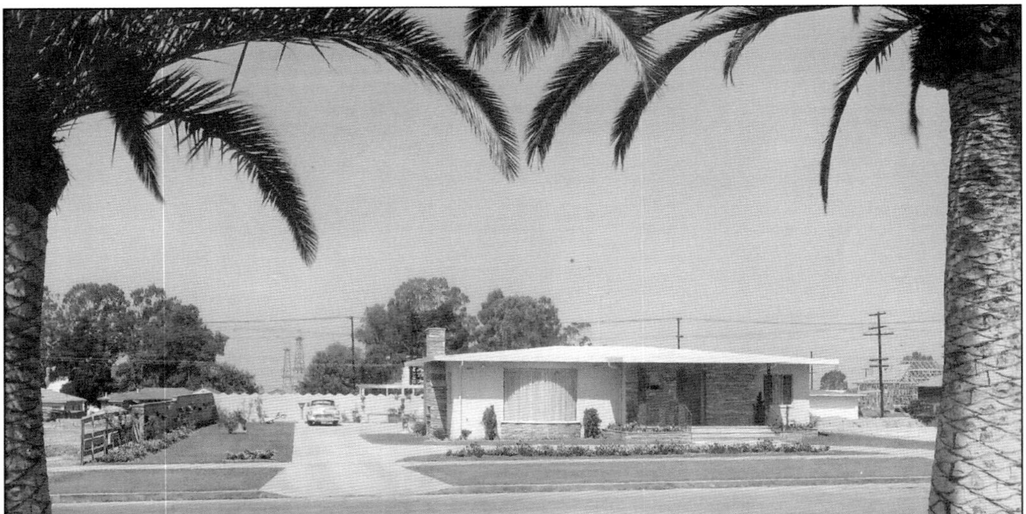

3733 PACIFIC AVENUE. In this 1950s photograph of a home on Pacific Avenue, oil wells are still visible to the left of the house, indicating that drilling on the outskirts of the neighborhood continued. (Courtesy of Jon St. Jacques.)

Six

Clubs, Institutions, and Community

From its beginning, the Los Cerritos neighborhood had a strong sense of community. The young bachelors established the first club in the neighborhood with a clubhouse overlooking Los Cerritos Park. Known as the El Rodeo, it was active until many of the young men were called off to World War I or succumbed to marriage. A club founding member, Oliver Sweningsen, continued annual meetings of the club until 1974, when 8 of the original 122 members were still living. Swensingsen died the following year. No other record of meetings could be found.

By 1927, the Los Cerritos Improvement Association was formed. Charles R. Rowett, often called the "Mayor" of Los Cerritos, was its first president. He strongly opposed oil drilling in the neighborhood and worked to ensure the neighborhood was beautified. The Los Cerritos Improvement Association incorporated in October 1940 and again in 1991 to address issues related to traffic, crime, and noise. In 2010, the organization became the Los Cerritos Neighborhood Association.

The sale of lots by the Virginia Country Club meant that many prominent Long Beach families moved into the neighborhood to live close to the club, which became a focal point of social activity. Residents who may have had connections through business or civic pursuits also socialized together. Families were also brought together by the activities of the Los Cerritos School. Today, summer months find residents down at Los Cerritos Park, enjoying the Long Beach Municipal Band concerts. A July 4th parade has been held every year for decades, attracting several thousand residents who walk, bike, or drive their classic cars, suitably attired in red, white, and blue. The parade has intensified the spirit of camaraderie in the neighborhood, and it is not unusual during summer weekends to find street closures for block parties.

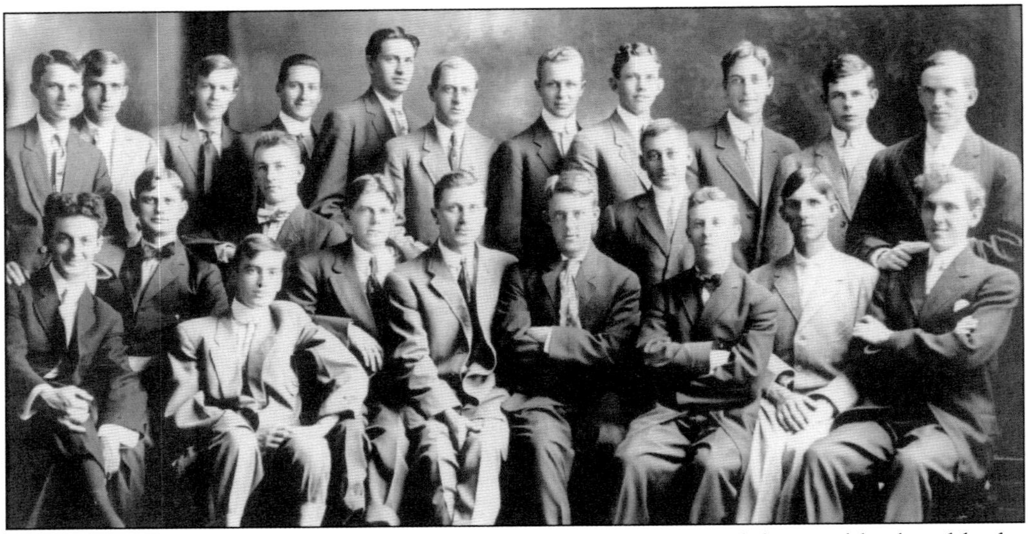

El Rodeo Club. Formed in May 1909 so that the young men of the neighborhood had a meeting place, this club's charter members were Lee Cronk, Roger Roe, Frank Long, Ray Darcy Clarence Meacham, Everett Burk, Mark Schilling, Forest Boughman, William Sweningsen, Fred Hudson, Richard Bixby, Irving Fordham, William Store, Phillip Bixby, Walter Housworth, Oliver Sweningsen, Alec Lawson, Frank Vail, Peter Fraser, and Wilber Downs. Dick Bixby came up with the name El Rodeo. (HSLB.)

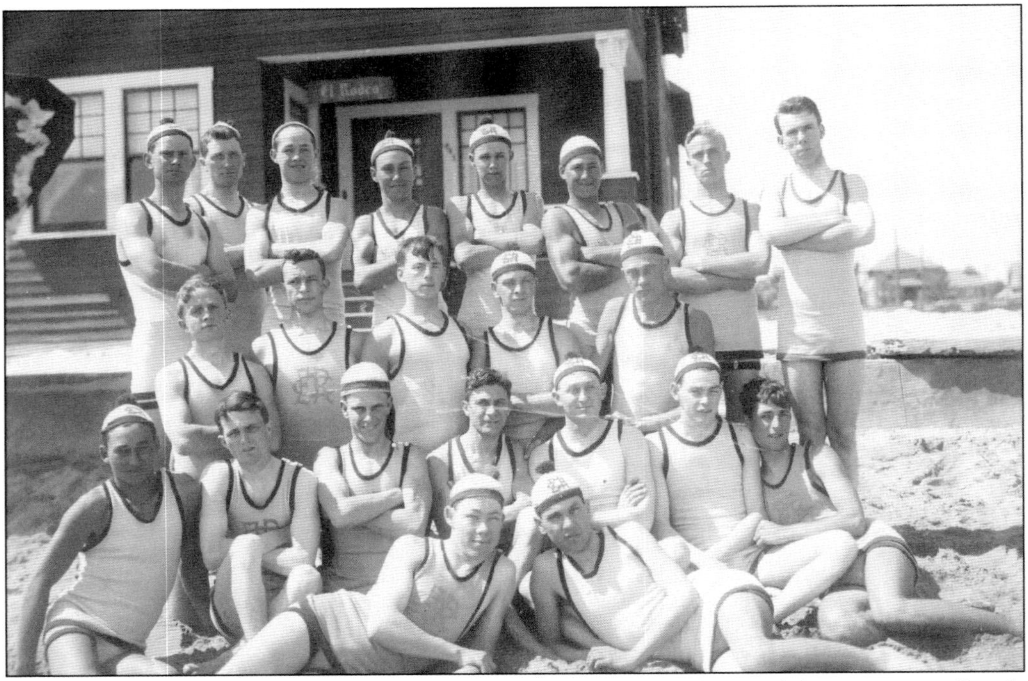

Club Members at the Beach. The club members initially leased a beach house in Long Beach west of the Virginia Hotel. Shown here are, from left to right, (first row) Charley Glenn and Jack Rothwell; (second row) Larry Darby, Lee Cronk, Walker Saunders. Bert Walp, ? Lockhart, Dane Anderson, and William Sweningsen; (third row) Cecil Schilling, Clem Nadeau, Bill Blake, Al Vivian, and Stanley Stoneacker; (fourth row) ? Stone, Oliver Sweningen, Carl Brunn, Don Darby, Frank Long, Raymond Darby, Clyde Hammer, and Ed Loy. (HSLB.)

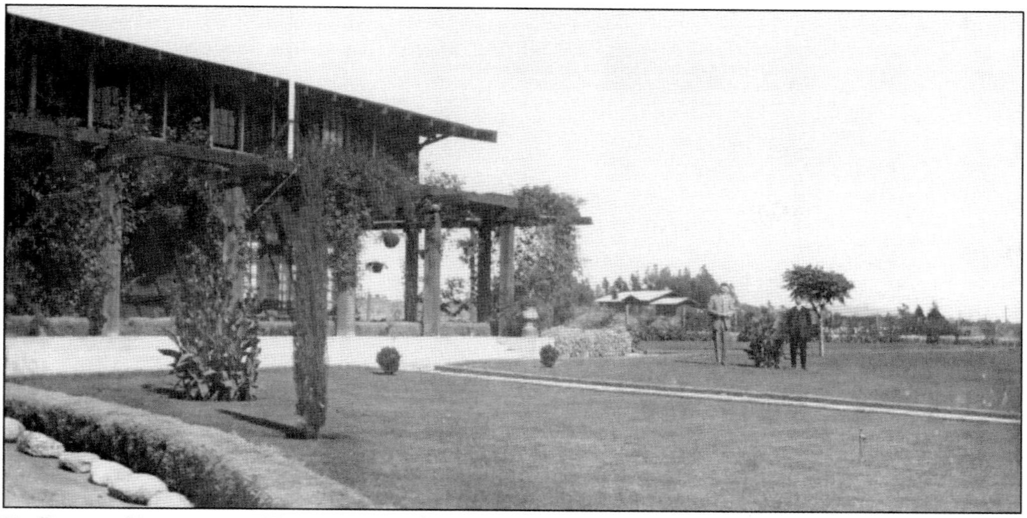

El Rodeo Clubhouse. To raise enough money to build a clubhouse, members enlisted female help in selling subscriptions to the *Herald Examiner*, and won $4,000 and a few acres on Bellflower Boulevard, which they sold. Mrs. George H. Bixby donated four acres of land for the clubhouse, on Country Club Drive, just across the street from Los Cerritos Park. (HSLB.)

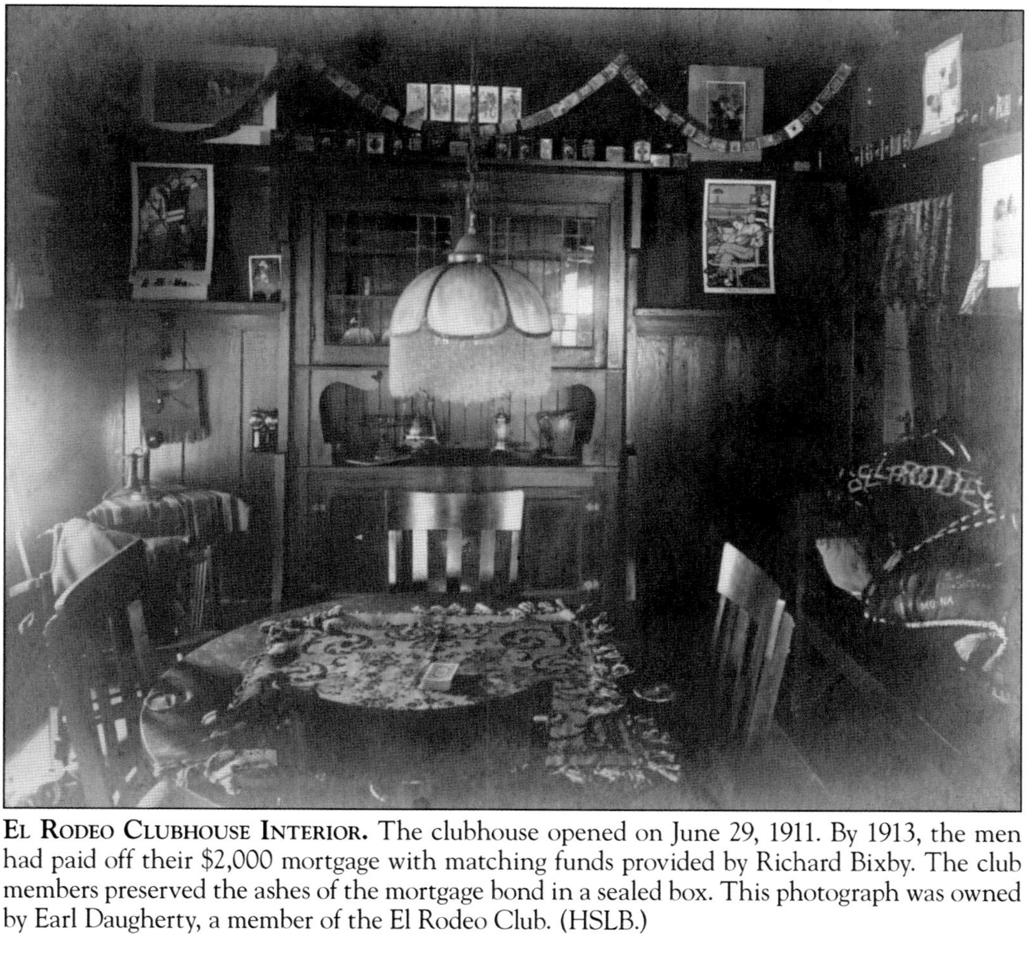

El Rodeo Clubhouse Interior. The clubhouse opened on June 29, 1911. By 1913, the men had paid off their $2,000 mortgage with matching funds provided by Richard Bixby. The club members preserved the ashes of the mortgage bond in a sealed box. This photograph was owned by Earl Daugherty, a member of the El Rodeo Club. (HSLB.)

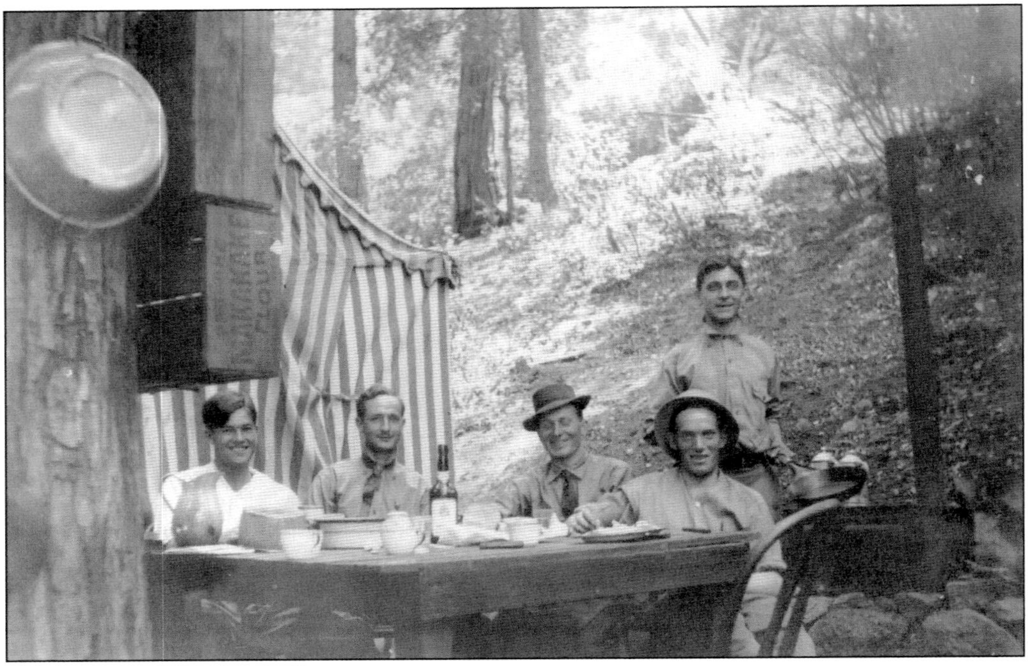

Club Members on Mount Wilson. The El Rodeo Club engaged in numerous activities, including camping on Mount Wilson. Bert Walp is holding a frying pan. Oliver Sweningsen is wearing a hat. Sweningsen, the club's first president, held yearly reunions. In 1949, the reunion included 30 former members; 25 members came in 1967. The 1974 reunion was attended by seven members: Charles V. Harris, J.R. Holton Sr., Donald Darby, S.W. and Oliver Sweningsen, Lee Cronk, and George Vogeley.

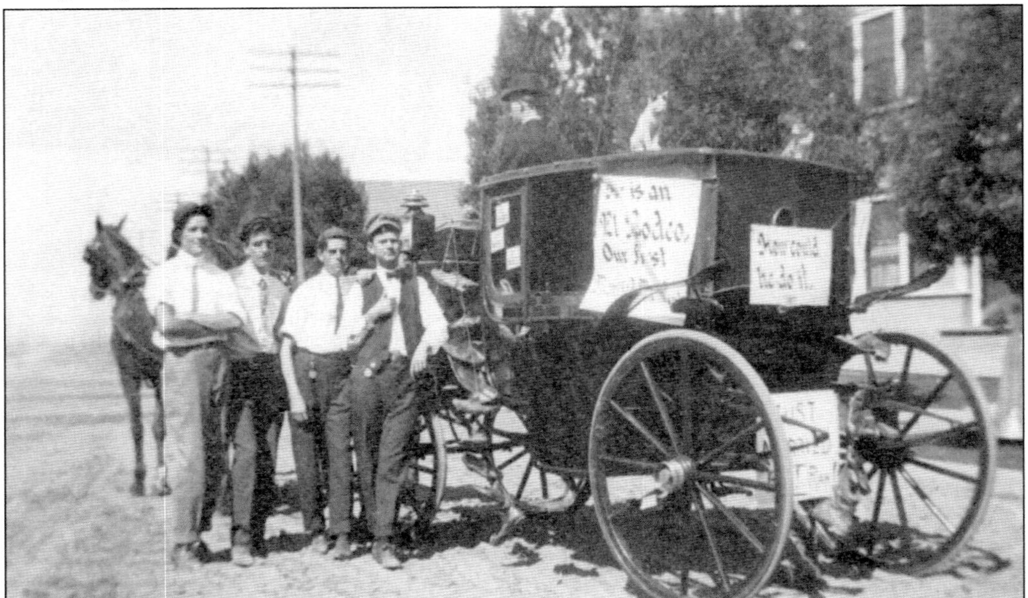

How Could He Do It? Members of the El Rodeo Club disqualified themselves from membership by falling in love. Here, club members poke fun at their fallen comrades. Between marriage and World War I, club membership dwindled from 112, and the clubhouse closed in 1918. (HSLB.)

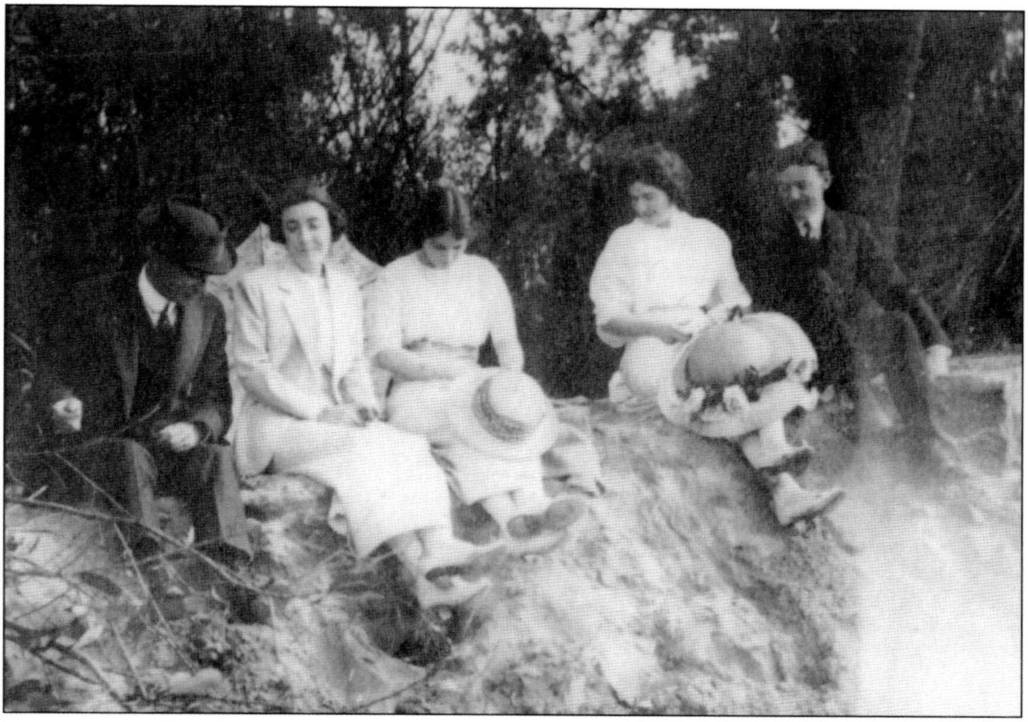

PICNIC BY THE LOS ANGELES RIVER. Adults and children often spent time along the banks of the Los Angeles River. In this photograph are, from left to right, Oliver Sweningsen, Edwine Vignes Sweningsen, Amelia Vignes, Marie Vignes Sans Souci, and Fred Sans Souci. (Courtesy of Ellen Collins.)

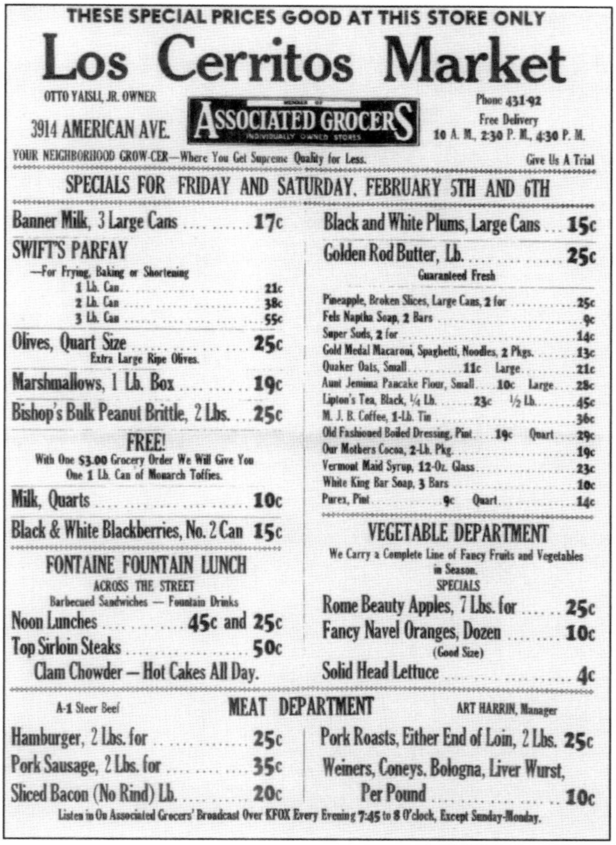

LOS CERRITOS MARKET. Residents were fortunate to have a grocery store in the neighborhood, located at 3912 American Avenue (now Virginia Road), later 3923 Long Beach Boulevard. The early proprietors were brothers Walter C. and Otto Yaisli, who operated the market for 24 years. Otto was the owner, and Walter and his wife lived in an apartment above the store. (Courtesy of Carol Conley.)

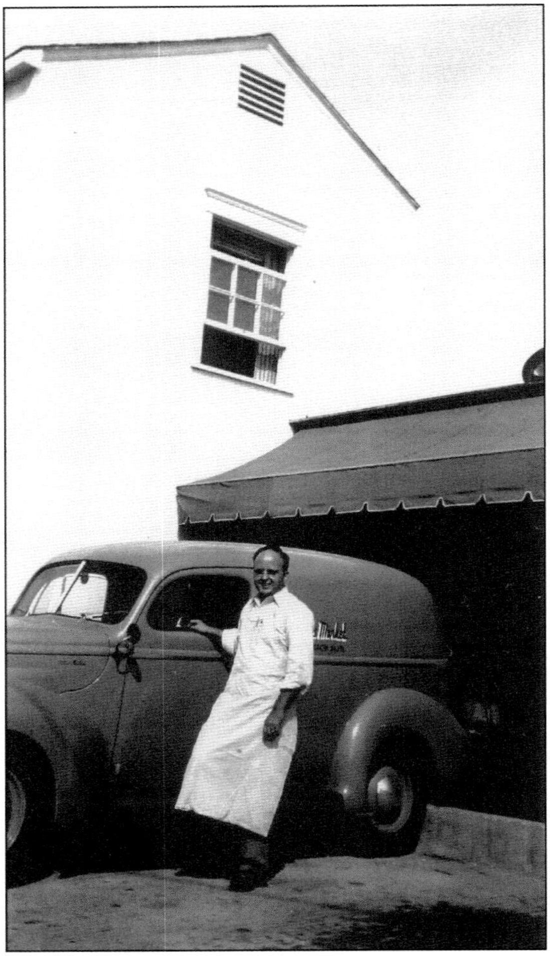

OTTO YAISLI. Yaisli, here posing next to his delivery truck, brought groceries to the homes in the neighborhood. About $350 to $400 worth of groceries were delivered each month to the Bixby and the Dudley family at the Bixby mansion. Yaisli also leased a portion of his buildings to a beauty salon and jewelry store. (Courtesy of Carol Conley.)

LONG BEACH EARTHQUAKE. Photographs of the 1933 Long Beach earthquake tend to be of downtown Long Beach, but private homes also sustained damage. The Merrell home at 4201 Chestnut Avenue lost its chimney. Many Los Cerritos residents took to living in tents in their yards until the aftershocks subsided. Bricks from fallen buildings were used in the construction of many patios in Los Cerritos. (Courtesy of Janet Watts.)

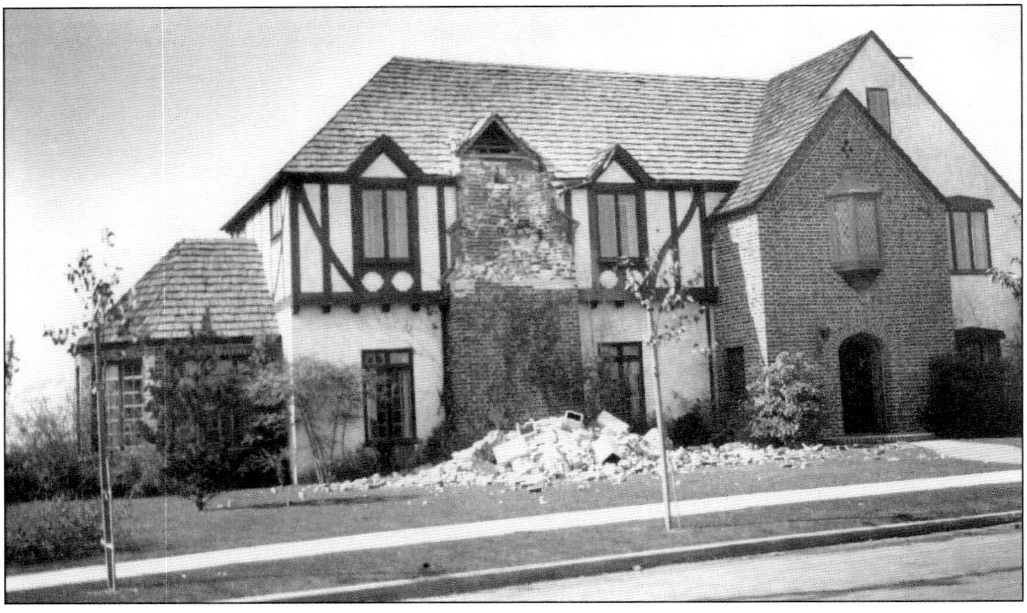

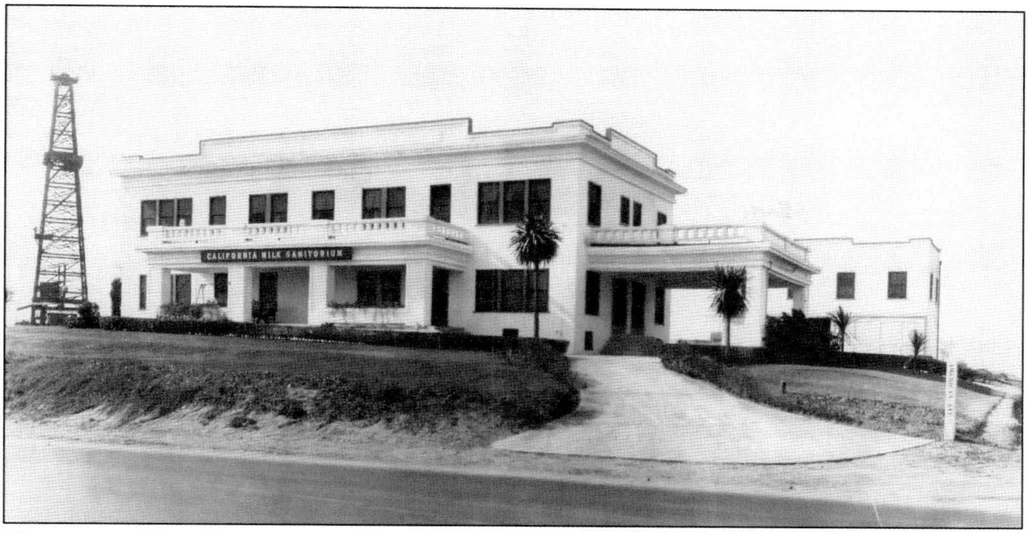

CALIFORNIA MILK SANITORIUM. The first institution established for the exclusive treatment of noncontagious diseases such as anemia, gout, arthritis, and ulcers through the use of milk, the sanitorium was constructed about 1919 at the corner of American Avenue and Wardlow Road. It moved in 1926 to 4010 Virginia Road. Several eminent physicians swore by the success of milk treatments, and the sanitorium drew patients from around the country. (HSLB.)

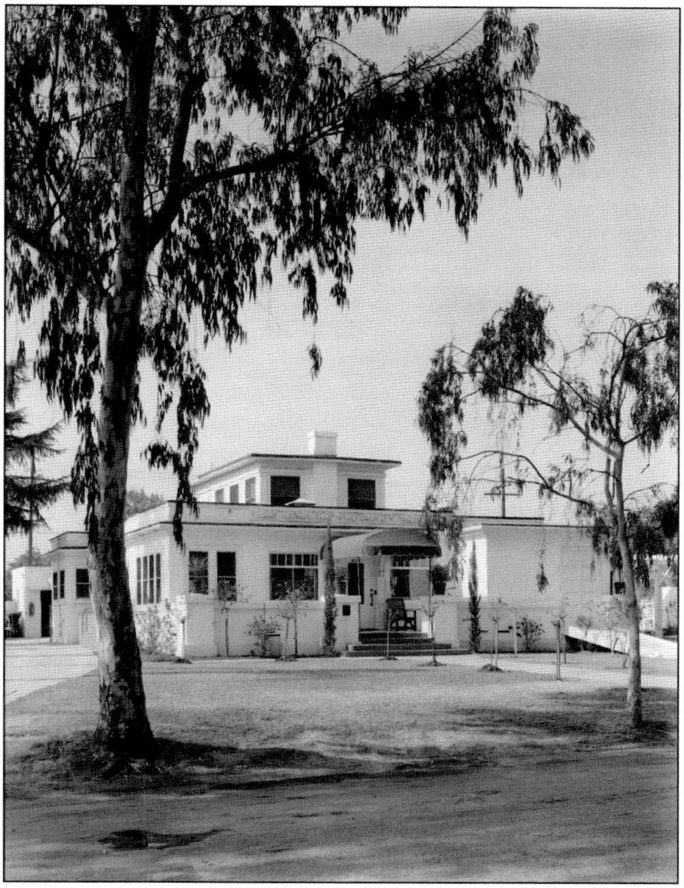

LOS CERRITOS MATERNITY HOSPITAL. Located at 4005 American Avenue (now Virginia Road), the Los Cerritos Maternity Hospital was convenient for expectant mothers in Los Cerritos. It was acquired by Pacific Hospital in 1944. (HSLB.)

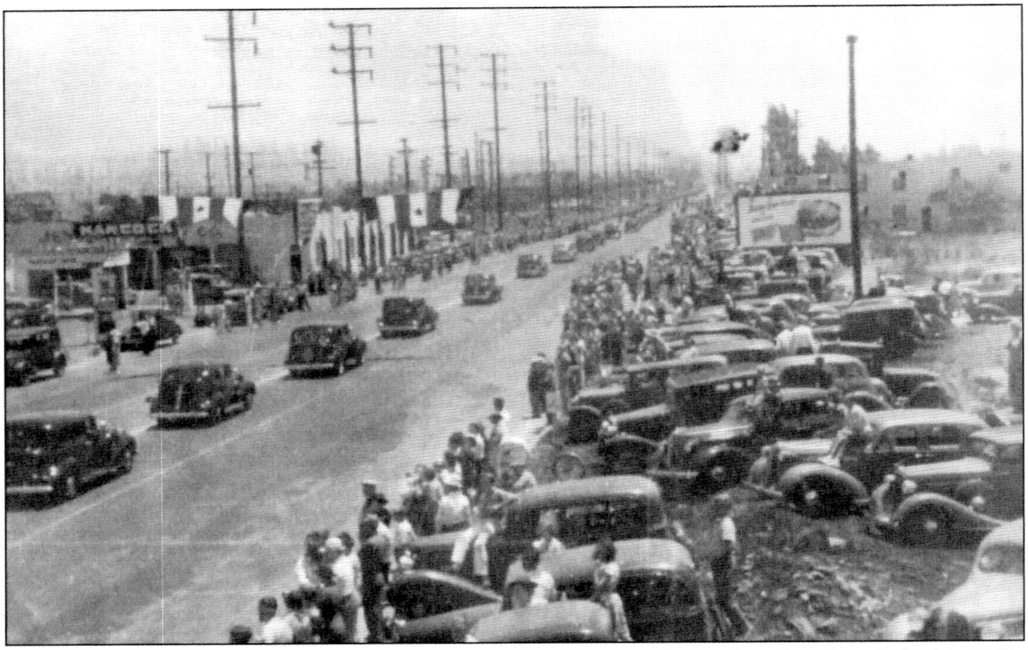

President Roosevelt on Wardlow Road. Hundreds lined Wardlow Road on July 16, 1938, to watch Pres. Franklin Roosevelt's motorcade drive by on the way to San Diego. Although the president only drove through Long Beach, he would return in September 1942 for an inspection tour of Douglas Aircraft.

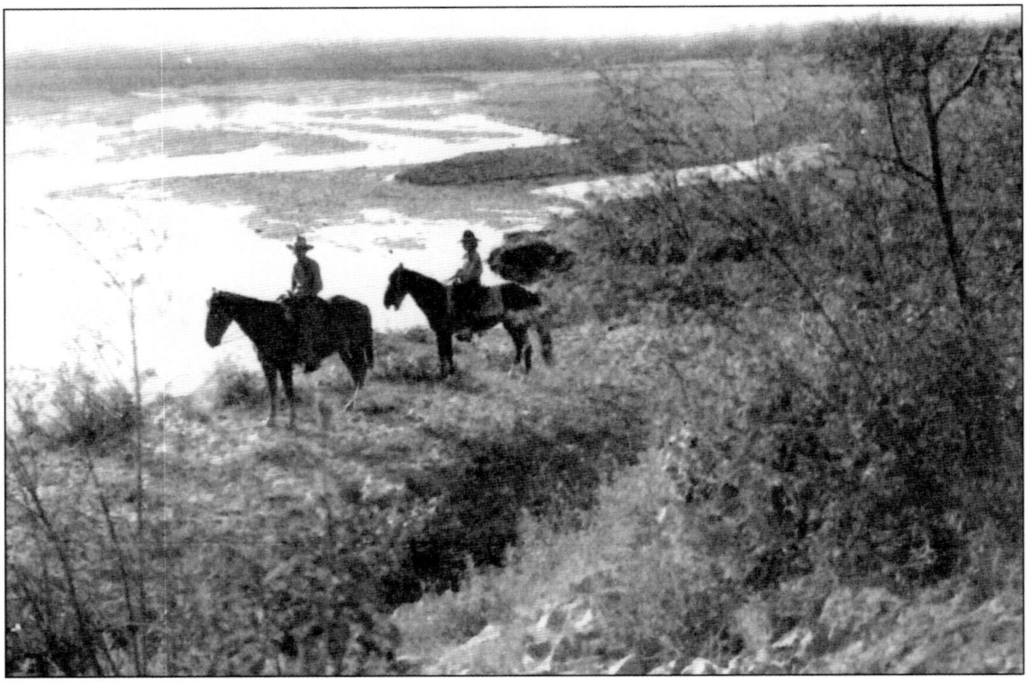

Horseback Riding along the Los Angeles River. Many families in Los Cerritos kept horses stabled along the river. This photograph, taken between 1937 and 1939, shows the approximate location of current homes on Devon Place. On the left is John B. Merrell. He is accompanied by his sister Marjorie Merrell. (Courtesy of Marjorie Merrell Bartlett.)

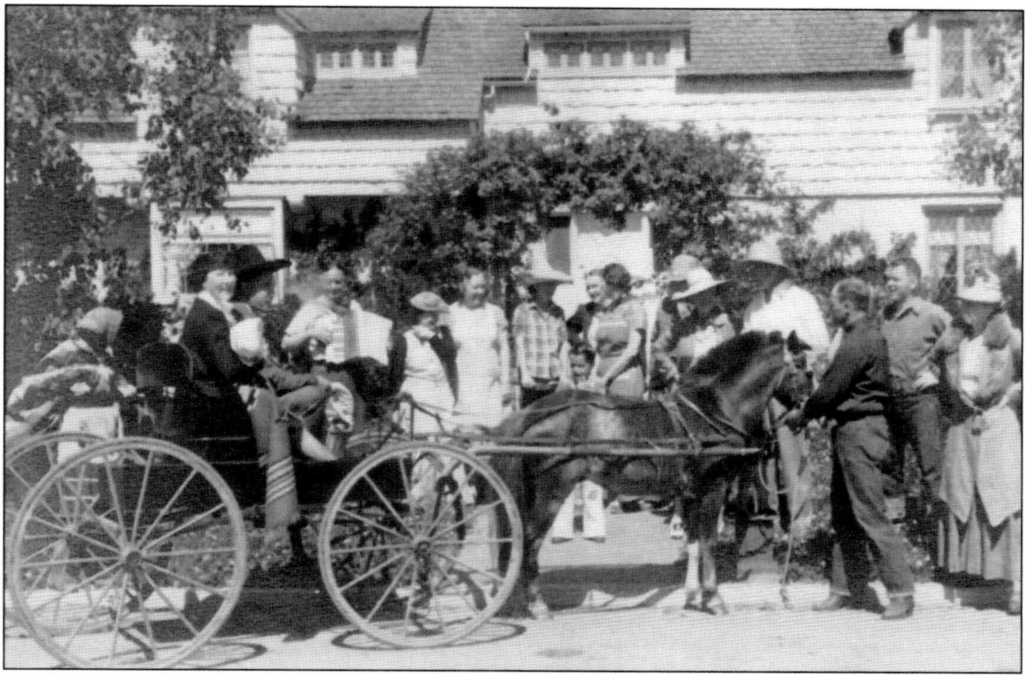

Neighbors at the Jimerson/Knatz-Mulvey Home. Neighbors greet John and Glen Jimerson (holding a baby) in a horse-drawn wagon in front of 4181 Country Club Drive in this late-1930s photograph. (Courtesy of Gary Holland.)

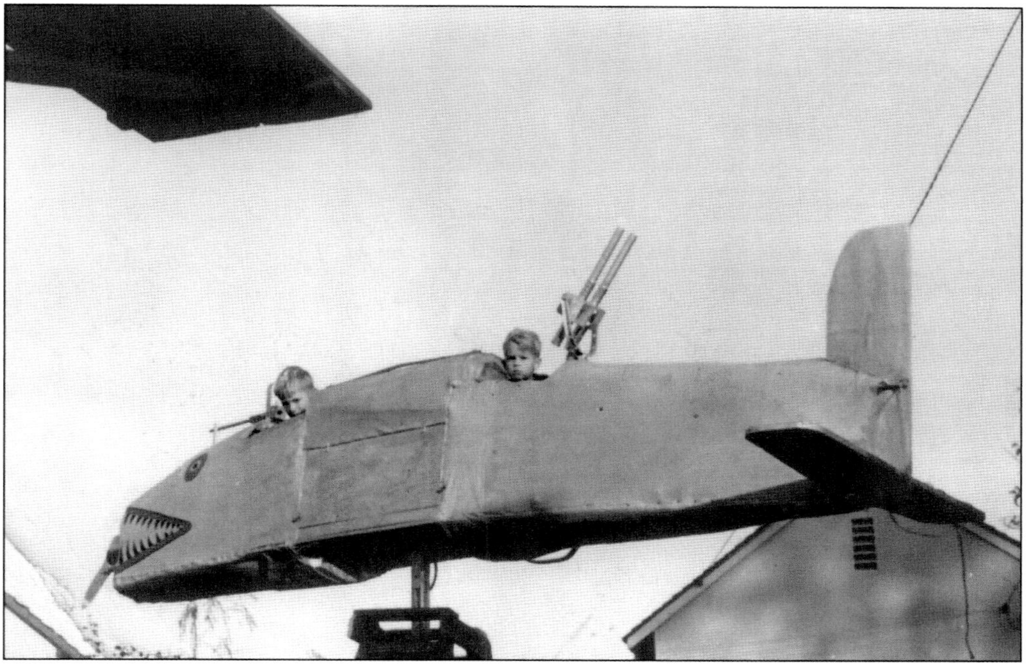

World War II Toy Plane. Manley Natland constructed this full-sized toy airplane during World War II for his kids. It was equipped with toy machine guns and decorated with teeth dangling a cigar. Taking advantage of his oil background, Natland constructed it on a derrick-like structure for elevation over the rooftops.

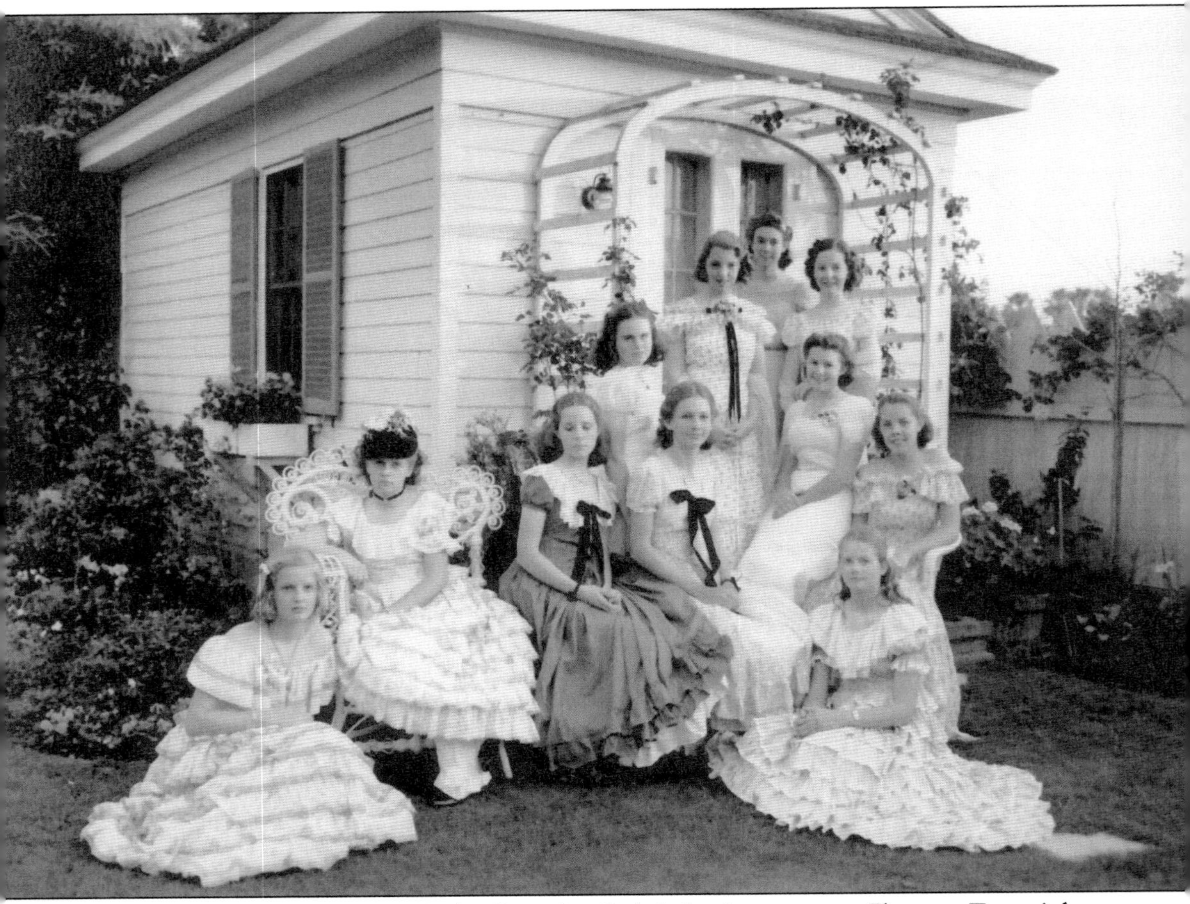

Campfire Girls Tea. In 1940, the Campfire Girls helped serve tea at Florence Turner's house at 4299 Country Club Drive. Pictured from left to right are (seated on the lawn) Barbara Enloe and unidentified; (seated on chairs) Marjorie Merrell, Cynthia Taves, Carolyn Clock, Jeane Whisenank, and Janet Wilkinson; (standing) Janice Campbell, Margaret Wilkinson, Betsy Taves, and Barbara Condit. (Courtesy of Margaret Wilkinson Mahannah.)

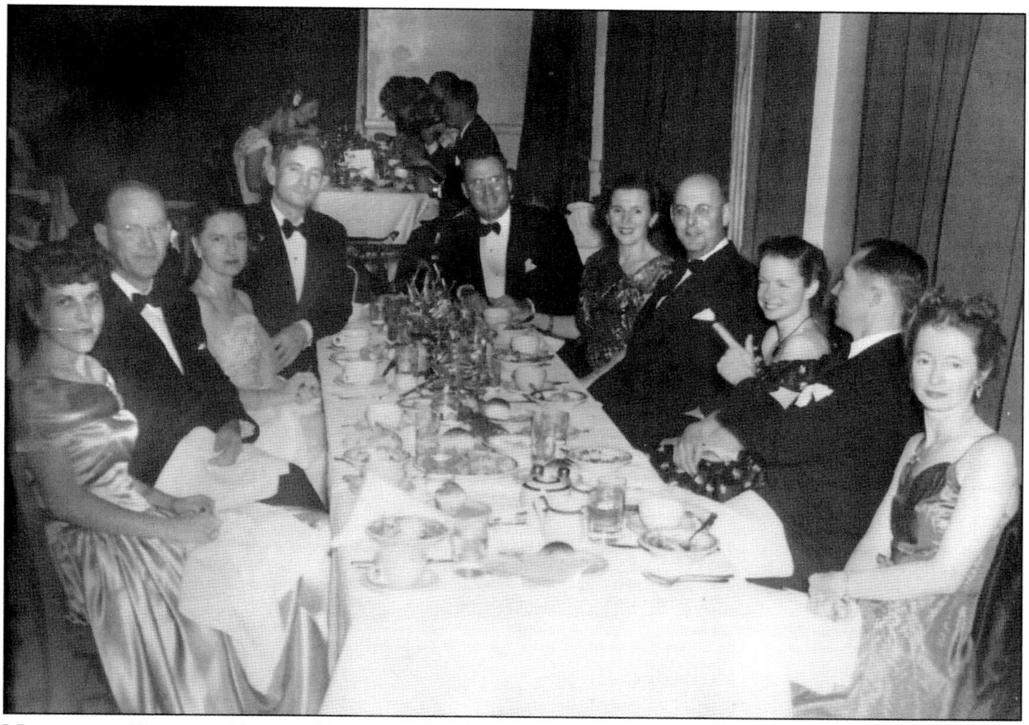

NEIGHBORS DINNER. Pictured here at the Sky Room in 1942 are some of the notable citizens of Los Cerritos. They are, from left to right, Dorothy Combs, Stender Sweeney, Josephine Sweeney, Manley Natland, Eldridge Combs, Frances Clock, Henry Clock, Ruth Hubbell, Maurice Hubbell, and Dorothy Natland.

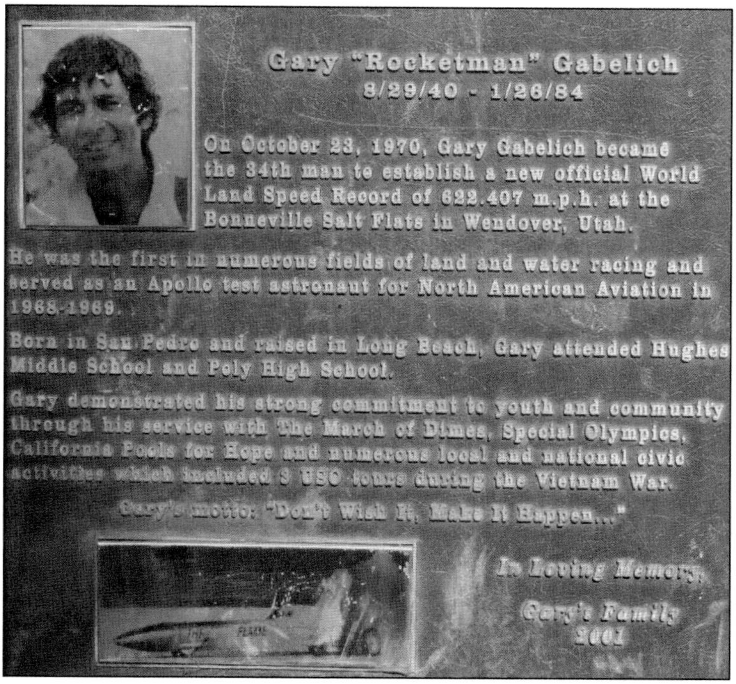

"ROCKETMAN" GARY GABELICH. Gary Gabelich set the land speed record with his rocket-powered vehicle *Blue Flame* on October 23, 1970, averaging a speed of 622.3 miles per hour. Gabeich died in a motorcycle accident in 1984. In 1985, the Long Beach City Council approved dedicating a portion of the Los Cerritos park to his memory. Gabelich was the husband of Rae Gabelich, councilwoman for Los Cerritos from 2004 to 2012. (Courtesy of John Mulvey.)

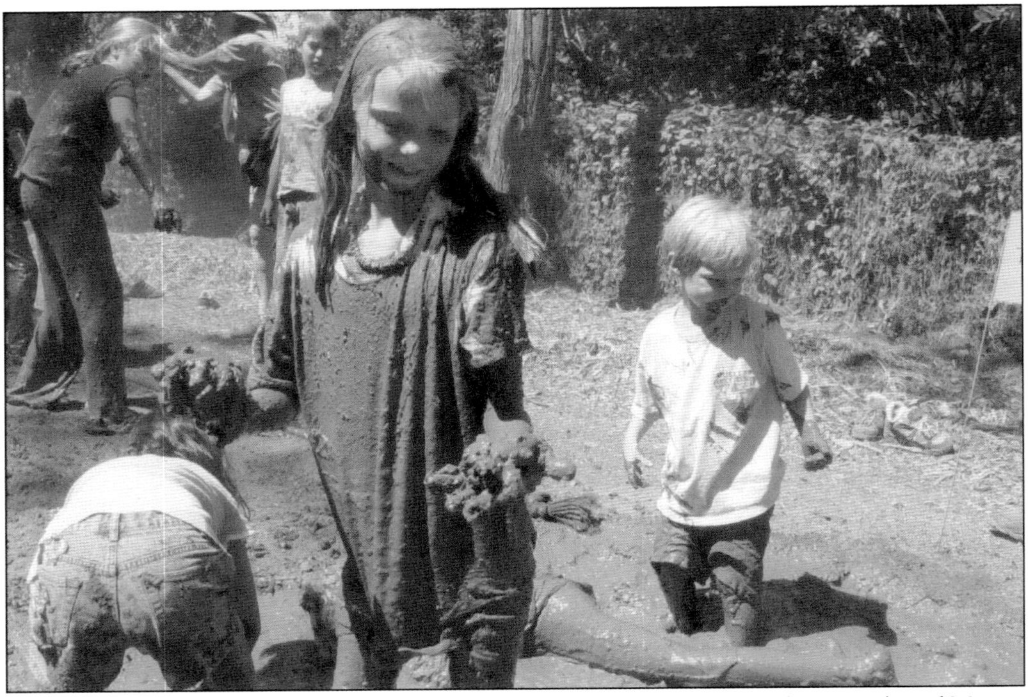

Mud Mania. The perfect venue for children who like to play in the dirt is the annual Mud Mania. Rancho Los Cerritos was constructed of adobe brick, and this event allows adults and children the opportunity to make adobe bricks, plaster a wall, and make a tiny adobe house. (RLC.)

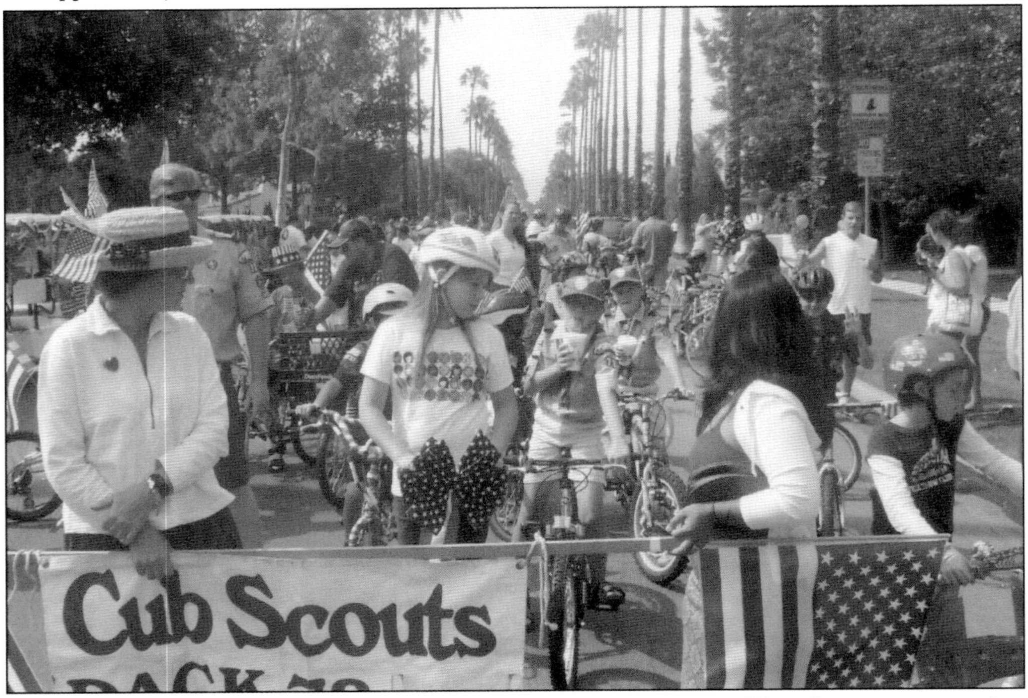

Kids in Red, White, and Blue. For over 30 years, Los Cerritos neighbors have come together to sponsor their own annual July 4th parade. With bikes decorated, hundreds of Los Cerritos children line up at the start of the 2005 annual parade. (Courtesy of John Mulvey.)

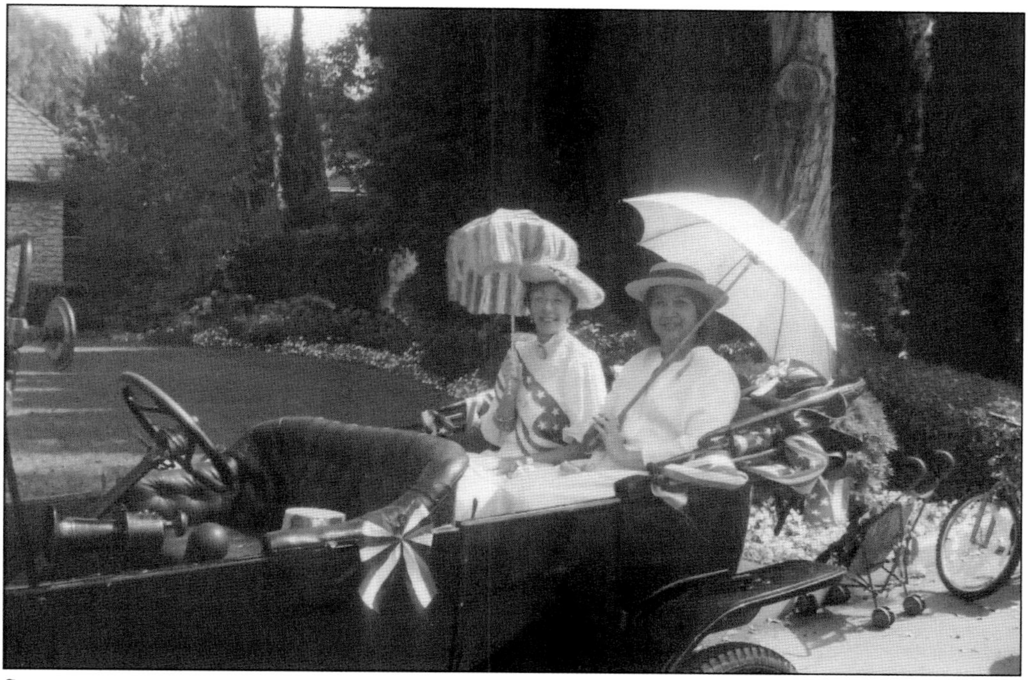

SUFFRAGETTES. Los Cerritos residents Geraldine Knatz (left) and Lillian Kawasaki, dressed as suffragettes, await the start of the 2005 parade in a Model T owned by Craig Carter. (Courtesy of John Mulvey.)

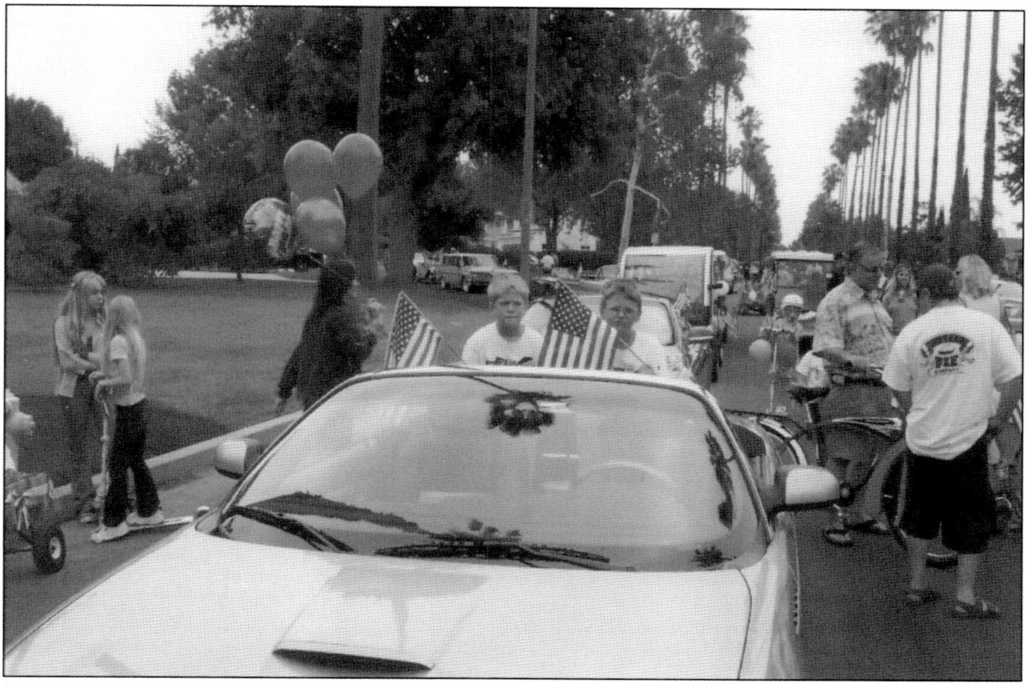

START OF JULY 4TH PARADE. J.R. (left) and Patrick Mulvey await the start of the 2004 parade in a Thunderbird owned by Jan Hower. (Courtesy of John Mulvey).

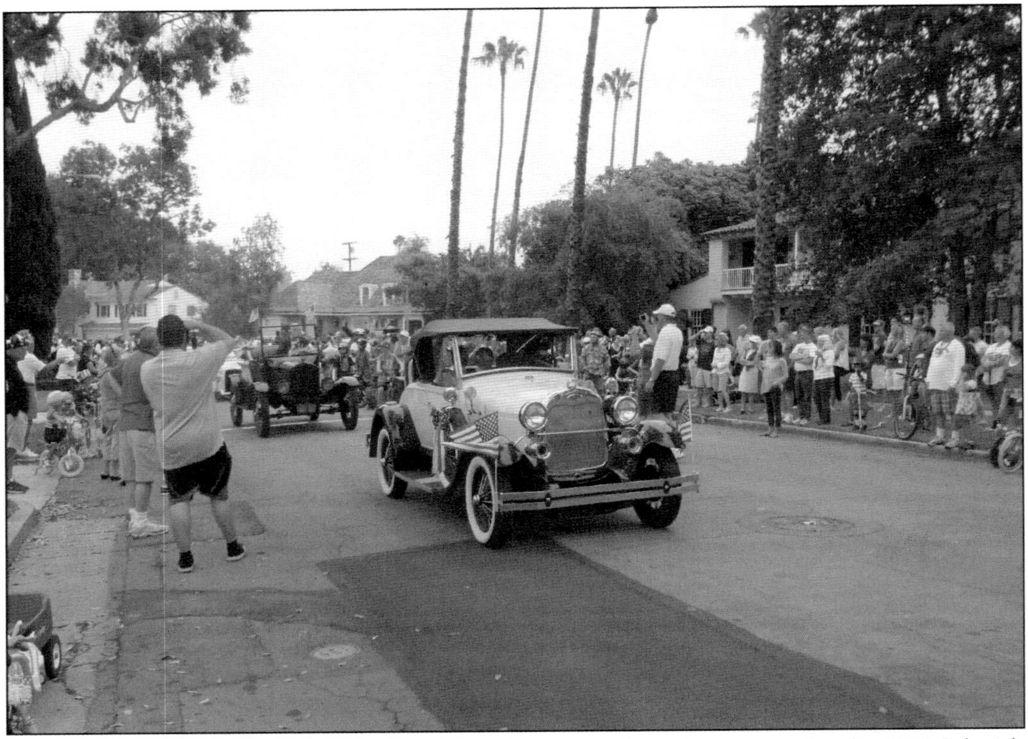

From Model Ts to Muscle Cars. Neighbors bring out their vintage cars for the 2013 July 4th parade. (Courtesy of John Mulvey.)

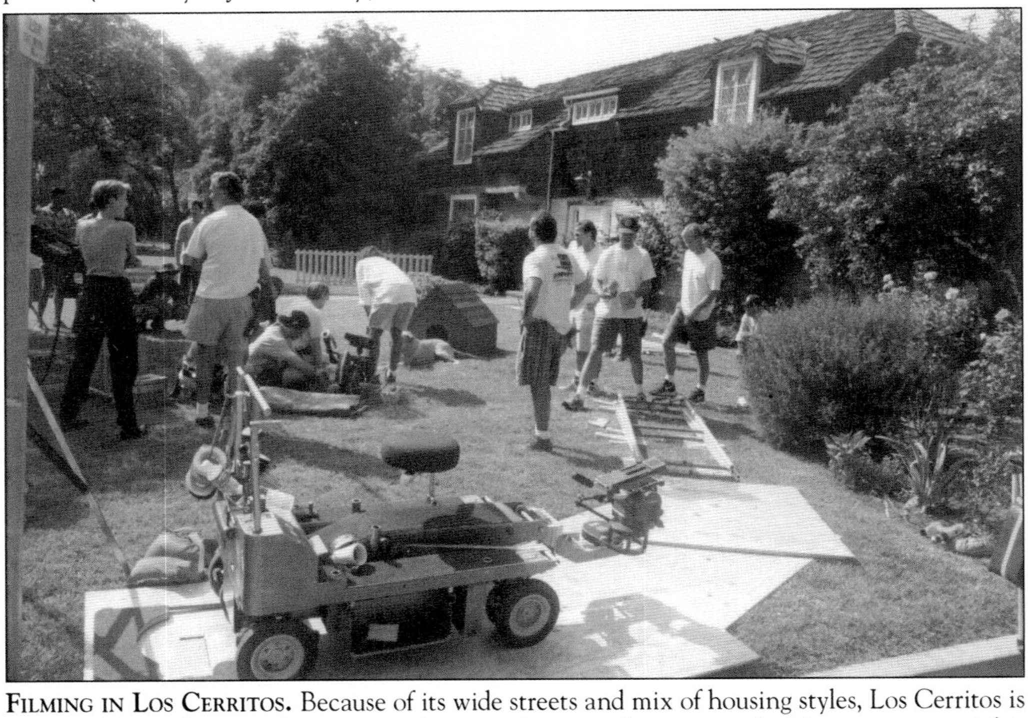

Filming in Los Cerritos. Because of its wide streets and mix of housing styles, Los Cerritos is a prime filming location for movies, television shows, and commercials. Here, a commercial is being shot at 4181 Country Club Drive. (Courtesy of John Mulvey.)

Seven

VIRGINIA COUNTRY CLUB

The Virginia Country Club was incorporated in November 1909 with 119 charter members. The members assessed themselves a $25 initiation fee and monthly dues of $2.50 to cover the annual rent payment of $1,200 to the Alamitos Land Company for their first site, now Recreation Park in Long Beach. Many charter members were residents of Los Cerritos, including Ralph H. Clock, James F. Craig, and Walter Desmond. Beset by financial difficulties, a 1912 agreement between the club and the Seaside Investment Company paid the club in exchange for club privileges for guests of the Virginia Hotel. As the club approached the termination of its 10-year lease with the Alamitos Land Company, the club considered the acquisition of the Recreation Park site, as well as an area including the Rancho Los Cerritos adobe. It finally agreed in June 1920 to a 20-year lease of 135 acres with an option to purchase near the rancho adobe. On August 31, 1921, the new clubhouse and golf course were dedicated. The club was able to purchase the land after receiving a fee of $150,000 from Shell Oil for drilling rights. An agreement with Associated Oil Company paid a fee of $75,000, which was used to improve the clubhouse. On September 10, 1927, the Spanish hacienda-style clubhouse was formally opened.

The early records of the club have little reference to women's activities. In 1920, a woman, Mrs. Fred Leavens, was hired as a hostess and assistant secretary for $125 per month. At the club board meeting of September 21, 1921, a letter from the board of the YWCA about women smoking in the clubhouse was received and filed. The club's own history, published in 1928, included a quote from Charles Cushing's series in *Country Life* on the subject of country clubs: "It has brought our women out of stuffy houses and out of their own hopeless, aimless selves; has given color to their cheeks, vivacity to their movements, charm and intelligence to their conversations."

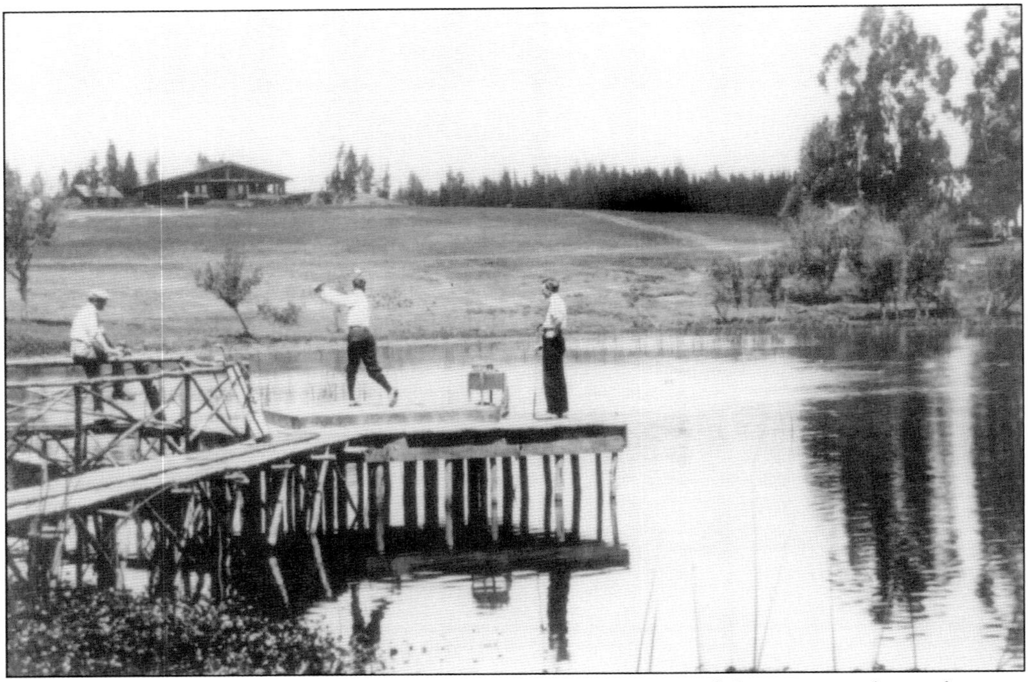

ORIGINAL VIRGINIA COUNTRY CLUB. The first Virginia Country Club course was located in east Long Beach, now Recreation Park. The club was famous for its wooden platform tee, 260 yards long and uphill. Pictured here at the 16th hole in this 1912 photograph are, from left to right, A.M. Goodhue, president; Bert Paul Sr.; and George Martin, the club's first professional. (VCC.)

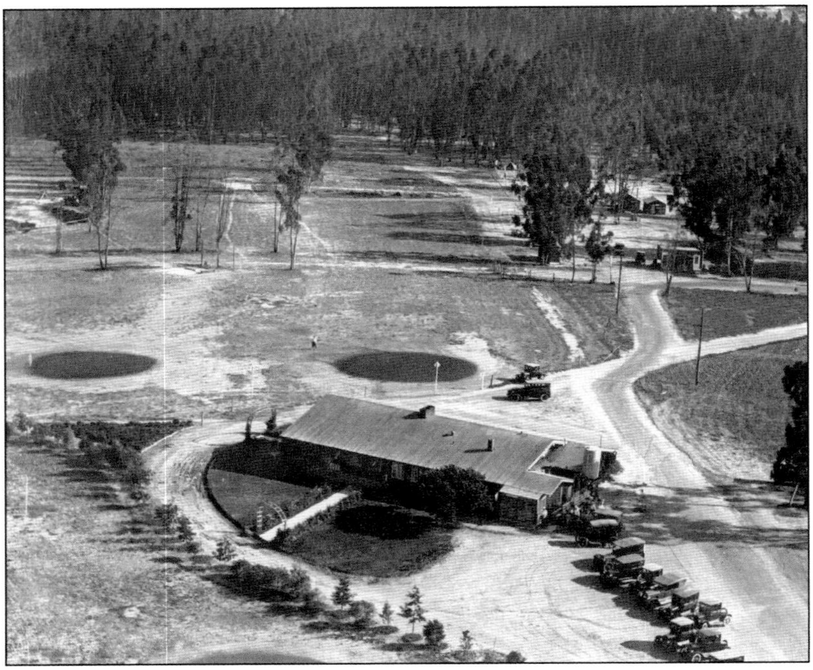

ORIGINAL CLUBHOUSE. The club leased the Recreation Park site for 10 years beginning January 1, 1910, from the Alamitos Land Company. The Land Company spent $3,500 constructing the clubhouse and $2500 improving the grounds. (VCC.)

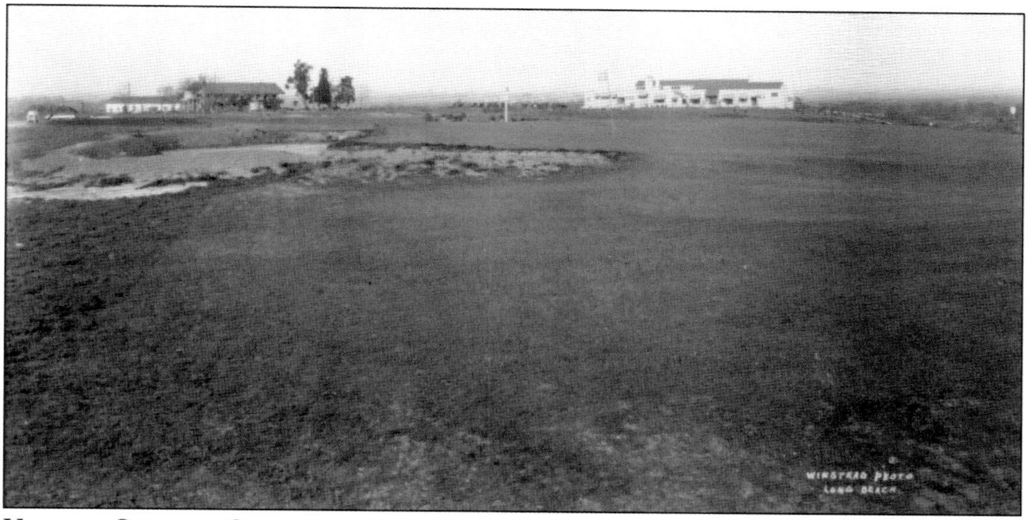

VIRGINIA COUNTRY CLUB. An early proposal for the new country club was 100 acres of land, including the old rancho adobe and the home of George H. Bixby, which would have been converted into a clubhouse. The rancho adobe would have been reserved by the Bixby family. Ultimately, the club selected 135 acres next to the rancho. This 1928 photograph shows the proximity of the clubhouse to the old rancho. (RLC.)

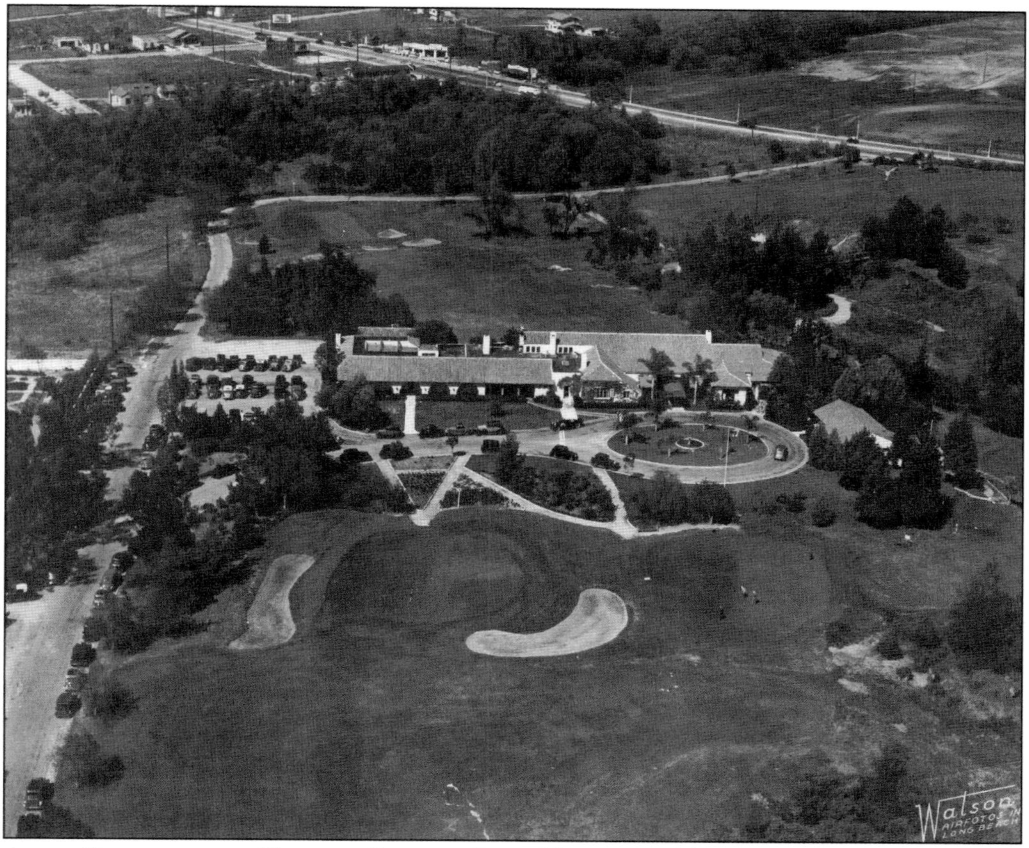

AERIAL PHOTOGRAPH OF VIRGINIA COUNTRY CLUB. This image of the Virginia Country Club shows the early layout of the buildings and parking. The rancho adobe is on the far right. (VCC.)

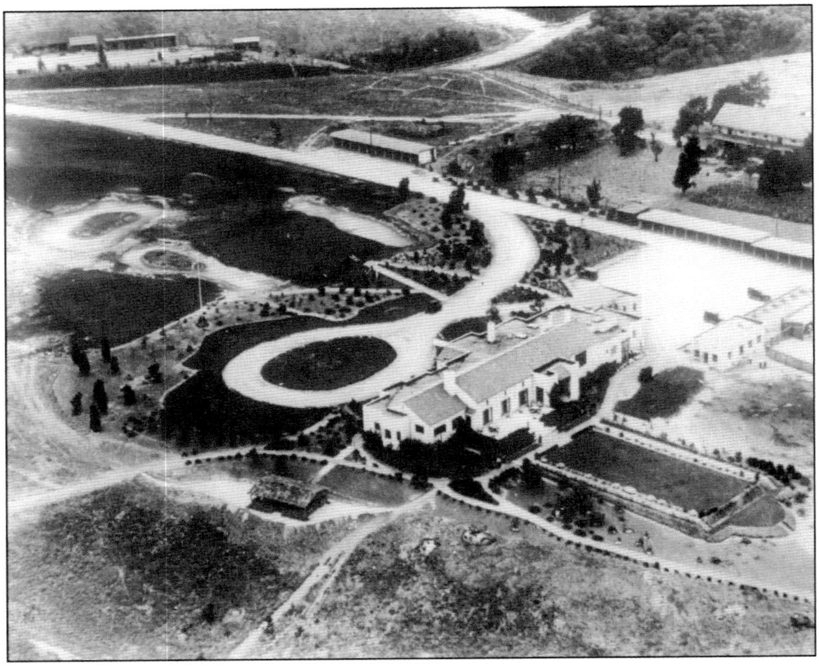

Country Club and Stables. The club was founded when horses were the primary means of transportation. In 1910, club records show a purchase of a horse from Fred Bixby for $250 for use on the grounds. The club provided places for members to park their cars or their horses. (VCC.)

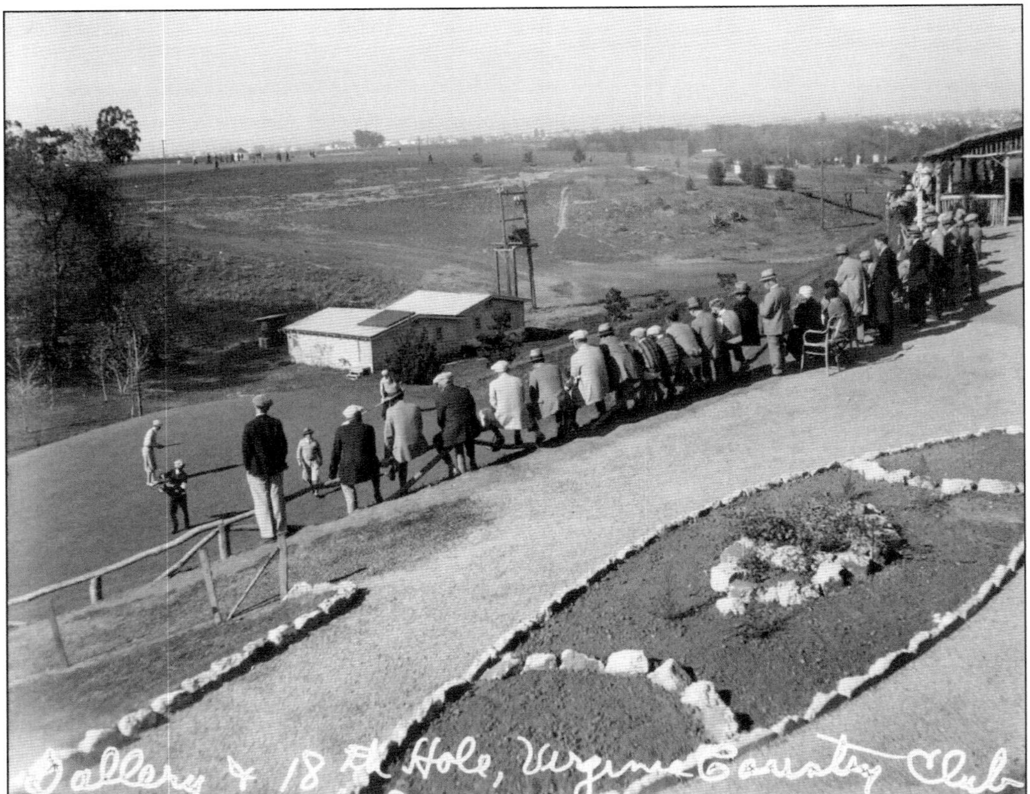

The 18th Hole at Virginia Country Club. Members watch as a player tackles the 18th hole green. The first Long Beach Open Tournament was held on January 23, 1926. (VCC.)

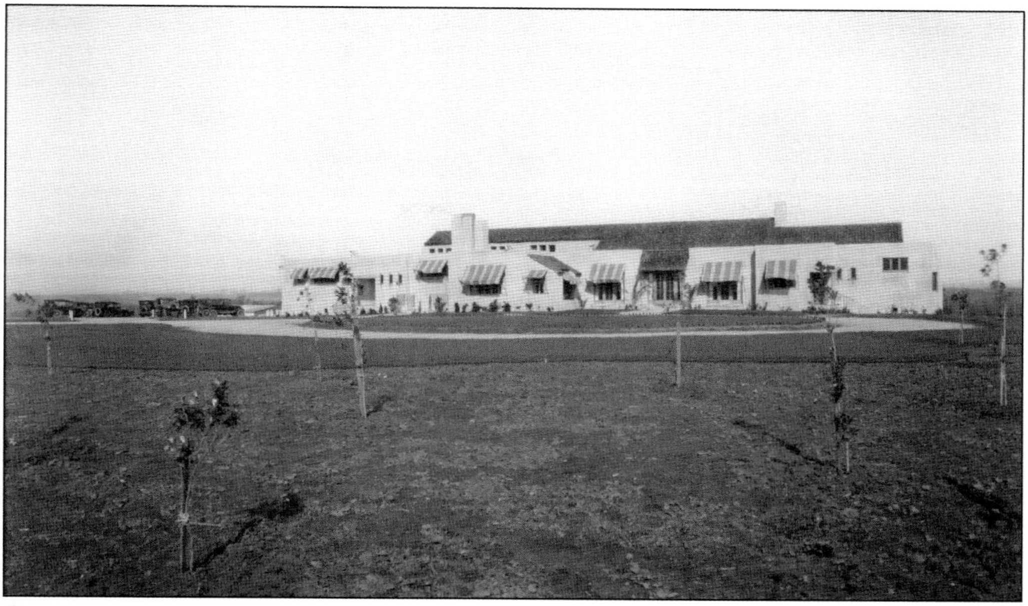

Clubhouse at Official Opening. After having a successful first tournament in 1926, the members hired C.T. McGrew and Sons to remodel and expand the clubhouse. The official opening of the Spanish hacienda-style clubhouse was September 10, 1927. (VCC.)

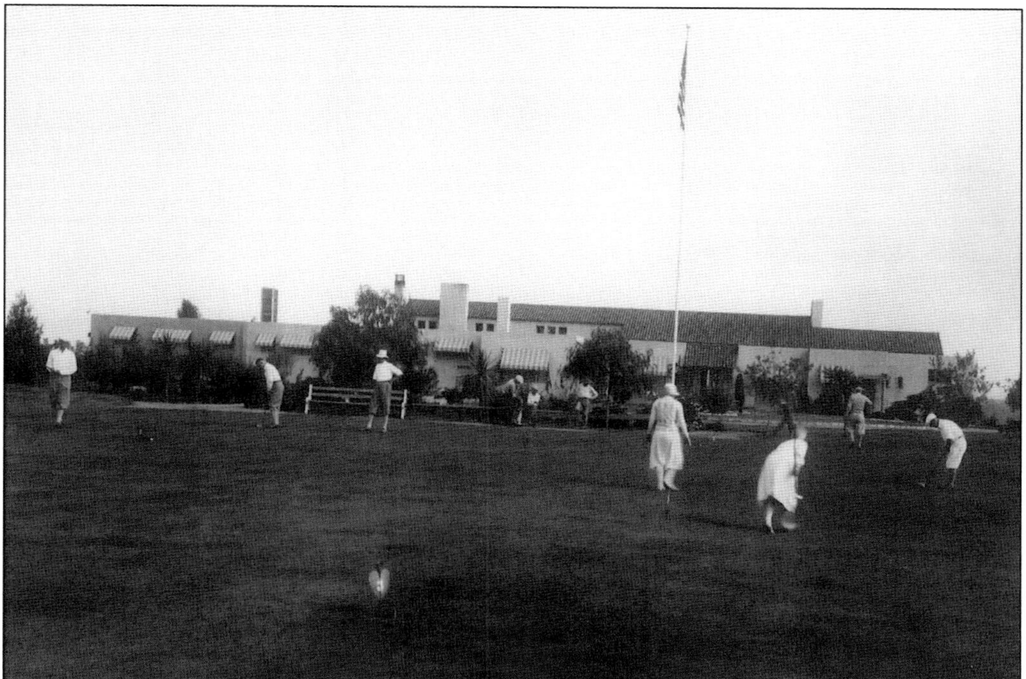

Female Golfers at Virginia Country Club. This early-1920s photograph shows women playing the Virginia Country Club Course. According to club records, as cars became more common, the use of the club by women increased. (RLC.)

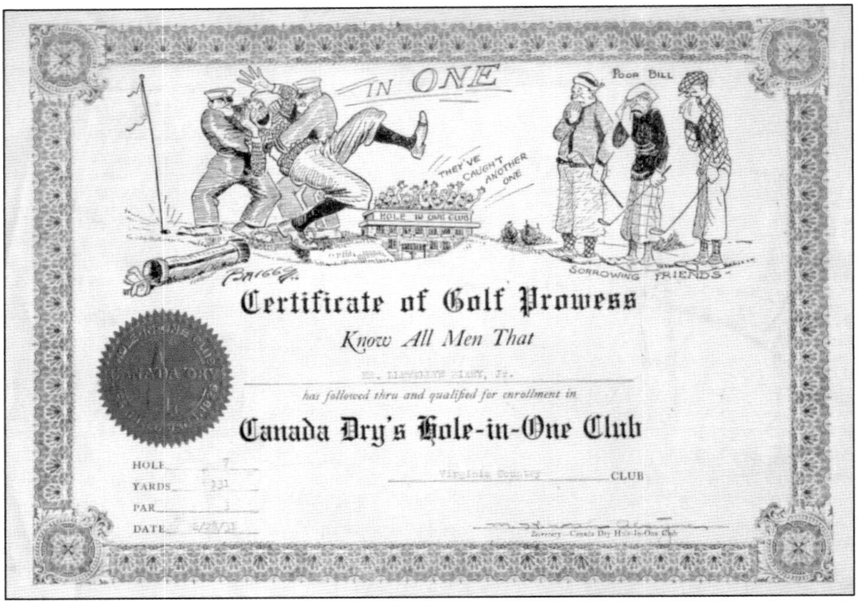

IN ONE

POOR BILL

THEY'VE CAUGHT ANOTHER ONE

HOLE IN ONE CLUB

SORROWING FRIENDS

Certificate of Golf Prowess

Know All Men That

MR. LLEWELLYN BIXBY, Jr.

has followed thru and qualified for enrollment in

Canada Dry's Hole-in-One Club

HOLE 7

YARDS 331

PAR

DATE

Virginia Country CLUB

Secretary Canada Dry Hole-in-One Club

LLEWELLYN BIXBY HOLE-IN-ONE. On February 28, 1931, Llewelyn Bixby Jr. earned his Canada Dry Official Hole-in-One certificate for his golf prowess. (VCC.)

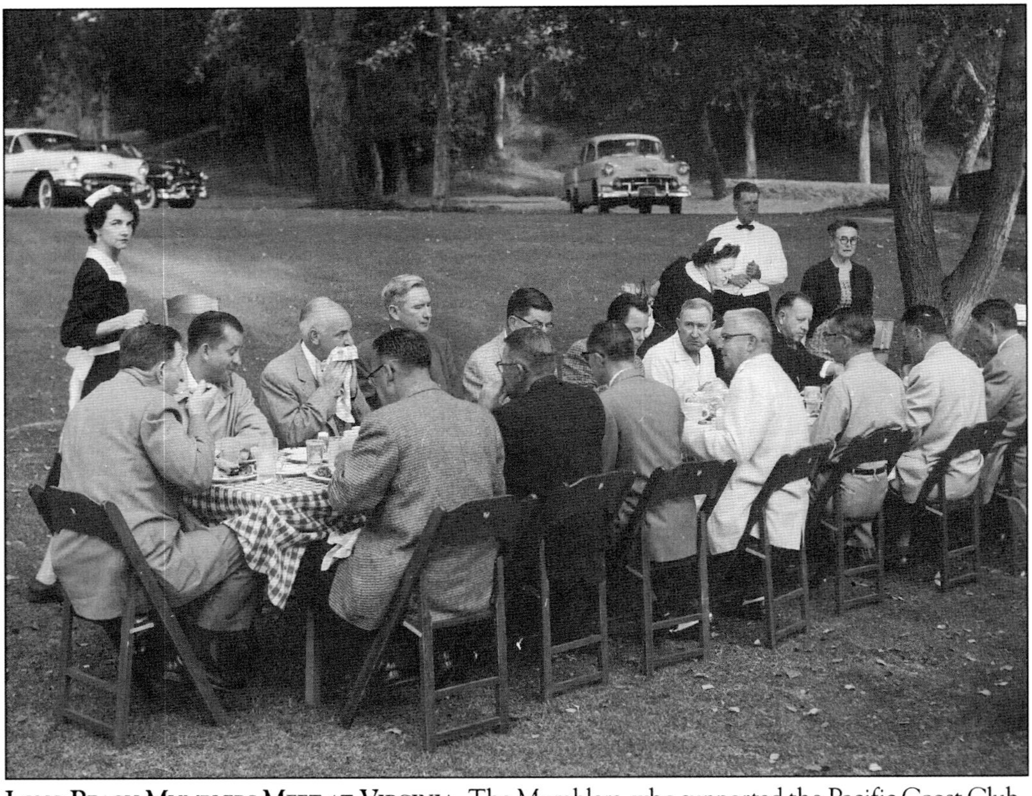

LONG BEACH MUMBLERS MEET AT VIRGINIA. The Mumblers, who supported the Pacific Coast Club, meet here at the Virginia Country Club in the 1950s. Pictured are (at the left end) Red Thompson; (background row, facing forward) Neil Ensch, Bob Reid, Joe Bishop, Gerald Houts, and James G. Craig Jr., Fred Kerns, and George Craig; (foreground row, with backs to the photographer) Emmet Sullivan, Earle Sullivan, Eldredge Combs, Latham Brightman, Frende Combs, unidentified, and Laurence Houts. Standing in the right rear is club manager Pearl McInnis. (VCC.)

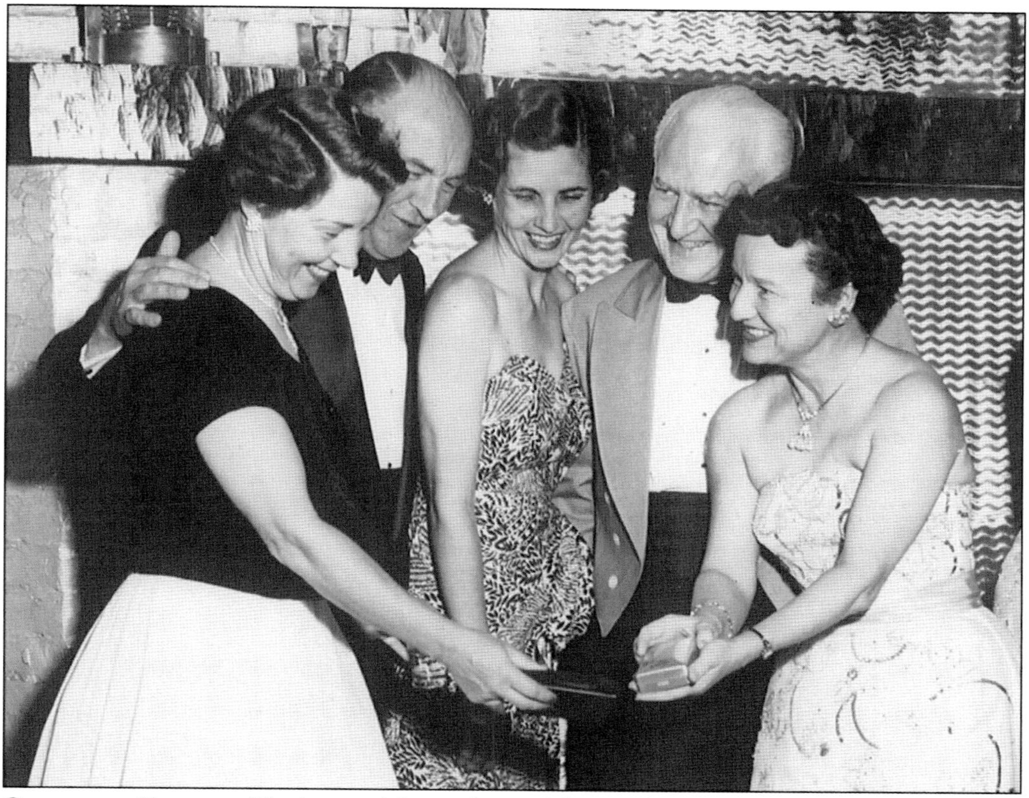

Couples at Virginia. The happy club members celebrating here are, from left to right, Dorothy McGrew, Milton McGrew, unidentified, Vernon Fay, and Corrine Fay. (VCC.)

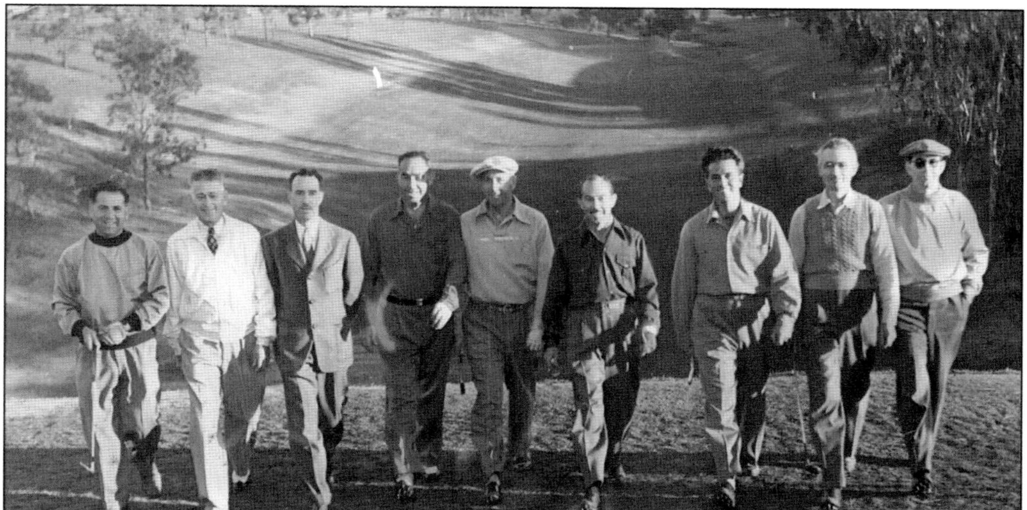

Team Match Players. Seen at hole No. 1, the members of the 1939 team are, from left to right, Joe Rodgers, Harry Graham, John Halbert, Len Pulley, Harry Witz, Bob McCrystal, Wendell Schooling, Franklin Robinson, and an unidentified nonplayer. (VCC.)

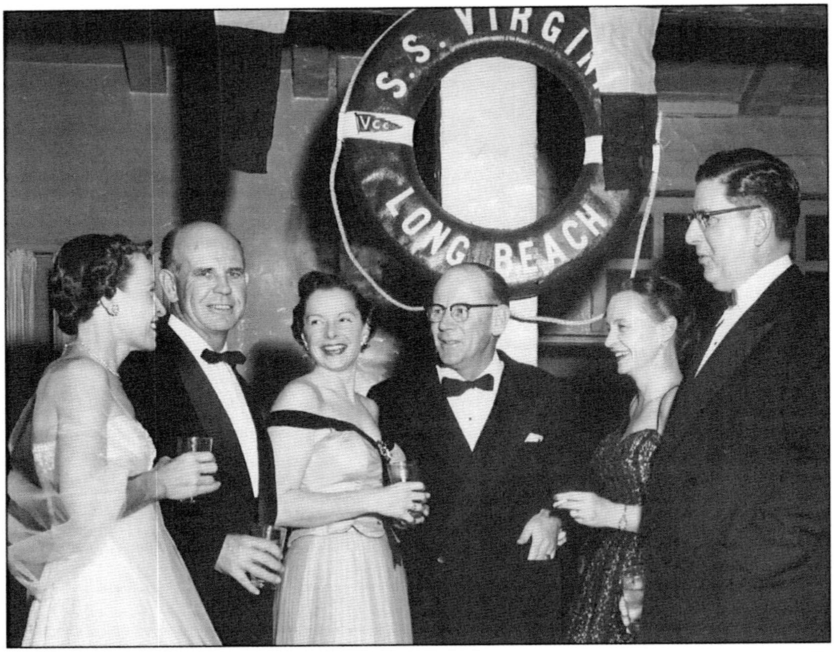

The SS *Virginia*. This c. 1950 photograph of a cruise-themed evening at Virginia County Club shows, from left to right, Opal Evans, Denny Evans, Ruth Hubbell, Maurice Hubbell, Grace Houts, and Dr. Gerald Houts. (VCC.)

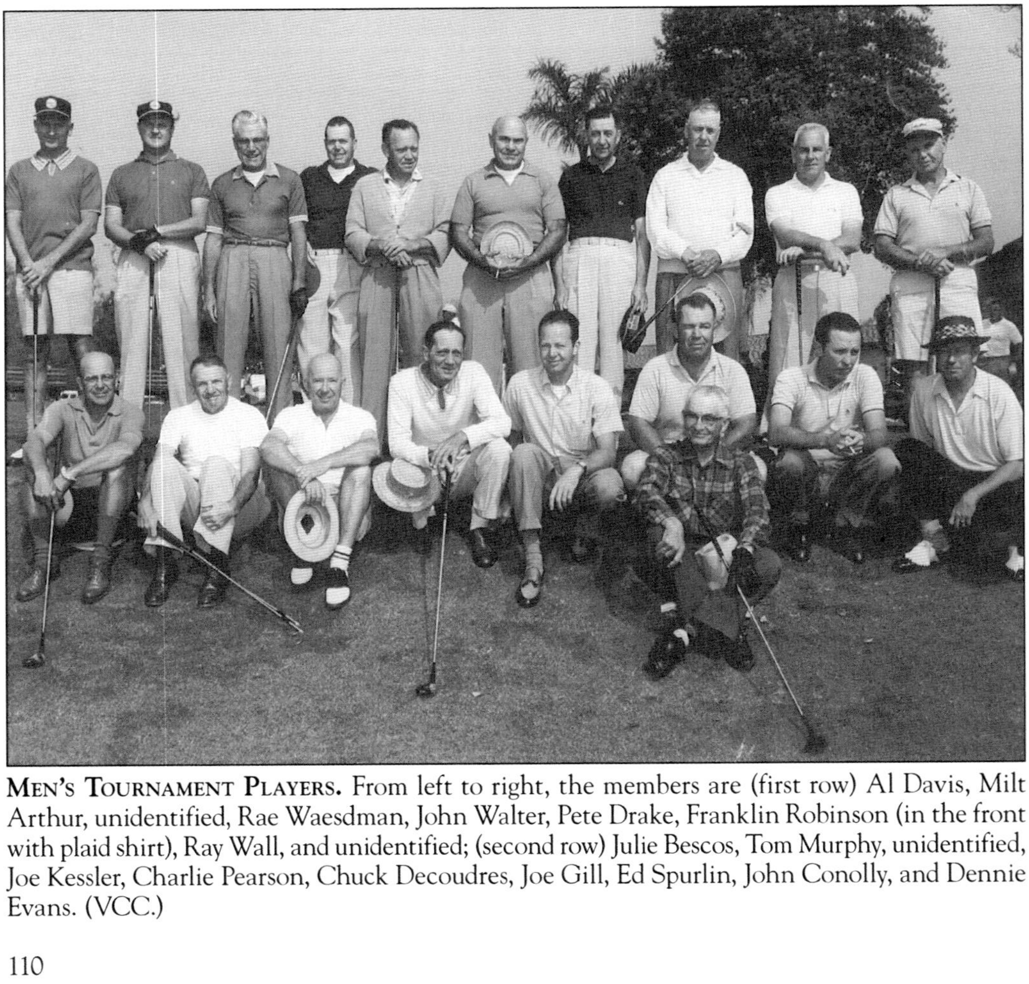

Men's Tournament Players. From left to right, the members are (first row) Al Davis, Milt Arthur, unidentified, Rae Waesdman, John Walter, Pete Drake, Franklin Robinson (in the front with plaid shirt), Ray Wall, and unidentified; (second row) Julie Bescos, Tom Murphy, unidentified, Joe Kessler, Charlie Pearson, Chuck Decoudres, Joe Gill, Ed Spurlin, John Conolly, and Dennie Evans. (VCC.)

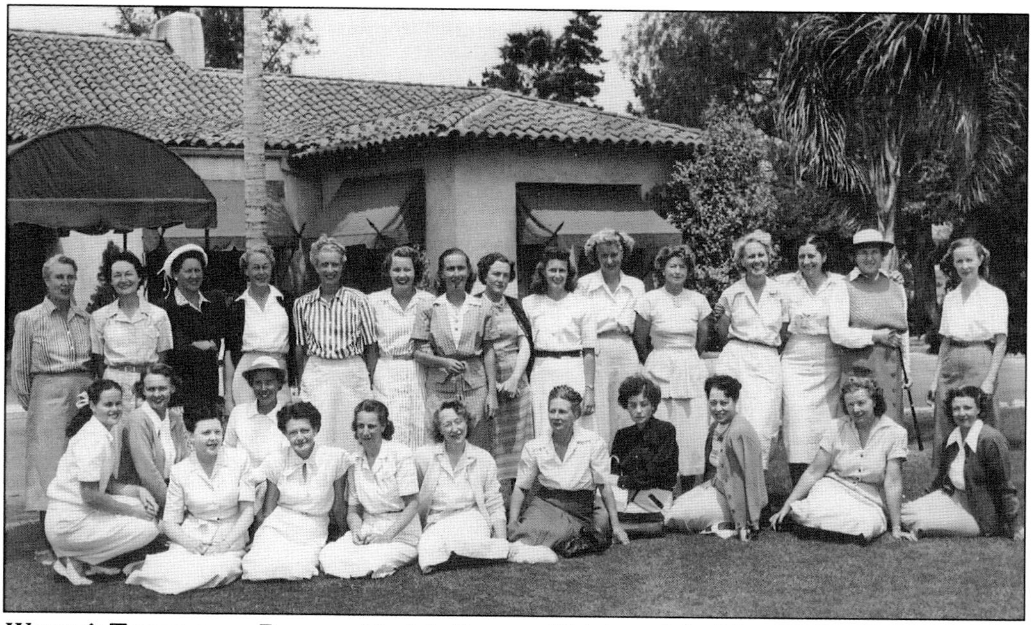

WOMEN'S TOURNAMENT PLAYERS. Virginia Country Club joined the Women's Southern California Golf Association when it was created in 1933. Only a few of the woman in this photograph are identified. On the far right in the first row is Janice Campbell. In the second row, second from left, is Louise Montague; fourth from left is Charlotte Waldwagel; and second from right is Joanne Borce. (VCC.).

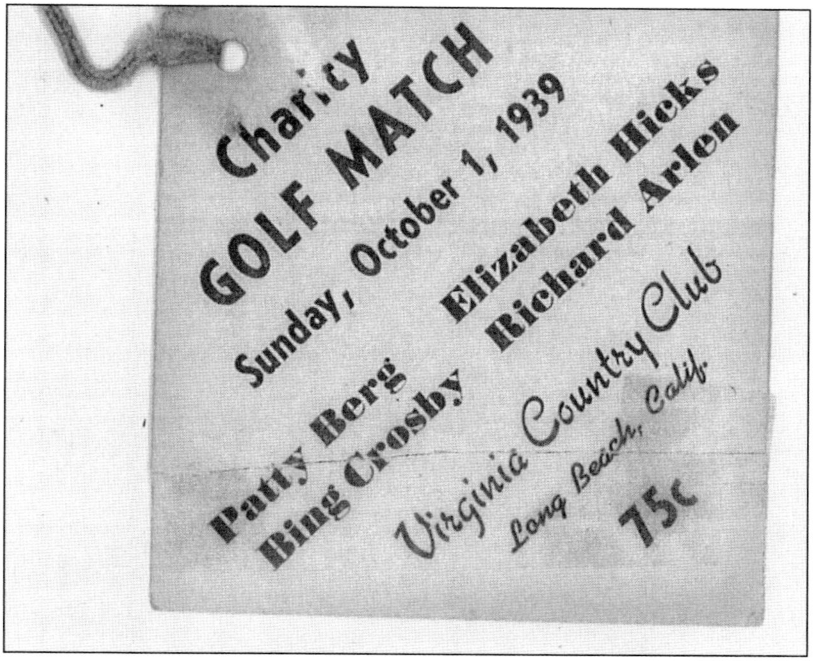

CHARITY TOURNAMENT. On October 1, 1939, the club held a charity tournament in which Bing Crosby played along with Patty Berg, a pioneer in women's golf and winner of 15 major championships during the 1940s to 1960s. Also attending were actors Richard Arlen and Elizabeth Hicks. (VCC.)

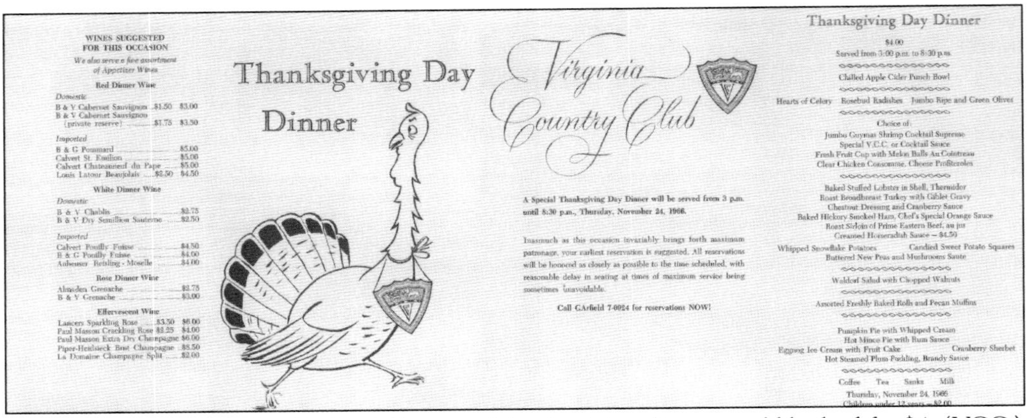

WINES SUGGESTED
FOR THIS OCCASION

We also serve a fine assortment of Appetizer Wines

Red Dinner Wine

Domestic

B & V Cabernet Sauvignon .$1.50 $3.00
B & V Cabernet Sauvignon (private reserve) .$1.75 $3.50

Imported

B & G Pommard .$5.00
Calvert St. Emilion .$5.00
Calvert Chateauneuf du Pape .$5.00
Louis Latour Beaujolais .$2.50 $4.50

White Dinner Wine

Domestic

B & V Chablis .$2.75
B & V Dry Semillion Sauterne .$2.50

Imported

Calvert Pouilly Fuisse .$4.50
B & G Pouilly Fuisse .$4.00
Anheuser Reisling - Moselle .$4.00

Rose Dinner Wine

Almaden Grenache .$2.75
B & V Grenache .$3.00

Effervescent Wine

Lancers Sparkling Rose .$3.50 $6.00
Paul Masson Crackling Rose $2.25 $4.00
Paul Masson Extra Dry Champagne $6.00
Piper-Heidsieck Brut Champagne .$8.50
La Domaine Champagne Split .$2.00

Thanksgiving Day Dinner

Virginia Country Club

A Special Thanksgiving Day Dinner will be served from 3 p.m. until 8:30 p.m., Thursday, November 24, 1966.

Inasmuch as this occasion invariably brings forth maximum patronage, your earliest reservation is suggested. All reservations will be honored as closely as possible to the time scheduled, with reasonable delay in seating at times of maximum service being sometimes unavoidable.

Call GArfield 7-0024 for reservations NOW!

Thanksgiving Day Dinner

$4.00
Served from 3:00 p.m. to 8:30 p.m.

Chilled Apple Cider Punch Bowl

Hearts of Celery Rosebud Radishes Jumbo Ripe and Green Olives

Choice of:
Jumbo Guymas Shrimp Cocktail Supreme
Special V.C.C. or Cocktail Sauce
Fresh Fruit Cup with Melon Balls Au Cointreau
Clear Chicken Consomme, Cheese Profiteroles

Baked Stuffed Lobster in Shell, Thermidor
Roast Broadbreast Turkey with Giblet Gravy
Chestnut Dressing and Cranberry Sauce
Baked Hickory Smoked Ham, Chef's Special Orange Sauce
Roast Sirloin of Prime Eastern Beef, au jus
Creamed Horseradish Sauce – $4.50
Whipped Snowflake Potatoes Candied Sweet Potato Squares
Buttered New Peas and Mushrooms Saute

Waldorf Salad with Chopped Walnuts

Assorted Freshly Baked Rolls and Pecan Muffins

Pumpkin Pie with Whipped Cream
Hot Mince Pie with Rum Sauce
Eggnog Ice Cream with Fruit Cake Cranberry Sherbet
Hot Steamed Plum Pudding, Brandy Sauce

Coffee Tea Sanka Milk

Thursday, November 24, 1966
Children under 12 years – $2.00

THANKSGIVING MENU. In 1966, a full-course Thanksgiving dinner could be had for $4. (VCC.)

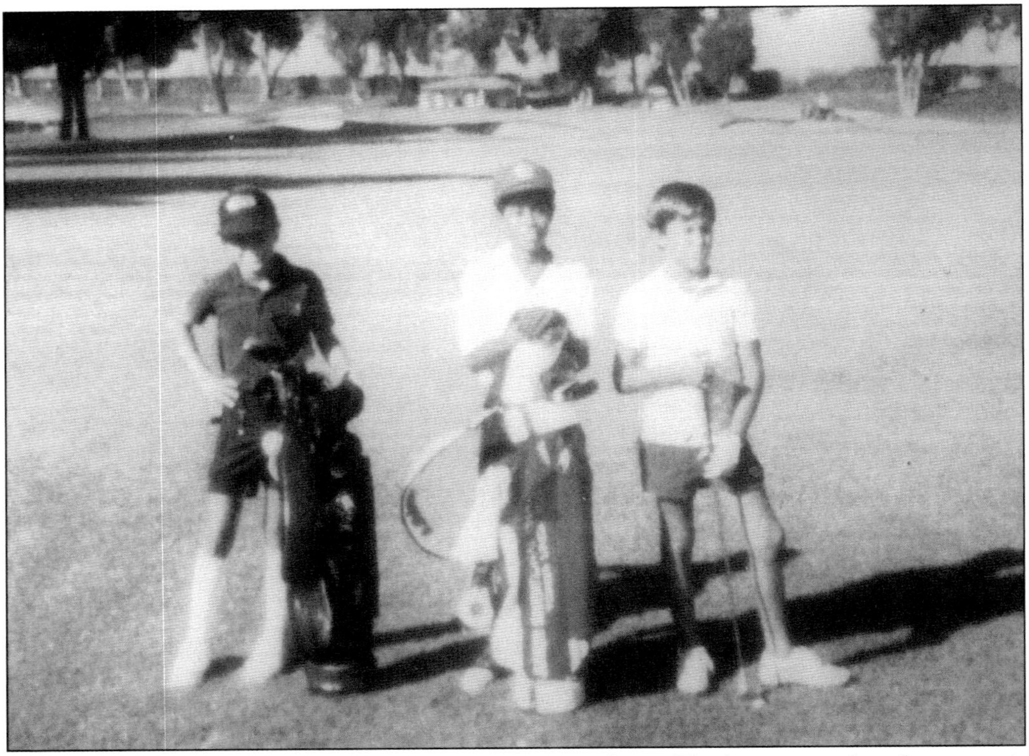

A YOUNG TIGER WOODS PLAYS AT VIRGINIA COUNTRY CLUB. The boy pictured in the center is Tiger Woods, who played at many Long Beach golf courses when he was growing up, including Virginia County Club. (VCC.)

Eight

Family Homes of Los Cerritos

The neighborhood of Los Cerritos not only has homes of Long Beach pioneers who figured prominently in the area's history, but it also is a prime filming location, making a tour through the neighborhood somewhat like a trip through Universal Studios' back lot. From the beginning, the neighborhood attracted prominent physicians, attorneys, and businessmen, many of who purchased lots close to the Virginia Country Club. Homes designed by noted architects such as Paul Revere Williams, Kirtland Cutter, Edward Killingsworth, James R. Friend, Hugh Gibbs, Kenneth Wing, and Charles and Henry Greene can be found in Los Cerritos. Prevalent styles are Craftsman, Colonial Revival, Monterey, and Tudor Revival. A gated community of homes known as La Linda was developed on the land that was part of the 10-acre grounds that originally surrounded the 1890s George H. Bixby home.

The pattern of the subdivisions is predominately responsible for the social and architectural contrasts found today. The northern subdivisions had large lots, 75 feet wide by 150 feet deep, with a 50-foot setback from the street. The resulting deep lawn helps to create a stately setting for a two-story home. The subdivisions in the southern part of the neighborhood are the more typical 50-foot-wide lots with standard 20-foot setbacks from the curb. The result was a socioeconomic stratification of the neighborhood, with the larger, more expensive homes located in the area north of San Antonio Drive, and the more modest homes with smaller square footages located in the southern part of the neighborhood.

Although many still refer to the northern part of the neighborhood as "Virginia Country Club" to distinguish it from the rest of Los Cerritos, over time, the earlier socioeconomic stratification from north to south has blurred. New construction and significant remodeling, often using two adjacent lots, has transformed many smaller dwellings into larger homes. The neighborhood today is an eclectic mix of homes of various sizes and styles, including some mansions.

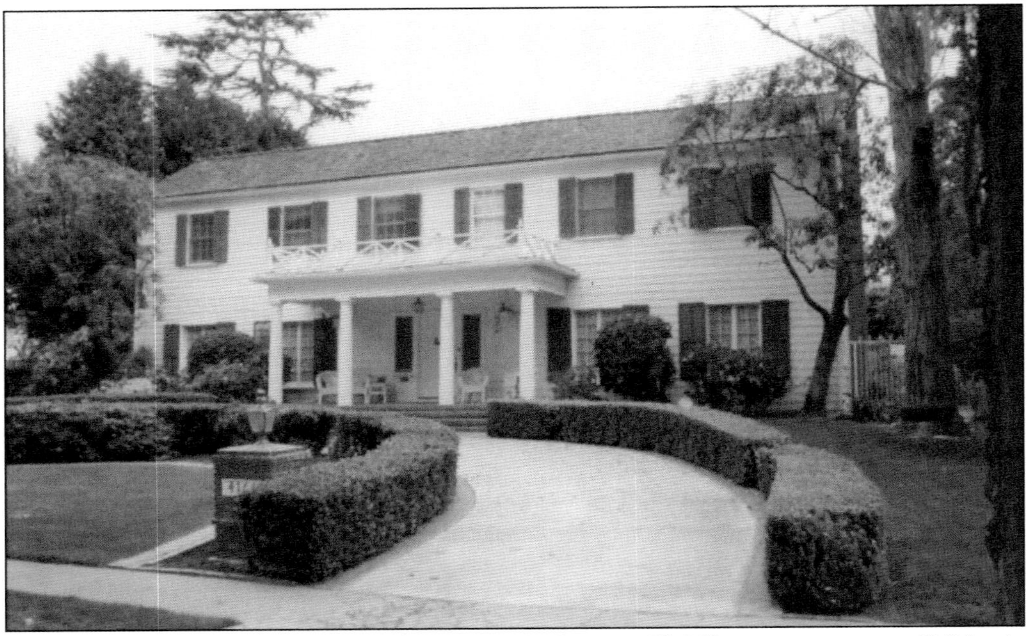

"Ferris Bueller House." This 1928 home, at 4160 Country Club Drive, is a two-story California adaptation of a Colonial Revival with fluted Doric columns at the entry portico. The movie *Ferris Bueller's Day Off* was filmed here, as were *Red Dragon* and *Not Another Teen Movie*. Long Beach mayor Burton W. Chase moved into this home in 1951. (Courtesy of John Mulvey.)

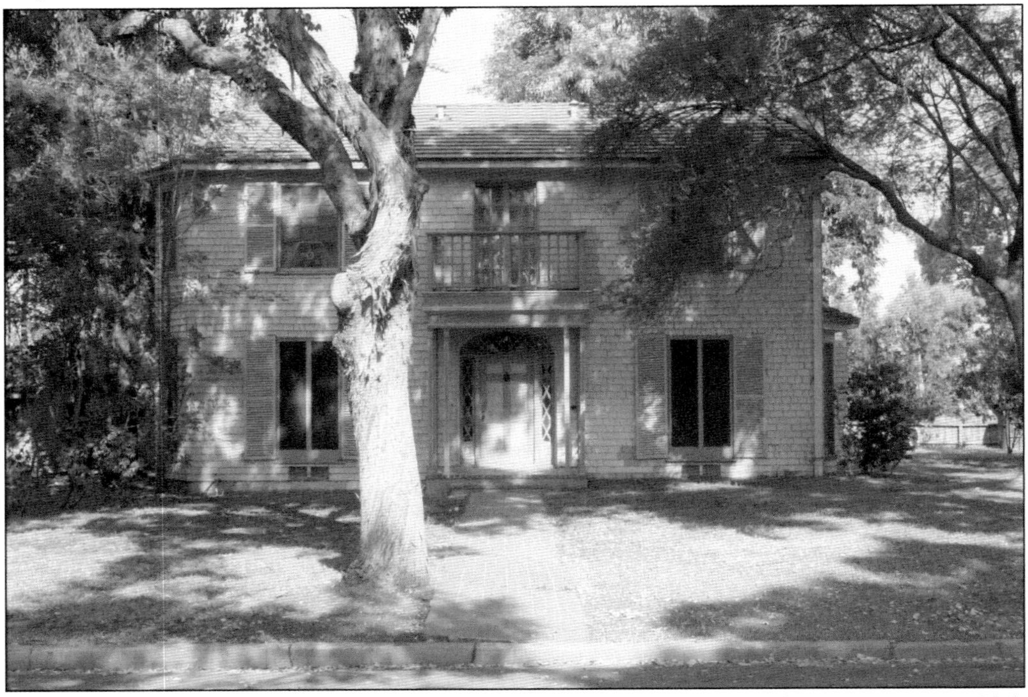

Charles Windham Home. This 1930s Colonial Revival home was moved to 4165 Country Club Drive in Los Cerritos from Sixty-first Place on the peninsula in Long Beach due to storm threats. Charles Windham's father was the mayor and city manager of Long Beach and is known as the "Father of the Port of Long Beach." *American Pie 2* was filmed here. (Courtesy of John Mulvey.)

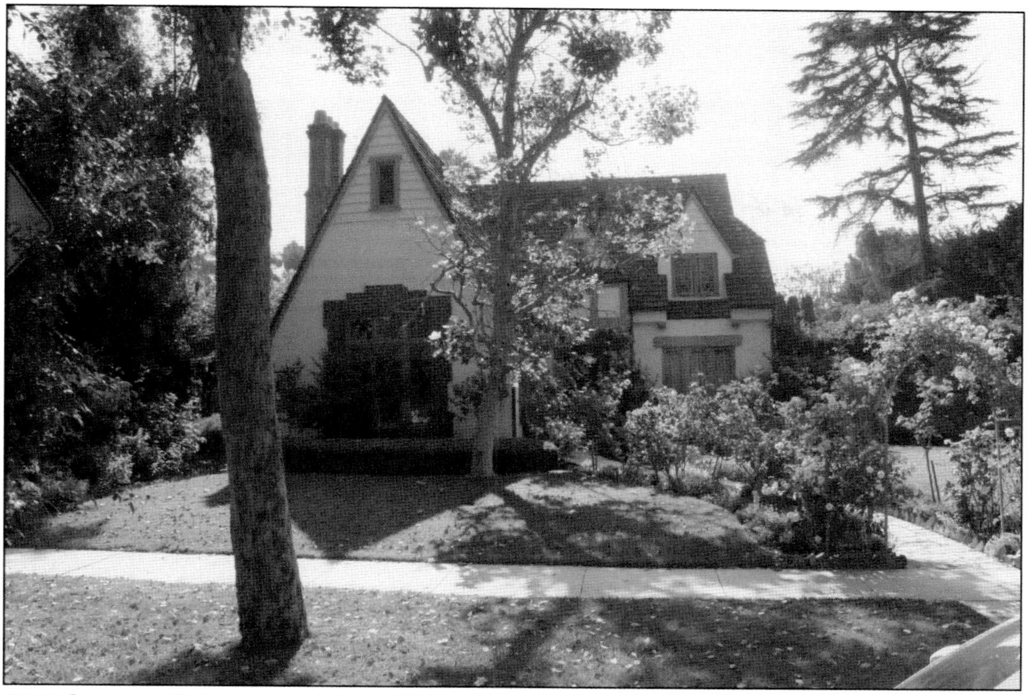

4170 Country Club Drive. This 1932 home was built for Gus Walker, president of the Farmers & Merchants Bank. (Courtesy of John Mulvey.)

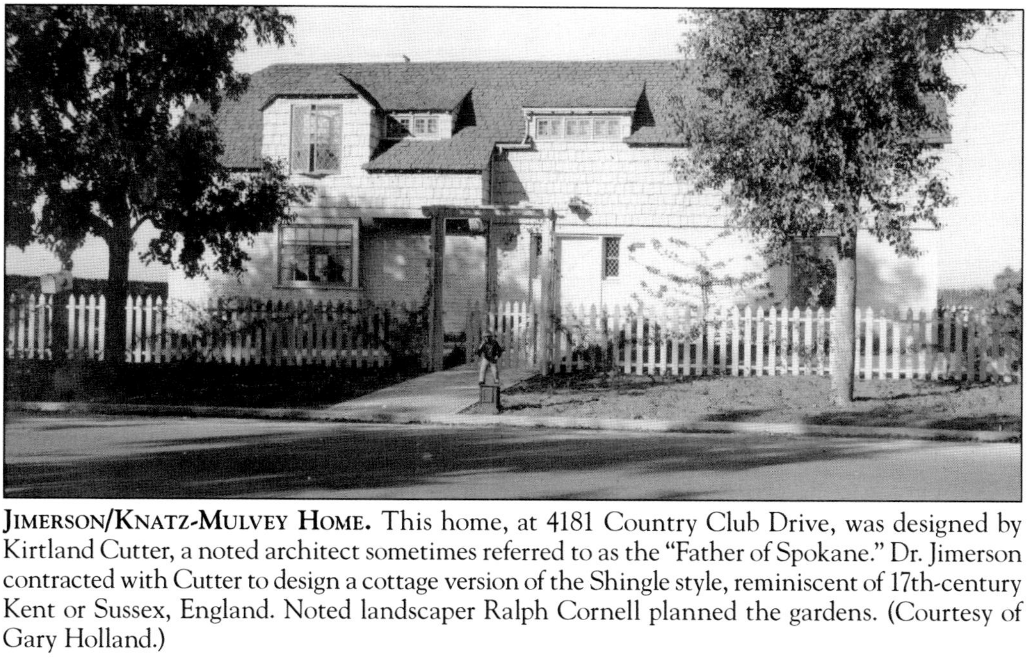

Jimerson/Knatz-Mulvey Home. This home, at 4181 Country Club Drive, was designed by Kirtland Cutter, a noted architect sometimes referred to as the "Father of Spokane." Dr. Jimerson contracted with Cutter to design a cottage version of the Shingle style, reminiscent of 17th-century Kent or Sussex, England. Noted landscaper Ralph Cornell planned the gardens. (Courtesy of Gary Holland.)

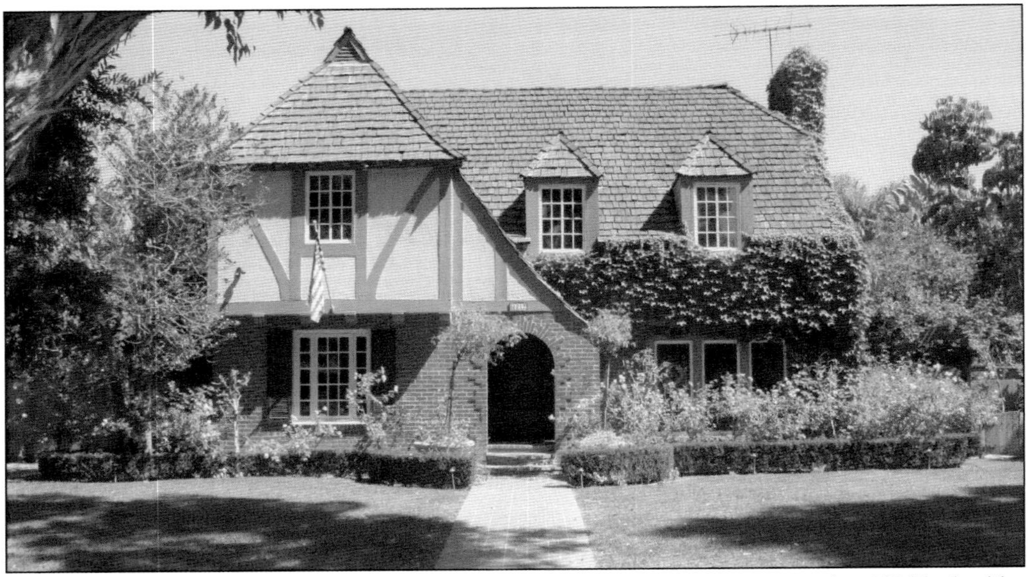

4212 Country Club Drive. This English Tudor Revival home was constructed in 1935 by builder Fred W. Wood. Architect Hugh Davies assisted in the design of this home for Lester Callahan, president of Wood-Callahan Oil Company. (Courtesy of John Mulvey.)

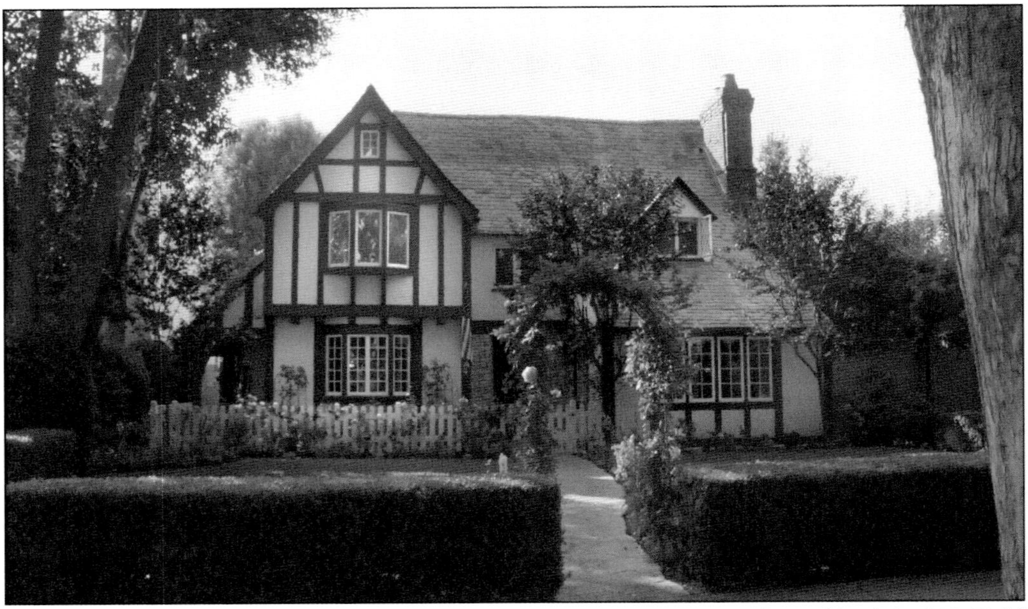

Don Wallace Home. This home was designed by architect H. Roy Kelly and built by J.H. Kuhl Jr. in 1929 for attorney Donald C. Wallace. Wallace's father was William H. Wallace, a pioneer Long Beach banker and former assistant city manager. Donald Wallace operated his radio station, WGAM, from this home at 4214 Country Club Drive. (Courtesy of John Mulvey.)

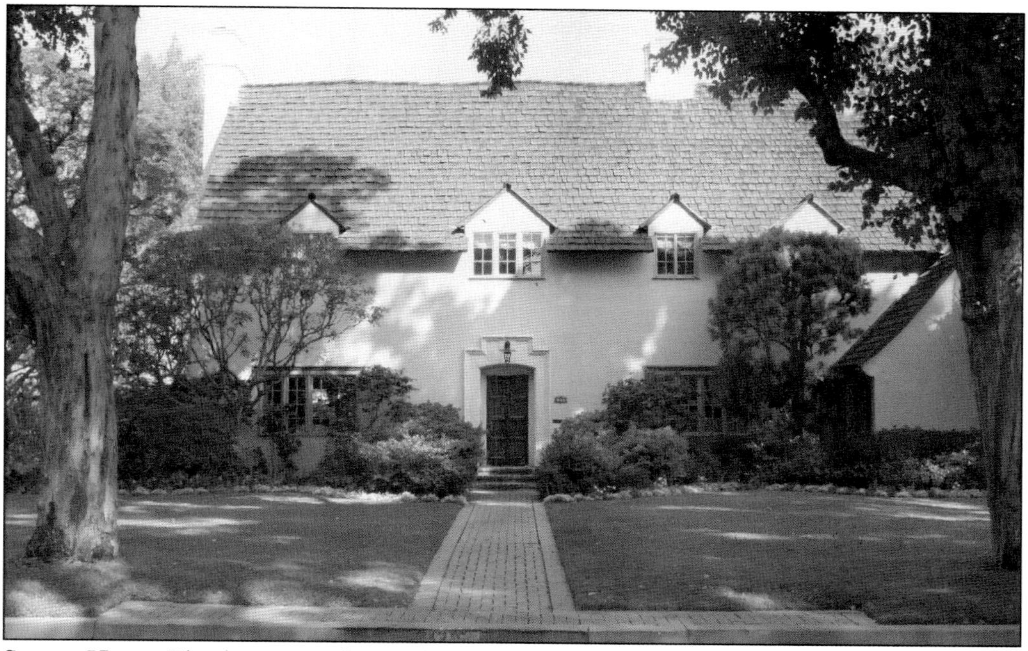

Settle Home. This home was designed by architect Kenneth Wing and built by E.G. Short for Dr. and Mrs. Frank B. Settle. The residence, at 4215 Country Club Drive, passed to the Macrate family in 1951. The picturesque massing of this home suggested a Tudor style, along with its double chimney, steeply pitched roof, and many dormers. (Courtesy of John Mulvey.)

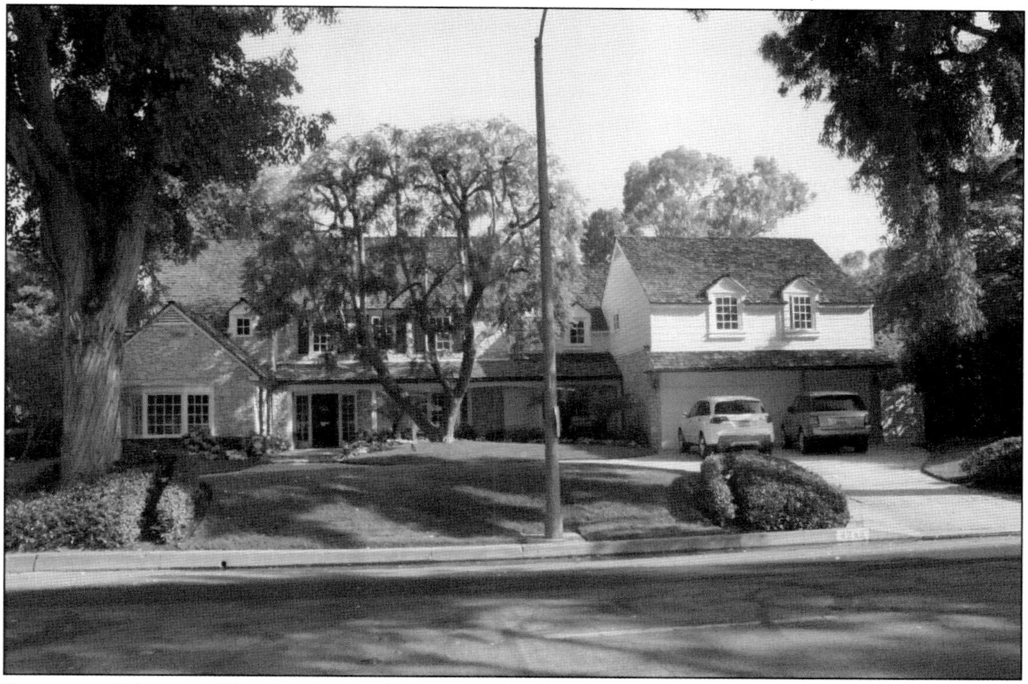

Standlee Martin Home. This is the home of Standlee Martin, owner of Martin Oldsmobile, at one time the largest automobile dealership in the city. Designed by James Friend and built by Winchester Stacey in the Period Revival style, the house is located at 4243 Country Club Drive. (Courtesy of John Mulvey.)

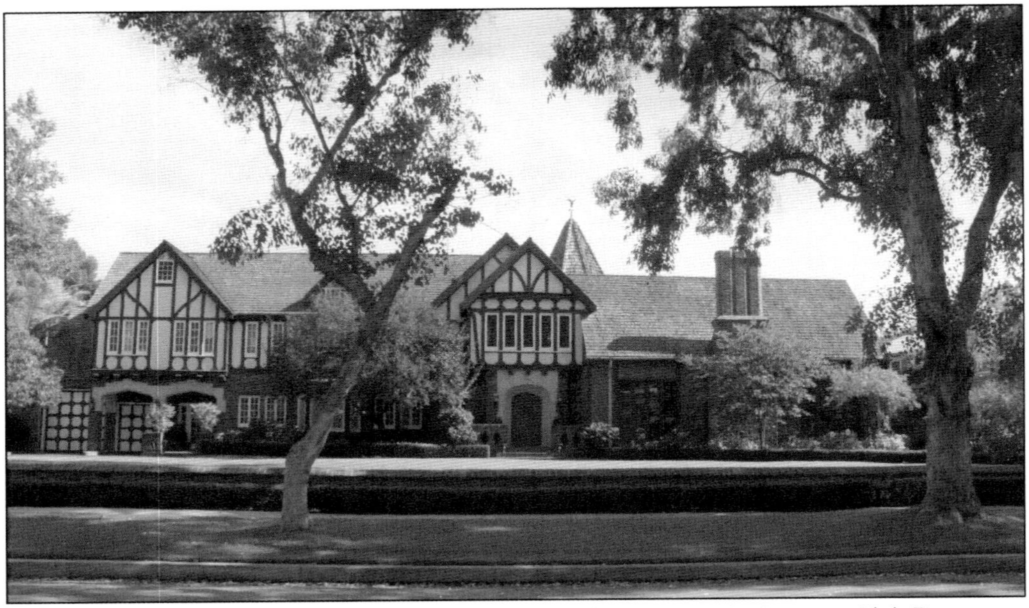

Babb/Pray/Dawson Home. This 1927 Tudor Revival home, at 4252 Country Club Drive, was designed by architect Clarence Aldrich for William E. Babb, manager of the telephone company. The Prays used the home as a center of social life for wealthy Long Beach citizens. William Dawson, who served as the first general manager of the agency that would become the Long Beach Convention and Visitors Bureau, and his wife, Vicki, later acquired the home. (Courtesy of John Mulvey.)

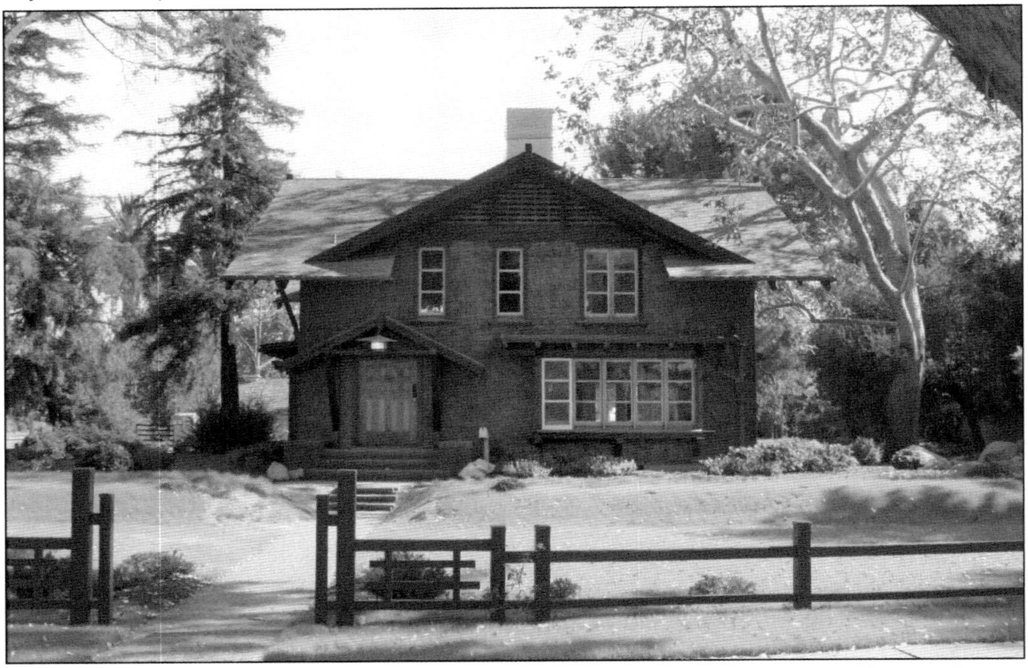

Jennie Reeves/Townsend Home. This house was designed and built by the architects Greene and Greene for Jennie Reeves in 1904. It was moved to Country Club Drive by Dr. Raymond Townsend and then to Los Cerritos by his wife, Ada Campbell Townsend. The home, at 4260 Country Club Drive, is in the National Register of Historic Places. (Courtesy of John Mulvey.)

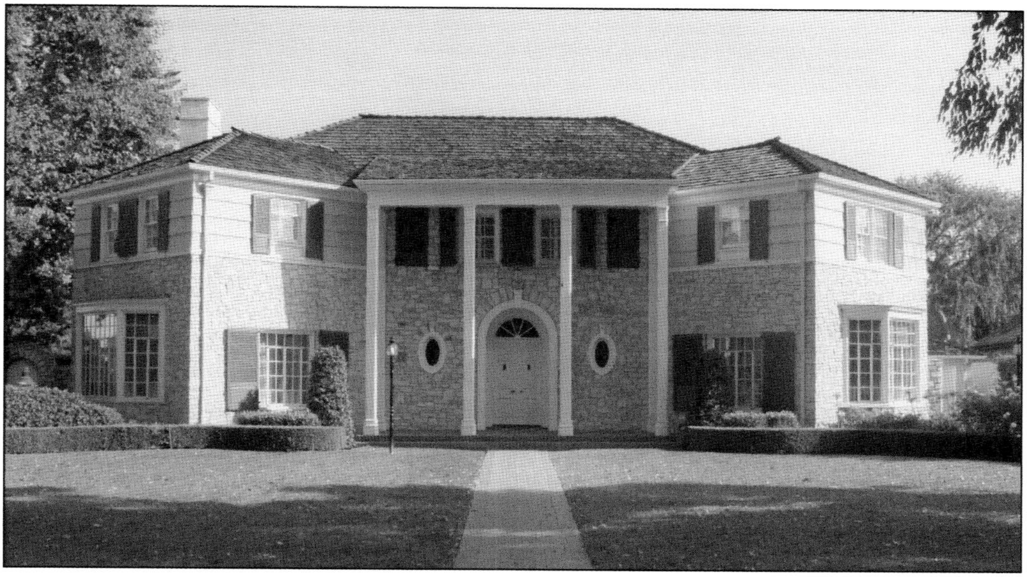

Home at 4265 Country Club. This home is the only residence in Long Beach designed by noted architect Paul Revere Williams, the first black registered architect in California. Built in 1941 by Albert Reingardt, it was owned by J.W. Wood of Wood-Callahan Oil Company. (Courtesy of John Mulvey.)

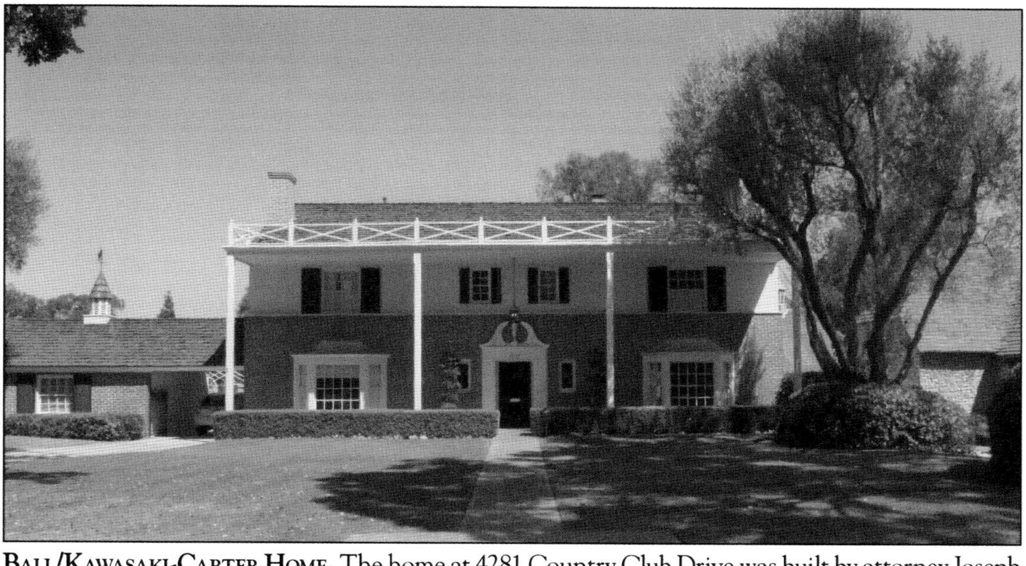

Ball/Kawasaki-Carter Home. The home at 4281 Country Club Drive was built by attorney Joseph A. Ball in 1940. Ball is best known for his role as senior counsel on the Warren Commission that investigated the assassination of Pres. John F. Kennedy and for defending Watergate figure John D. Ehrlichman and automaker John DeLorean. The home was purchased by Lillian Kawasaki, an elected director on the Water Replenishment District, and Craig Carter. (Courtesy of John Mulvey.)

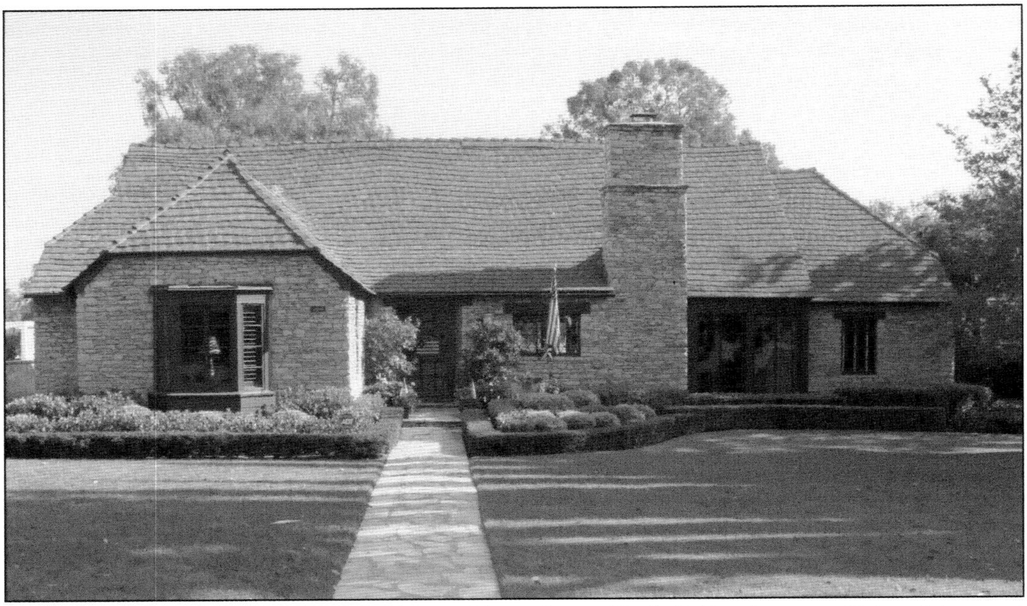

Newton Bass Home. This home was designed by architect Hugh Gibb, who started his architectural firm in Long Beach in 1934. Constructed by the Russel Mangum Company in 1940, the style is Period Revival. The structure has a T-shaped clipped gable with slate sidings. The owner of the home, located at 4285 Country Club Drive, was Newton T. Bass, an oil producer with the company of Bass, Goodnight & Westland. (Courtesy of John Mulvey.)

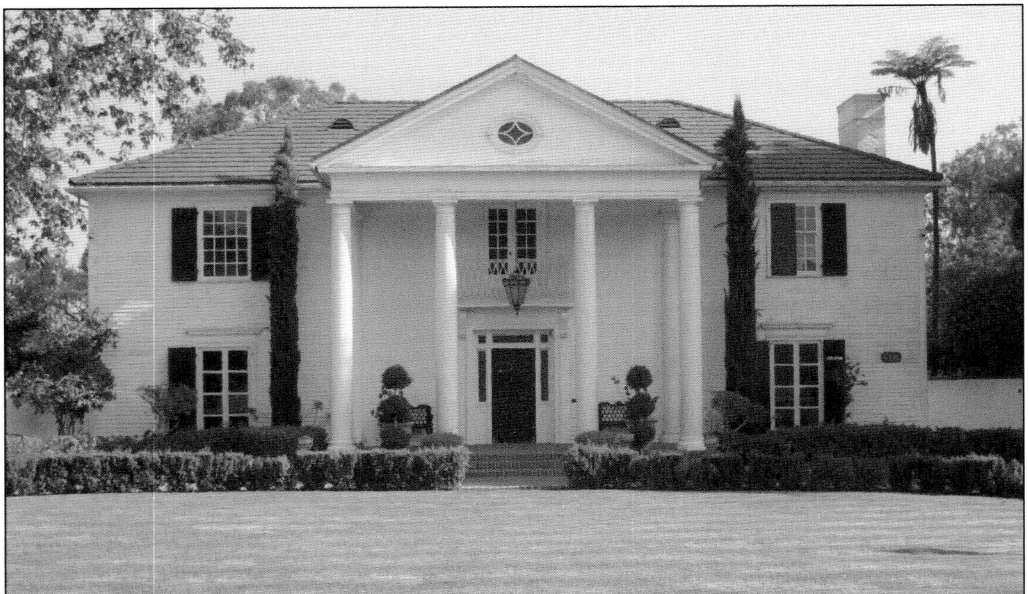

Paul McCrery Home. This 1940 Georgian Revival home was designed by architect Edward Killingsworth and built by E.G. Short for Paul R McCrery, the owner of the McCrery Music Company. The establishment opened on Pine Avenue in 1924 and operated for 34 years. Another musician, pianist Dephine Smith, occupied this house, located at 4291 Country Club Drive. (Courtesy of John Mulvey).

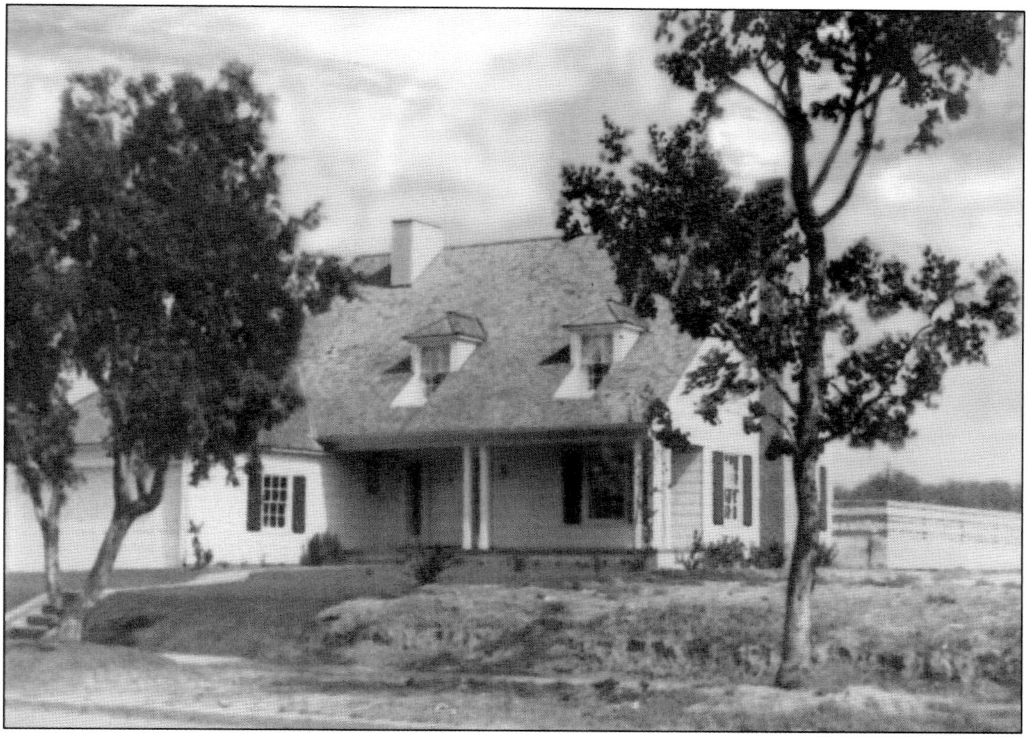

Reese/Marks Home. This Dutch Colonial home, built by W. Tosh, was copied from a house featured in the February 1939 *Sunset* magazine. The Berkeley Women's Club, working with architect John B. Anthony, canvassed 300 women to determine the "must haves" and "don't wants" in home features, and *Sunset* magazine sold the house plans. The house, located at 3860 Country Club Drive, is pictured here in 1940. (Courtesy of Mary Marks.)

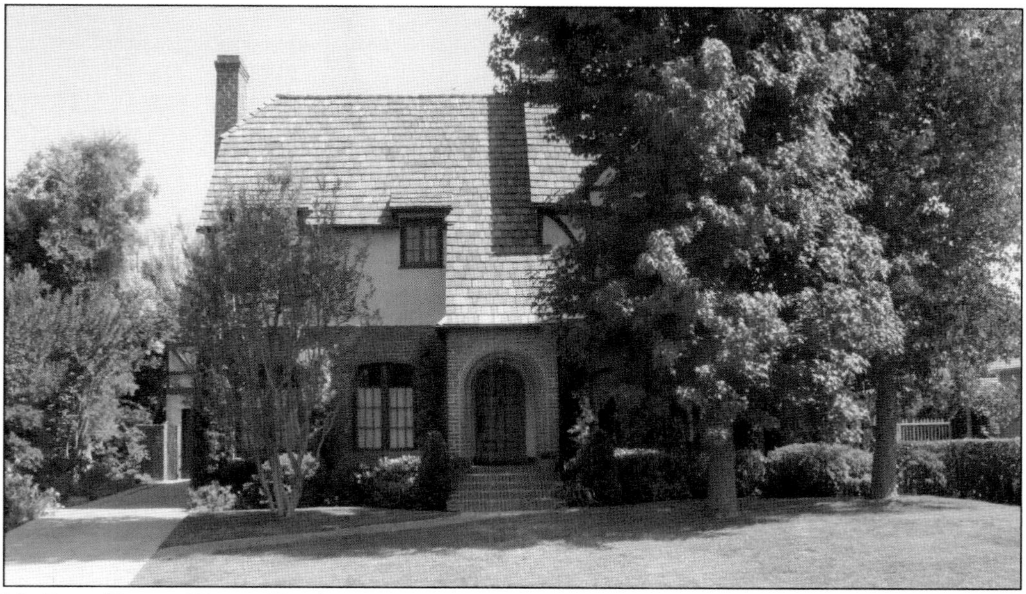

McGrew/Baker Home. This home, at 165 East Roosevelt Road, was built and occupied by Milton McGrew in 1929. McGrew was part of the C.T. McGrew & Sons Construction Company, which built many of the homes in Los Cerritos. (Courtesy of John Mulvey.)

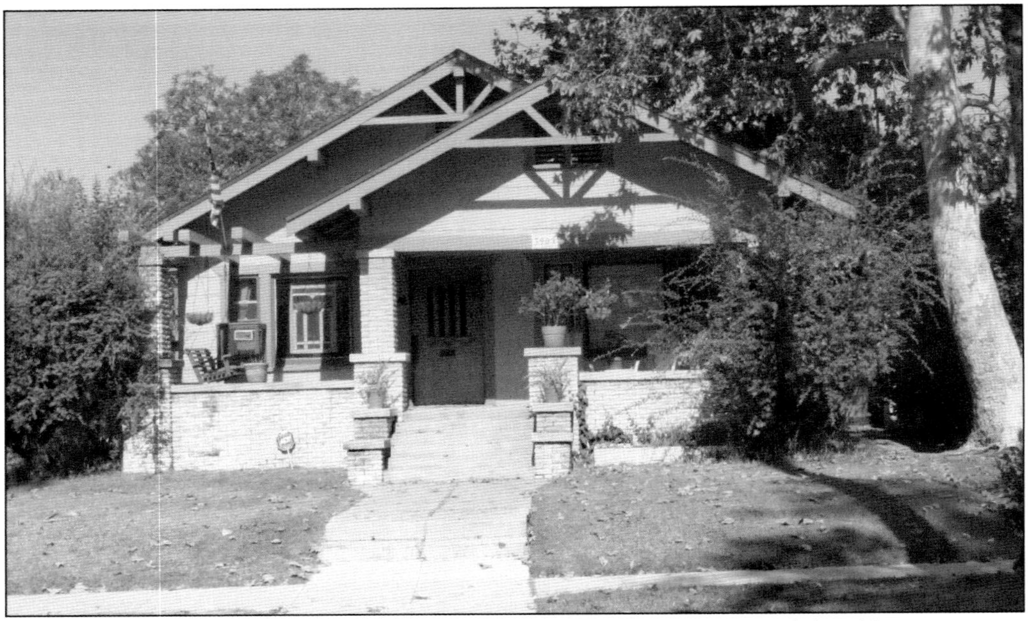

Mahieu/Heckman Home. This structure, at 3903 Pine Avenue, is one of the oldest remaining homes in Los Cerritos, built in 1914. It is an example of a California bungalow with a modest chalet influence. Early residents were A.A. Mahieu and H.H. Heckman, owner of the gas station on Broadway in Long Beach. (Courtesy of John Mulvey).

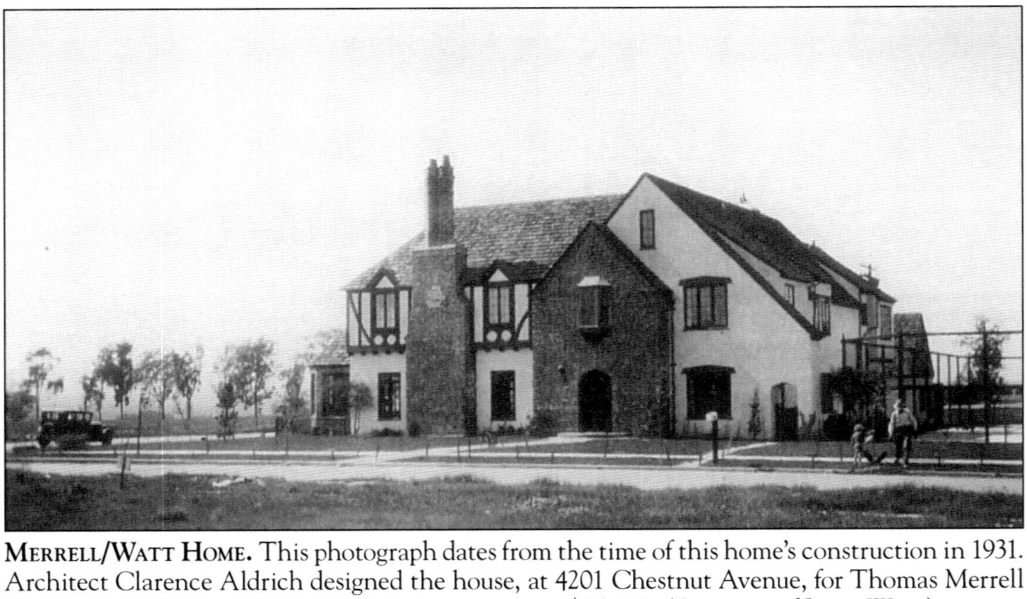

Merrell/Watt Home. This photograph dates from the time of this home's construction in 1931. Architect Clarence Aldrich designed the house, at 4201 Chestnut Avenue, for Thomas Merrell and his wife, Ruth Craig. The construction cost was $35,000. (Courtesy of Janet Watt.)

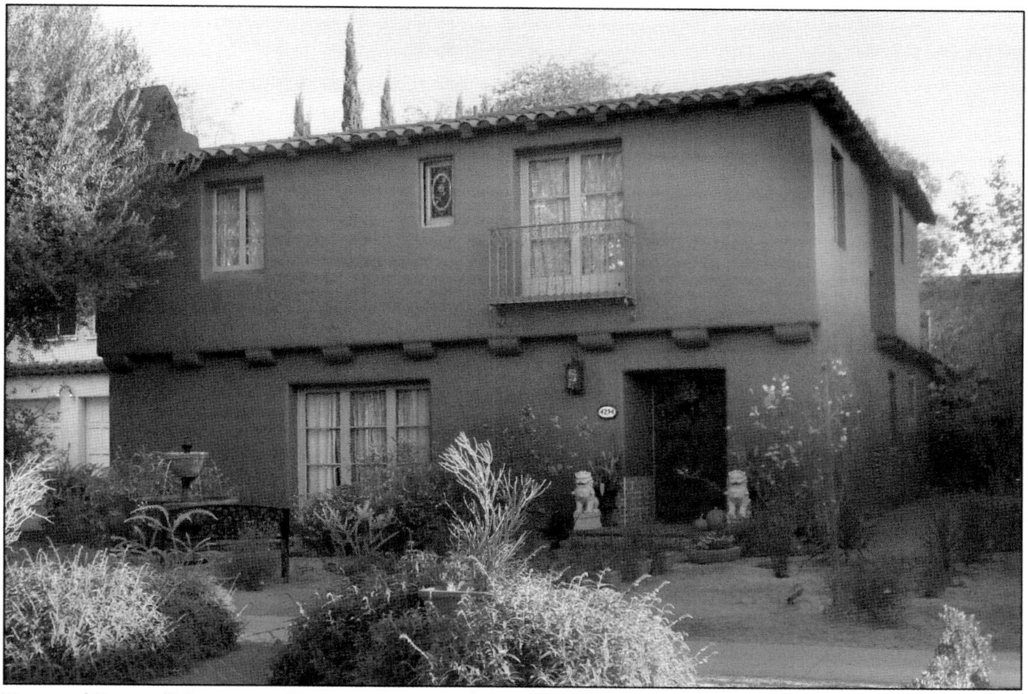

Davies/Combs/Marsocci-Flores Home. The house at 4254 Chestnut Avenue was built in 1928 for architect Hugh Davies, who designed homes and civic buildings, including Poly High School. He was the designing architect for the Pacific Southwest Exposition, held in Long Beach in 1928. In 1936, the home passed to Eldridge. E. Combs, who drilled oil wells in Los Cerritos. Combs's company, the Termo Oil Company, still operates in Signal Hill. (Courtesy of John Mulvey.)

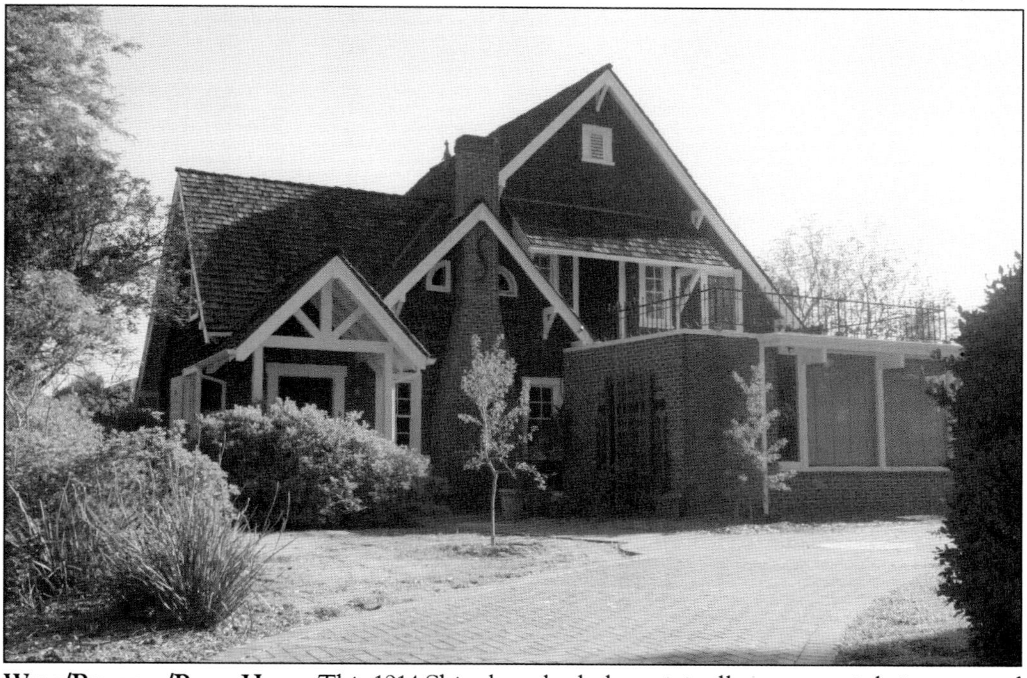

Walp/Burrell/Price Home. This 1914 Shingle-style chalet, originally one story, is being restored by the Price family. It is located at 3808 Cedar Avenue. (Courtesy of John Mulvey.)

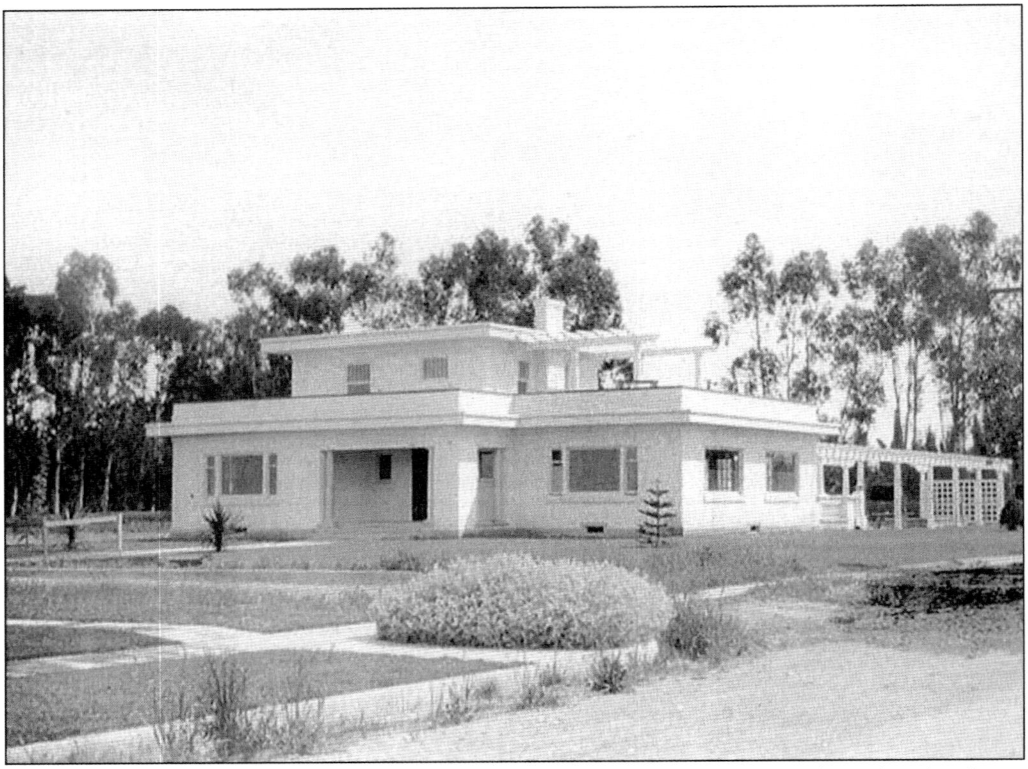

Carson/Jablonski Home. This image shows the home at 3800 Weston Place shortly after it was constructed in 1917 by C.T. McGrew and Sons in the Italian Mediterranean Revival style. (Courtesy of the Jablonski family.)

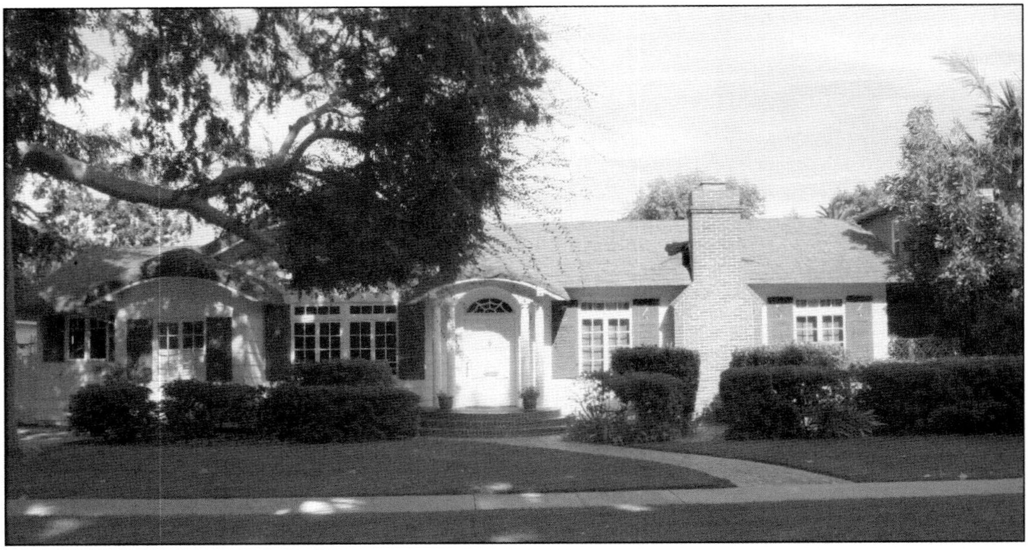

Walker Home. This Colonial Revival home at 3838 Weston Place, with a gable roof with rolling edges, was built in 1924 by Earl L. Chessman for attorney Charles Z. Walker. Charles was the son of Charles J. Walker, the founder of Farmers & Merchants Bank. (Courtesy of John Mulvey.)

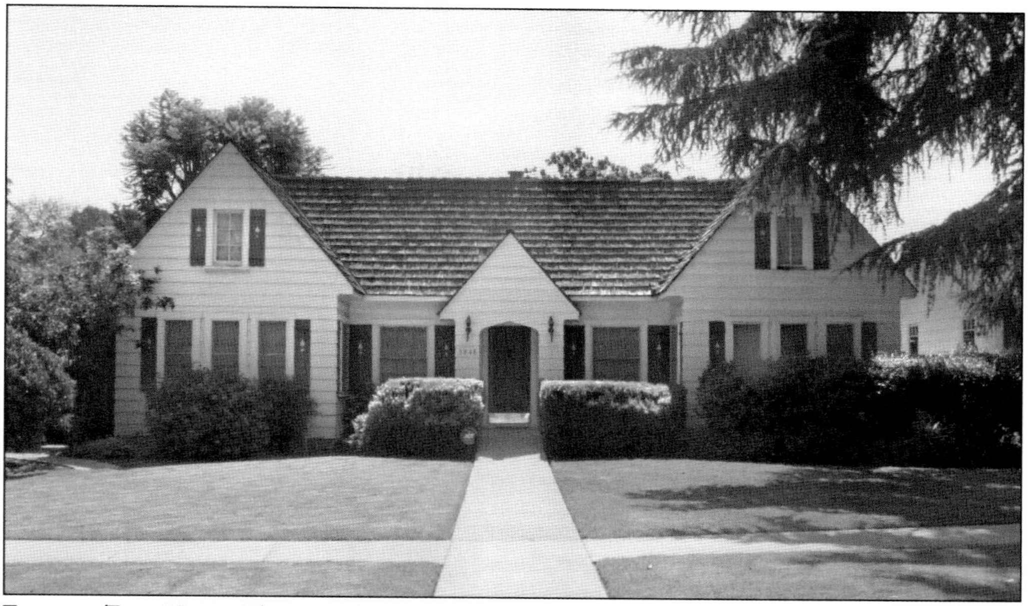

Freeman/Reid Home. This Period Revival home was built in 1921 for C.W. Freeman, who built rigs for Standard Oil Company. It later passed to Will J. Reid, who headed Inter-Insurance Exchange of the Tuna Fisherman of Southern California, which sold insurance to fisherman. Reid later invested in Hancock Oil Company. This home is located at 3846 Weston Place. (Courtesy of John Mulvey.)

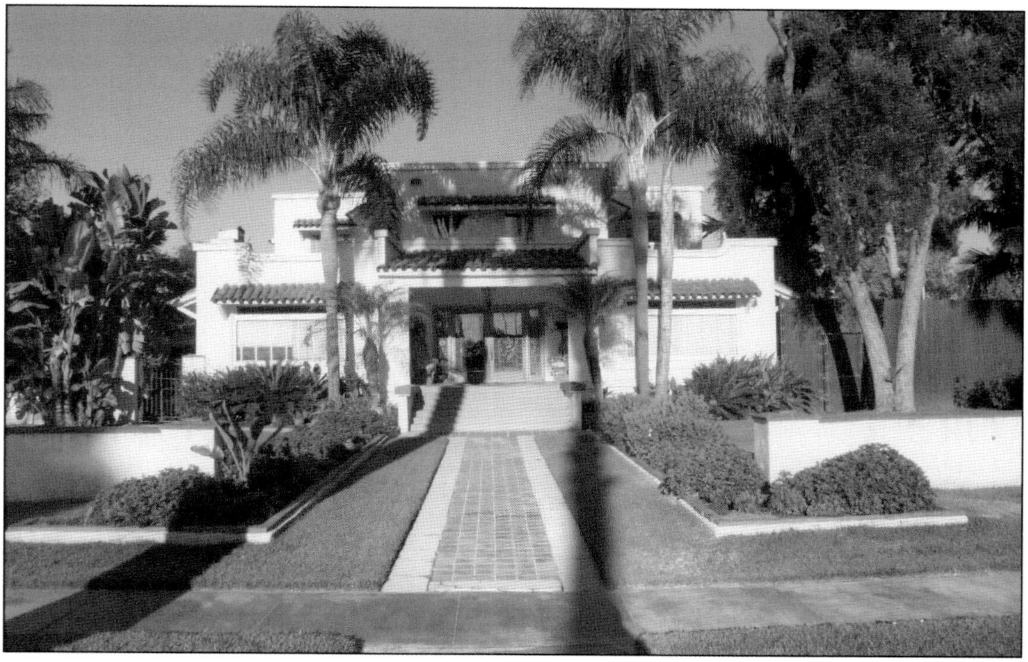

Desmond Home. This 1916 home, located at 3855 Pacific Avenue, is a Spanish Mediterranean Revival building. Early residents were H.G. Johansing, who was in the insurance business, and attorney Walter J. Desmond. Desmond was the father of city attorney Gerald Desmond, who obtained restitution for the City of Long Beach in the battle over land subsidence due to oil operations. The Gerald Desmond Bridge is named for him. (Courtesy of John Mulvey.)

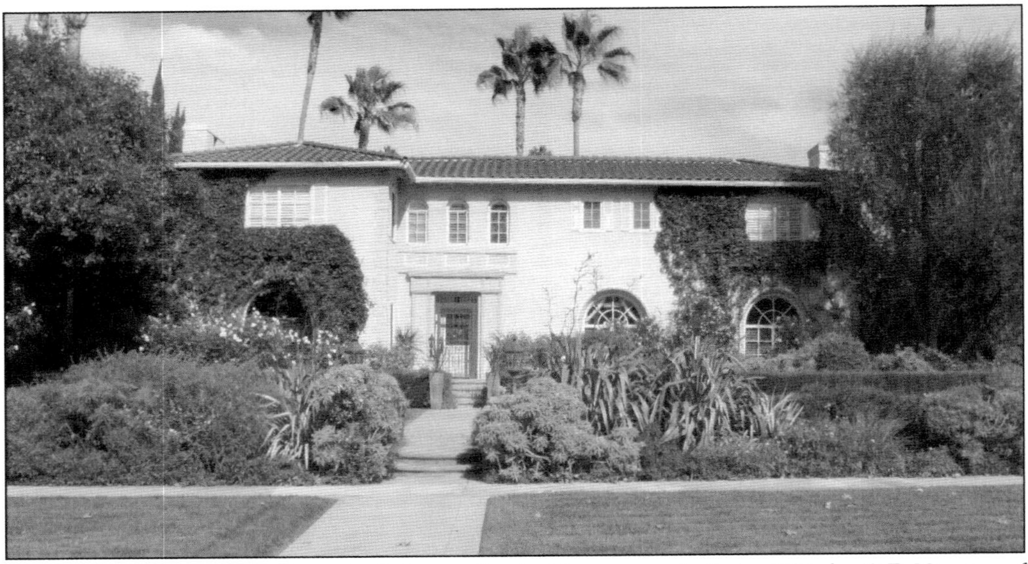

W.H. CREE HOME. This Spanish Colonial Revival home was built in 1929 for C.F. Higgins of Higgins & Grey Wrecking. William H. Cree, an attorney with Cree and Brooks, lived at the home, located at 4256 Pacific Avenue, during the 1940s. (Courtesy of John Mulvey.)

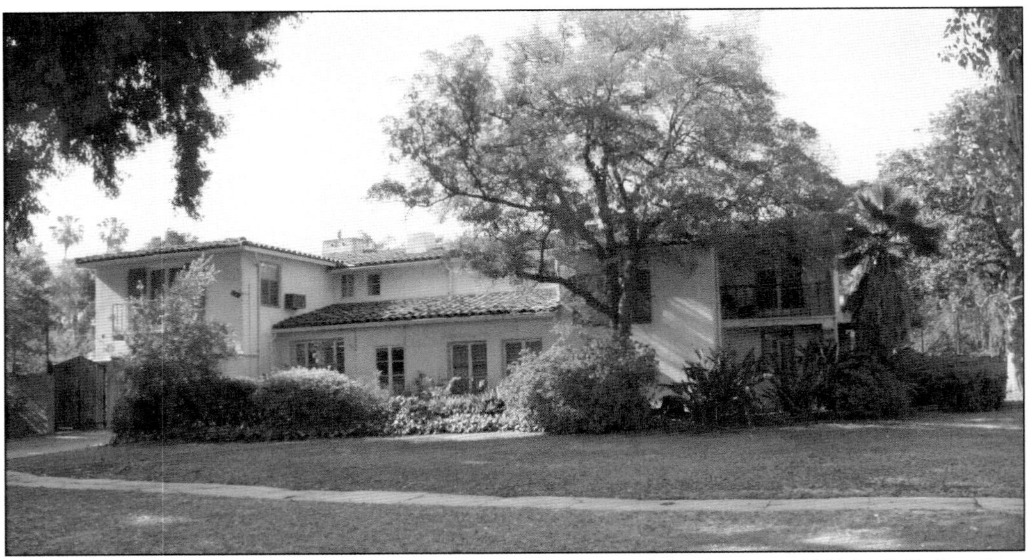

D.P. CONDUIT/DENIO/COMBS HOME. Kirtland Cutter designed this home in 1929 for D.P. Conduit, the first attorney to open an office in Long Beach in 1893. In the 1930s and 1940s, the home was occupied by Elon Denio, who also started a law practice in 1893. In 1891, Denio was elected to the city board of trustees and then became its chairman (mayor) in 1896. The home, at 4282 Pacific Avenue, passed to Frende and Georgia Combs. (Courtesy of John Mulvey.)

Bibliography

Andriesse, Ann. "Los Cerritos: The Development of a Neighborhood." *The Branded Word*. Long Beach, CA: Rancho Los Cerritos, summer 1987.

Brokate, Kristen. *The Bixby Family and Changes in Land Use in Southern California. 1850–1900.* Thesis. California State University at Long Beach, 1992.

Case, Walter. *Long Beach and Vicinity, Volume 1.* Chicago, IL: S.J. Clarke Publishing Company, 1927.

———. *The History of Long Beach.* Long Beach, CA: The Press Telegram Publishing Company, 1935.

Grobaty, Tim. 2012. *Location Filming in Long Beach.* Charleston, SC: History Press, 2012.

Long Beach Heritage. *A Kirtland K. Cutter Long Beach Salon and Tour.* Long Beach, CA: 1999.

———. *Gems of Los Cerritos Home Tour.* Long Beach, CA: 2003.

Matthews, Henry C. *Kirtland Cutter, Architect in the Land of Promise.* University of Washington Press, 1988.

Mullio, Cara, and Jennifer M. Volland. *Long Beach Architecture: The Unexpected Metropolis.* Santa Monica, CA: Hennessey and Ingalls, 2004.

Perkins, Jan Davis. *Don C. Wallace, Wireless W6AM Amateur Radio's Pioneer.* New York, NY: The Vestal Press, 1991.

Pope, Jean, and Harry Pope. *History of La Linda Drive.* Long Beach, CA: La Linda Drive Association, 2001.

Quam-Wickham, Nancy. "'Cities Sacrificed on the Altar of Oil': Popular Opposition to Oil Development in 1920s Los Angeles." *Environmental History,* Vol. 3, No. 2. Cary, NC: April 1998.

Simkins, Harold. *Long Beach Cultural Heritage Survey, Los Cerritos Survey.* Long Beach, CA: City of Long Beach, 1981.

State Oil and Gas Supervisor. *Summary of Oil Field Operations,* Vol. 12, No. 8. San Francisco, CA: California State Mining Bureau, 1927.

Washburn, Josephine. *History and Reminiscences of the Holiness Church Work in Southern California and Arizona.* 1912.

Discover Thousands of Local History Books Featuring Millions of Vintage Images

Arcadia Publishing, the leading local history publisher in the United States, is committed to making history accessible and meaningful through publishing books that celebrate and preserve the heritage of America's people and places.

Find more books like this at
www.arcadiapublishing.com

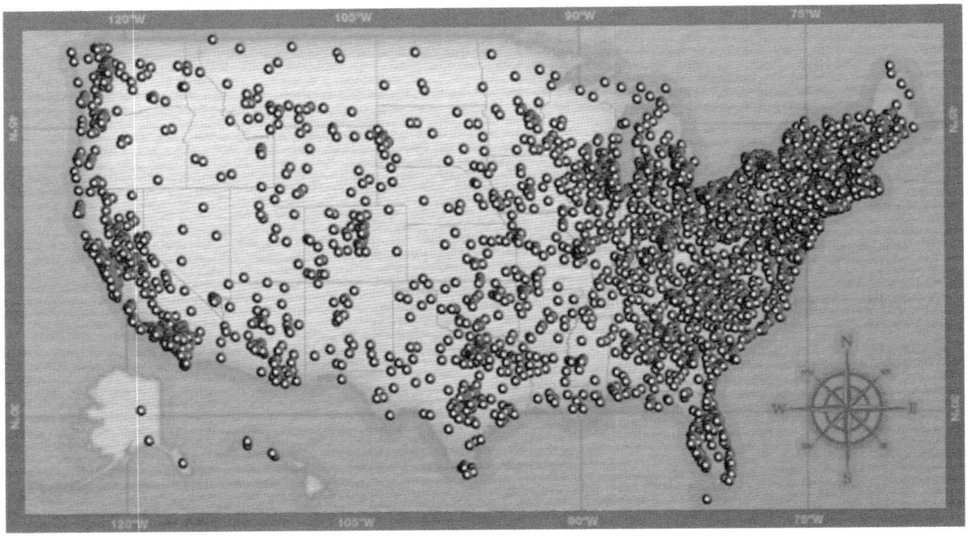

Search for your hometown history, your old stomping grounds, and even your favorite sports team.

Consistent with our mission to preserve history on a local level, this book was printed in South Carolina on American-made paper and manufactured entirely in the United States. Products carrying the accredited Forest Stewardship Council (FSC) label are printed on 100 percent FSC-certified paper.

MADE IN THE USA